Women in Contemporary France

Women in Contemporary France

Edited by
Abigail Gregory and Ursula Tidd

Oxford • *New York*

First published in 2000 by
Berg
Editorial offices:
150 Cowley Road, Oxford OX4 1JJ, UK
838 Broadway, Third Floor, New York, NY 10003-4812, USA

Berg is the imprint of Oxford International Publishers Ltd.

Library of Congress Cataloging-in-Publication Data

A catalogue record for this book is available from the Library of Congress.

British Library Cataloguing-in-Publication Data

A catalogue record for this book is available from the British Library.

ISBN 1 85973 353 0 (Cloth)
ISBN 1 85973 358 1 (Paper)

Typeset by JS Typesetting, Wellingborough, Northants.
Printed and bound in Great Britain by Biddles Ltd
www.biddles.co.uk

Contents

Notes on Contributors

Maggie Allison is Senior Lecturer in French Studies at the University of Bradford. Her research is in media analysis with particular emphasis on the representation of women in the political arena in Britain and France. She has co-edited two volumes recently: *In/visibility: Gender and Representation in a European Context* (with R. Cleminson), special issue of *Interface: Bradford Studies in Language, Culture and Society*, vol. 3 (1998) and *Forty Years of the Fifth French Republic: Actions, Dialogues and Discourses* (with O. Heathcote) (Bern: Peter Lang, 1999). Her chapter on comparative representations of women politicians during the French and British elections of 1997 has appeared in O. Krakovitch and G. Sellier (eds) *Représentations des femmes de pouvoir: mythes et fantasmes* (Paris: L'Harmattan, 2000).

Kate Beeching is a Senior Lecturer in Linguistics and French at the Faculty of Languages and European Studies, University of the West of England, Bristol. She is preparing her Ph.D. on 'Parenthetical Remarks in Women's and Men's Speech in Contemporary French' at the University of Surrey/Université de Paris X-Nanterre and has research interests in sociolinguistics and the spoken language. Recent publications include 'The social significance of gender-linked features of French' in *Women in French Studies*, 7 (September 1999) and 'Le rôle de la particule pragmatique "enfin" dans le discours des hommes et des femmes' in Armstrong, N., Bauvois, C. and Beeching, K., *Femmes et français* (Paris: L'Harmattan, 2000).

Máire Fedelma Cross is Head of French at the University of Sheffield, where she teaches aspects of contemporary French politics and history at postgraduate and undergraduate level. She has co-authored *The Feminism of Flora Tristan* (Berg, 1992) and *Early French Feminisms 1830–1940* (Elgar, 1996). She contributes regularly to the journals *Modern and Contemporary France*, *European History Quarterly*, *French Studies*, and is a member of the Editorial Board of *Modern and Contemporary France*.

Notes on Contributors

Marion Demossier is a Lecturer in French and European Studies at the University of Bath. Her research interests are in social anthropology and rural studies. Her publications include *Vignerons, propriétaires et négociants en Bourgogne* (Dié, 1994) and *Homme et vin, une anthropologie du vignoble bourguignon* (Presses Universitaires de Dijon, 1998).

Jane Freedman has a *doctorat de sociologie politique* from the Université de Paris VII. She is Lecturer in French in the Department of Modern Languages at the University of Southampton. She has published *Femmes politiques: mythes et symboles* (L'Harmattan, 1997) and is the joint editor (with Carrie Tarr) of *Women, Immigration and Identities in France* (Berg, 2000).

Abigail Gregory is Lecturer in French at the University of Salford, where she offers a Final Year Undergraduate module on Women in the Labour Force in France. She is the co-author (with Jan Windebank) of *Women and Work in France and Britain* (Macmillan, 2000). She has published chapters in Jones, B. and Cressey, P (eds) *Work and Employment in European Society: Integration and Convergence* (Routledge, 1995) and (with J. O'Reilly) in Crompton, R., Gallie, D. and Purcell, K. (eds) *Changing Forms of Employment: Organisations, Skills and Gender* (Routledge, 1996). She has also published articles in *Work, Employment and Society*, *Gender, Work and Organisation*, *Formation Emploi* and the *Revue Française des affaires sociales*.

Gill Rye is Postdoctoral Research Fellow in French at Roehampton Institute, London and a College Teacher of contemporary French literature at University College, London. Her most recent publications include 'Time for Change: Re(con)figuring Maternity in Contemporary French Literature (Baroche, Cixous, Constant, Redonnet)', *Paragraph* 19:3 (1998) and 'Textual Genealogies: The Legacy of Mme de Meurteuil. Reading Relations in Christiane Baroche's *L'Hiver de beauté*', *French Forum*, 24 (January 1999).

Ursula Tidd is Lecturer in French in the School of Languages and an Associate Director of the European Studies Research Institute (ESRI) at the University of Salford. She is the author of *Simone de Beauvoir, Gender and Testimony* (Cambridge University Press, 1999). She has published chapters in Langford, R. and West, R. (eds) *Marginal Forms, Marginal Voices: Diaries in European Literature* (Rodopi Press, 1999) and in Horner, A. and Keane, A. (eds) *Body Matters: Feminism, Textuality,*

Corporeality (Manchester University Press, 2000), as well as articles on Beauvoir's writing in *Women in French Studies, Simone de Beauvoir Studies, New Readings* and *Hypatia: A Journal of Feminist Philosophy.*

Jan Windebank is Senior Lecturer in French Studies at the University of Sheffield. Her principal publications include *The Informal Economy in France* (Avebury, 1991), (with C.C. Williams) *Informal Employment in the Advanced Economies* (Routledge, 1998), (with A.Gregory) *Women and Work in France and Britain* (Macmillan, 2000) as well as several articles on domestic labour and childcare in France and Britain in *Women's Studies International Forum, Nouvelles Questions Féministes, Journal of European Social Policy* and *Journal of Social Policy.*

Introduction
Abigail Gregory and *Ursula Tidd*

In *Le Deuxième Sexe,* published in 1949, Simone de Beauvoir examined how patriarchal society constructs woman as a relative 'other' to the universal male subject and offered a groundbreaking analysis of diverse aspects of women's oppressive situation in patriarchal society. The immediate pre- and post-war situation of French women certainly justified her analyses: when Beauvoir began writing *Le Deuxième Sexe* in the late 1940s, French women had only just gained the right to vote (1944). Twenty years later, in 1965, women were legally allowed to work without their husband's permission. In 1967 contraception was authorized in the *loi Neuwirth*, and in 1975, the *loi Veil* permitting abortion – albeit on a trial basis of five years – came into force.

During the post-war period French women have made some progress towards equal status in many areas, and the legislative and institutional framework has followed in the wake of wider societal change and sought to improve women's status. Women's situation has evolved in the post-war period in many areas including paid work, parity of representation in French political life, the increasing recognition of their independent sexuality, their autonomous contribution to cultural production, their participation in, and representation by, the media. In parallel, the French language is evolving slowly to represent these different and often conflicting roles played by women in French society. An ever-burgeoning French and Anglo-Saxon literature, too abundant to detail here, has traced such developments over the post-war period in all of these fields.

This is not to say, however, that women in France have achieved equal status in all fields. Indeed, in the late 1990s, it is tempting to share Pierre Bourdieu's surprise concerning 'le paradoxe de la doxa' which entails that the established order of the world, with all its interdictions, prejudices and oppressions, should be for the most part unceasingly accepted and replicated (Bourdieu 1998: 7). For Bourdieu and feminist scholars before him, the pre-eminent example of such submission to the established order is the acceptance of male domination in and of society, which ensures that the oppression of women in French society is still much in evidence.

This book will demonstrate that, despite the deconstruction of sex and gender throughout the 1990s by some anglophone feminist and 'queer' theorists (for example, Butler 1990, 1993; Halberstam 1998), the oppressive consequences of these compelling fictions of sexual identity in 'the real' remain. In a theoretical climate in which traditional notions of femininity and masculinity appear to have given way to a multiplicity of genders, this study may seem outdated. Is it still possible to speak of 'women'? In the present discussion, we do not seek to reify 'women' as a gendered category of oppression or perpetuate the political mechanisms through which, as Monique Wittig has argued, the universalizing category of 'women' is produced (Wittig: 1992). We aim nevertheless to analyse both certain thematic aspects of women's material situation and the situation of distinct minority groups of women in France. The category of 'women' is employed, then, to denote a diverse range of women whose experiences are in many ways distinct, yet who continue nevertheless to be positioned economically, politically, legally, historically, and culturally as women by patriarchal ideology; a process of positioning that, in turn, has structured the ways in which they have become self-conscious. As such, then, the category of 'women' is used as a contingent, yet necessary, material category of analysis in this study.

One might interpret the increased range of opportunities currently available to women as evidence that sexual oppression is now consigned to history, but, as Bourdieu notes, 'les changements visibles des conditions cachent en effet des permanences dans les positions relatives' ('visible changes in conditions actually conceal the persistence of relative inequalities') (Bourdieu 1998: 97). For this reason, despite certain high-profile legislative and political advances in the situation of women, it remains necessary to assess more precisely the situation of women in French society. Are women now effectively represented in politics and in paid work? What is the situation of rural women in today's France? How are women represented by the media? Do they achieve parity with men in the division of unpaid work and leisure? How have their new roles been reflected in the evolution of the French language?

In the 1990s, there were few attempts to draw together diverse facets of women's contemporary situation and contribution to French society and to respond to these questions. While there is a burgeoning literature in French focusing on both more mainstream aspects of women's condition, such as their place in paid work (Documentation Française, 1993; Hirata and Senotier, 1996; Maruani, 1998), in politics (Guigou, 1997; Halimi, 1997; Lang, 1995) in the media (Serdjénian, 1997) in education (Baudelot and Establet, 1992) their relationship to language (Yaguello

(1991) (1998); Singy, 1998) as well as on less publicized areas such as women in rural areas (Mouchtouris, 1994)), only a small number of works attempt to draw together more than one aspect of women's condition, and none deal simultaneously with mainstream and less mainstream issues. For the purpose of the Fourth World UN Conference on Women in 1995, the Documentation Française published a substantial critique of women's progress and persistent inequality in a wide range of areas including employment, education and training, health, their personal safety and wider representation in French society (Aubin and Gisserot, 1994), as well as a recent statistical overview of aspects of women's situation (INSEE, 1995). Likewise, Bihr and Pfefferkorn (1996) outline a number of areas in which women do not have equality of status in relation to men (in education, in the labour market, in the couple and family, in social mobility, in associative life and in politics, in their representation and in the media, in their sexuality and in the experience of old age), and Frischer (1997) focuses on a number of these same areas (women's representation, women's situation in paid work, women's sexuality) as well as others (for example, sexual harassment and single women) to argue that there has been a misogynist backlash against women. Frisque (1997) also draws together literature relating to women in the areas of employment, work and family life, women's bodies, sexuality and maternity, and politics, power and domination, but concentrates on reviewing the different approaches taken by different disciplines to these issues and seeks explanations for inequality, domination and the structuring of social relations. Similarly, in *Masculin/Féminin* (Héritier, 1996) a range of areas are studied, such as women's representation, masculine domination, sexual identity and the division of paid and unpaid work, to ascertain how gendered structures are established. Finally, Françoise Giroud's latest book (Giroud, 1999) constructs a picture of women's main concerns and priorities in contemporary France, primarily on the basis of opinion poll data.

In the Anglo-Saxon academic field, a number of recent works have examined single aspects of women's condition in contemporary France, sometimes in cross-national comparison. For example, in the area of work, Hantrais (1990) examines the reconciliation of family life and paid work among highly qualified French and British women, Dex, Walters and Alden (1993) study French and British mothers in paid work and Gregory and Windebank (2000) analyse French and British women's situations in paid and unpaid work. During the 1990s, studies written in English have appeared on French women in politics (Reynolds, 1998), French women and citizenship (Allwood and Wadia, 2000), and on women's literature in France (Holmes, 1996; Fallaize, 1993; Sellers, 1991). However, little recent work has sought to draw together more than one aspect of women's situation in contemporary France. A recent attempt is Rodgers' (1999) chapter in *Modern France* (Cook and Davie, 1999) which draws heavily on Aubin and Gisserot's work (1994) to discuss women's position in paid work, in education, in politics, their sexual stereotypes and recent legal advances in relation to violence against women and equality between spouses. However, the most wide-ranging review of women's condition in France published in English in the 1990s is *The Condition of Women in France 1945 to the Present. A Documentary Anthology,* edited by Claire Laubier (Routledge, 1990). Although examining a range of areas (language, work, politics and power, home-life and French women's writing), the space available for analysing women's contemporary situation is necessarily limited by the historical focus of the book and by the reproduction of key historical documents for language analysis. Its portrayal of contemporary French society is also now largely out of date, given the developments over the last decade relating to women in France. Our book will therefore be the first recent attempt to analyse women's situation in contemporary France. We intend to go further than simply a statistical overview of women's current situation in order to chart recent changes, or, in some cases, the lack of change. The book is an examination of the contemporary condition of women in France. It fills a gap in both the French and Anglo-Saxon literature by addressing both more mainstream issues (such as women's paid work, unpaid work and leisure and contemporary French women's writing) as well as areas that have, until now, been under-represented in published work written in English on French women: women in rural France, immigrant and exiled women in France, and the situation of French lesbians.

Inevitably, in offering a snapshot of the diversity of women's situation and their contribution to French society, we cannot hope to offer the depth of analysis found in books devoted to one aspect of women's situation. Instead we want to highlight this very diversity, setting out the 'bigger picture' relating to women's condition, and attempting to understand the broader factors influencing and impeding change.

To provide the context for the contributions in this book, it is first necessary to delineate some of the principal changes of a social, economic, legislative, political and cultural nature in France over the post-war period that have affected women's condition.

Introduction

Changes in France over the Post-War Period affecting Women's Condition

Numerous changes over the post-war period, many of which have also occurred in other industrialized countries, can be evoked to explain women's condition in contemporary French society. France has, for example, seen the post-war economic developments of mass consumerism and mass production under Fordist regimes combined with Keynesian economic policies to help develop education and the welfare state. Subsequently, it was also implicated in flexible accumulation under post-Fordism and the spreading of neo-liberal ideologies (Jenson, Hagan and Reddy, 1988). These industrial, political and economic changes have contributed to a transformation in the nature of employment and the replacement of a dominant model of full-time, permanent employment, characteristic of the immediate post-war period with a more extensive use of temporary, short-time and part-time working in countries where high levels of unemployment have been common after the oil crises of the 1970s (Bielanski, 1994).

As in many other industrialized countries, France has also undergone massive social changes, which have occurred as women have exercised greater control over their fertility. This has been due to wider access to contraception, abortion and assisted conception techniques, the related fall in marriage rates and family size, rising divorce rates and changes in family structures (notably, the growth in one-parent families) (Rogers 1999; Rubery 1988: 234). Related in part to the changes mentioned above is the growth in women's access to education and paid work, which has contributed to the reconceptualization of women's roles and perceptions of themselves in French society (Giroud, 1999). In addition, France, as an EU member country, has also been subject to the requirements of European law, notably in the area of equal opportunities for women, although in a number of cases France has pre-empted or exceeded the requirements of this legislation at European level with its own national measures (Hantrais, 1990, 1995).

Although all of these areas would justify fuller analyses, the present discussion will focus on two forces that we consider to have had a very significant impact on women's position in contemporary France: legislative changes and the second-wave feminist movement. These areas deserve special consideration because they have entailed legal and ideological challenges to the patriarchal infrastructure of French society that have resulted in an improved status for women.

Legislative Changes in the Post-War Period

Women in France, like many of their counterparts in the industrialized world, have gained significant rights during the post-war period. The principle of equal rights with men was inscribed into the Constitution in 1946 (and subsequently incorporated into the 1958 Constitution), but took many years to be translated into specific laws aiming to initiate equality between men and women in different areas. Although the pace of enactment of some legislation, notably laws relating to civil rights and the right to vote, has been slower in France than in some other EU countries such as the UK,[1] this has not been the case for much of the EU equal opportunities legislation. Here, France has frequently taken the lead and has sought to bring the rest of the EU in line with its practices. This was very clearly the case for equal pay legislation (Hantrais, 1990). Today, however, it has been argued that women have achieved equality with men in most areas *in principle* (Aubin and Gisserot, 1994; Rodgers, 1999). We shall now briefly outline some of the major gains in French women's rights during the post-war period in terms of control over their bodies, civil rights and rights within marriage, paid work and education, referring to Rodgers' summary of legislative changes where indicated in the text (Rodgers, 1999).

Women's control over their sexuality and fertility has been a key area of progress. Following the legalization of contraception in 1967 (although advertisements for contraception were only allowed in 1991 as a result of government policy relating to AIDS), and the Veil Law decriminalizing abortion, from 1983 the cost of abortion could be reimbursed through the Social Security system. In 1993, in response to the increasingly vociferous and violent anti-abortion lobby, failure to respect the right to abortion became a crime (Rodgers, 1999).

In the area of civil rights, French women did not begin to gain greater equality with their spouses until the mid-1960s. After they had acquired the right to engage in paid work and to open a bank account in 1965, they then benefited from a law passed in 1970 that replaced the notion of paternal authority with parental authority over family decisions. In 1975, divorce by consent was introduced. In 1985, each spouse's right to engage in paid work and to dispose of their salary as they wish, as well as to control their own personal property, was made explicit in the Civil Code (article 225), and children gained the right to take the surnames of both parents. In 1987, an Act was passed to facilitate the joint exercise of parental power, and in 1993 the principle of joint parental authority was extended to all children, not only those whose parents were married (Rodgers, 1999).

In the area of paid work, significant advances were not made until the 1970s, despite France's early commitment to the principle of equal rights for women. The law on equal pay for the same job or work of equal value was enacted in 1972; 1975 saw the law against discrimination in recruitment without legitimate reasons, and the law proscribing the dismissal of pregnant women was passed in 1980. Following the election of the first post-war socialist government in 1981, some of the most significant measures to achieve sexual equality were enacted. Key among these was the 1983 *loi Roudy* (after Yvette Roudy, Minister for Women's Rights at that time), which applied the 1976 Equal Treatment Directive 76/207/EEC to the private sector in France, and in several respects (detailed by Hantrais, 1990: 95) contained some of the most far-reaching legislation in the EC. Two key features of the 1983 law were the promotion of equal opportunities through positive action, and the devolving of responsibility for implementing equality in employment through collective bargaining (Lanquetin, Laufer and Letablier, 1999). The latter measure entailed the obligation for companies with more than fifty employees to prepare an annual report comparing the general conditions of employment of women and men with regard to recruitment, promotion, training and working conditions, as well as the requirement to conduct negotiations over equal opportunity schemes, with the possibility that exemplary schemes, called *plans d'égalité*, would receive financial support from the state. In 1987 a further instrument, the *contrat pour la mixité des emplois*, was introduced. These contracts are designed to enable companies with less than 600 workers to receive funding from the state to help women to be recruited or promoted into posts where men make up 80 per cent of the workforce.

In addition to the application of the equality principle in these ways, the French state has also sought, particularly since the mid-1970s, to make women's parity with men in paid work a reality by addressing major sources of their inequality, such as the unequal distribution of domestic responsibilities (particularly childcare) between men and women, and by facilitating women's continuity in employment. Hence, in addition to the extensive development of state-provided child-care facilities over the post-war period,[2] labour law has also developed progressively to offer generous minimum maternity conditions for women when they have children that 'legitimize their intention to pursue employment and encourage them to remain with the same employer' (Hantrais, 1990:126).[3] Furthermore, measures developed principally in the 1980s, such as parental leave, childcare subsidies and career breaks are mainly taken by women and have become among the most generous in Europe.

As in many other EU countries in the post-war period, there has been a rapid growth in the numbers of girls in the French education system (Hantrais, 1990). Women's training programmes also saw a considerable expansion from the early 1970s (Comité d'Information Féminin, 1977; Juter-Loiseau and Guilloux, 1979). Post-war changes in the education system seeking to promote equality between women and men began in 1963 with co-education being deemed the norm, for example in *collèges d'enseignement secondaires* (one form of secondary schooling), and in 1975 the *loi Haby* introduced the obligation of mixed schooling in all primary and secondary education. Yvette Roudy included in her push for equality a promotional campaign to encourage girls to choose unconventional jobs and launched the first of a series of initiatives to make teachers and senior managers in education more aware of the inequalities faced by women. For example, the Circular of 22 July 1982 sought to raise awareness of inequalities in training between women and men. A first convention signed on 20 December 1984 between the Ministry of Education and the Ministry of Women's Rights aimed to improve women's training, career advice and entry into jobs in order to widen access to non-traditional employment (Bertrand and Bernadet, 1997). Then the law of July 1989 introduced new measures to widen access to non-traditional jobs. An agreement was made between the Secretary of State for Women's Rights and the Secretary of State for Technical Education to set up national plans to widen access from September 1990 onwards. In 1992, three-year plans were developed in each local education authority to encourage women into technical and scientific subjects. In 1996, an action programme was set up to include an awareness of gender-segregated trajectories in education in the teacher-training programme. In the same year an overhaul of school textbooks conveying out-of-date images of the sexual division of labour was undertaken.

These post-war legislative changes in women's control over their fertility and sexuality, their civil rights, improved conditions in paid work and education as well as the evolution of family structures have had a significant impact on women's rights and situation in contemporary France, but in what ways can these changes be attributed to second wave feminism?

The Role of Post-1968 Feminism

The 'big bang' for second-wave French feminism came with the May 1968 'événements', in which women participated significantly. Initially an assault on the French university system, which was perceived by 'soixante-huitards' as a reformist sausage factory providing a ready supply of unquestioning, qualified graduate fodder to be exploited within an advanced capitalist economy, May 1968 rapidly became a much wider political crisis in French society. Setting aside its broad political consequences, the ideological effects of May 1968 and women's experience of having participated in this anarchic period of French politics are more significant for our purposes here. Features of political organization during the May 1968 period and its aftermath were a rejection of hierarchical forms of organization and of conventional party politics, which were perceived as moribund and incapable of revolutionizing French society. Amid this atmosphere of political dynamism, many women began to glimpse new possibilities. Yet, as Claire Duchen has noted in her authoritative account of post-1968 French feminism, women realized quickly that any feminist revolution would not be instigated by male-dominated, radical left-wing groups because, there also, women were still confined to their traditional roles, servicing male activists who did not or would not recognize that 'the personal is political' (Duchen 1986: 6–8, 44). The Mouvement de libération des femmes (MLF) emerged, as a spontaneous collection of diverse groupings that eschewed formal organisation and hierarchy. Groups came together, mixed or women-only, to explore what it meant to be a woman in a capitalist patriarchal society and a range of feminisms emerged that rejected patriarchal-style party politics and reformist demands for 'women's rights'. Slowly, three broad tendencies came into existence, such as broadly materialist groupings, inspired by, but not aligned to, Marxism, which prioritized women's struggle against patriarchy, others rooted in French socialism who, in their fight for women's liberation, prioritized solidarity with the working class to fight capitalism (known as the 'tendance lutte des classes' or 'class struggle tendency') and a third grouping, 'psychanalyse et politique', which advocated the existence of a repressed female difference that would emerge once 'phallocratic' society had been dismantled.[4] This group of sexual differentialists, founded by Antoinette Fouque, declared itself regularly to be opposed to feminism, which it saw as a reformist attempt to replace men with women in society without dismantling the phallogocentric symbolic order or patriarchal discourse which operates through individual and collective unconscious practices and cultural habits to enforce patriarchal gender codes.

One of the key successes of the post-1968 feminist period was the campaign for abortion, which was conducted through a series of rallies and high-profile political actions, such as the 'Manifeste des 343'. This was published by *Le Nouvel Observateur* and in *Le Monde* on 5 April 1971, as a manifesto declaring that 343 activists, film stars, writers and public figures had broken the law and had had an abortion. Slowly, a campaign to legalize abortion got off the ground, orchestrated by figures such as Christine Delphy, Anne Zelensky and Gisèle Halimi and supported by Simone de Beauvoir and other well-known public figures. This resulted in the legalization of abortion in 1974 in the first ten weeks of pregnancy for a trial period of five years and in 1979, the law was given permanent status.

Meanwhile, other actions took place in the early 1970s, which were small but significant steps in the second-wave feminist struggle in France – such as the two-day rally on 13–14 May 1972 in Paris denouncing crimes against women, which drew over 5,000 women, some of whom testified to their experiences of male violence, sexuality and motherhood. Rape crisis centres and women's refuges were set up as well as a plethora of feminist newspapers and journals in which feminist political ideas were debated. Yet within the disparate groupings that constituted the MLF, there was much dissent and division over the most strategic way forward and deeply rooted fundamental differences emerged between factions such as 'psych' et po' and radical materialist feminists, such as Delphy, over notions of gender identity and women's situation in society more gene- rally. As Claire Duchen has argued, these ideological differences between various factions of the MLF in the 1970s fell broadly into three areas: the relation of women's struggle to the class struggle and the roots of women's oppression more generally, the existence (or not) of sexual difference and, lastly, the relative merits of heterosexuality and lesbianism as political strategies in patriarchal society (Duchen 1986: 18–25). By the mid-1970s, the MLF was increasingly fragmented, particularly after the success of the abortion campaign and in 1979, in a bizarre reactionary move, the 'psych' et po' tendency appropriated the MLF name as their trademark and registered the MLF as their company property.

It has been suggested that the second-wave feminist movement did not directly contribute to supporting the laws of the 1960s and 1970s emancipating women within the family, or make specific demands in support of independent women as regards family policy, because many revolutionary feminist subgroups eschewed legal change as a means of improving women's lot (Jenson, 1993). However, such a position perhaps fails to understand the radical critique of patriarchal structures and discourse implicit in post-1968 radical feminist politics, which largely rejected the reformist approach to fighting for women's rights pursued in France in the first half of the twentieth century (Duchen, 1986: 2–4).

It also overlooks the dearth of women in the upper echelons of the French political and legal infrastructure in the 1960s and 1970s who might argue for such legal reforms (Laubier, 1990: 75). Jenson argues, however, that the post-1968 feminist movement *was* influential in raising the consciousness of women as a group rather than as simply asexual members of the proletariate (Jenson, 1993).

This consciousness raising was evident in feminist direct action and in women's increased cultural production in the 1970s (Fallaize, 1993: 16–19). The 'clivage' between sexual differentialist and materialist feminisms was manifest in women's literary and theoretical writing from the 1970s onwards. During the 1970s, and into the early 1980s, there was a proliferation both of realist, testimonial literature by women exploring their lives as lovers, mothers, daughters, and writers and of texts that sought to explore women's psycho-social difference through experimental attempts to write the body in 'écriture féminine'. Simultaneously, a rich corpus of theoretical writing developed. Figures such as Hélène Cixous, Luce Irigaray and Julia Kristeva sought to theorize in their different ways how the feminine and the maternal might be reconceptualized to subvert phallogocentric notions of woman as 'other'. For, as Duchen has argued, 'it is as important to dismantle the givens of phallogocentric discourse as it is to demystify the structures of patriarchy' (Duchen, 1986: 84).

Since the 1970s, French radical materialist feminists, such as Monique Wittig, have provided inspiring fictional and theoretical critiques of the political institution of hetero-patriarchy, while Christine Delphy and other radical materialist feminists have continued to theorize the political workings of patriarchy and analyse diverse aspects of women's condition in politically influential and long-running journals such as *Nouvelles Questions Féministes*.

At the turn of the new millennium, feminist struggle and polemic are by no means moribund in France, as the recent debates surrounding measures to ensure political parity between women and men in the national parliamentary assemblies have demonstrated. But, as we will see, there is still much to fight for to ensure women's equal status in all areas of French society. The legislative advances and broader ideological shifts delineated above have ensured significant changes in women's situation in France, although these changes are not uniformly positive ones. Indeed, Christine Delphy has argued recently that any notion of continuous progress in women's situation constitutes a lie perpetuated by prevailing patriarchal ideology. Delphy notes evidence of a virulent backlash against women ensuring that their situation is increasingly precarious in the context of wider economic regression and greater social inequality (Rodgers, 1998: 119–20). So, what exactly is the situation of women in contemporary France?

Argument of the Book

The present collection of essays provides detailed evidence of women's position in French society. In the first six chapters, women's roles in areas such as paid work, unpaid work and leisure, media, politics, language and writing are explored. These areas have been chosen as key domains in which women's autonomy and representation in French society can be effectively measured and analysed. In the subsequent chapters, the situations of three specific groups of women are explored, namely, immigrant and ethnic minority women, lesbians, and rural women, with a view to portraying aspects of the condition of women in various minority groups in France.

In Chapter One, Abigail Gregory explores the situation of women in paid work in order to chart areas of progress in recent years and issues of concern. The chapter firstly examines perhaps the most optimistic feature of recent changes in women's position in paid work – growing activity rates – before moving onto issues of continuing concern: rising unemployment levels, the growth in atypical employment and continuing job segregation and pay inequality. Gregory argues that the situation for French women in the labour market is a mixed one, and that changes at national and supra-national levels as we enter the new millennium may present both new threats and new opportunities for Frenchwomen.

In Chapter Two, Jan Windebank examines a key and often neglected dimension of Frenchwomen's work – their unpaid work – and its relationship to leisure. She initially explores the issue of measuring women's unpaid work and leisure in contemporary French society. Then she outlines the poverty of leisure time confronting Frenchwomen, which is explained through a detailed analysis of both unpaid domestic work and community work. Windebank argues that women's entry into paid employment, far from being liberatory, has actually led to a triple burden on women of increasing responsibility for employment but little or no reduction in their unpaid domestic and community work commitments.

The third chapter contains a wide-ranging analysis of women in the media. Maggie Allison looks at the relative lack of visibility of women in the mainstream media over recent decades in France. She analyses how women continue to be subjected to sexist stereotyping and sexual harassment as a result of the non-application of existing legislation and prevailing masculinism. These are explored with reference to the 'esprit gaulois' phenomenon, which implicitly promotes the denigration of women and the myth of male sexual omnipotence, objectifying all women as available to the mediatized and sexualized male gaze. Allison then surveys how such sexist attitudes are reinforced or challenged in the mainstream and alternative women's press. Finally, she looks at women's media presence in the 1995 presidential election and the 1997 legislative election and at women's broader activity across the media sector with particular reference to the Association des Femmes Journalistes.

In Chapter Four, Máire Cross explores the role of women in French political life. She analyses why there are so few women politicians in the French political system. Tracing women's role in the modern French Republican system, she analyses the particularity of the French Republican universalist tradition, which has militated against women's presence in the political forum. Concentrating on women's recent attempts to break through the glass ceiling inherent in the political structure, Cross argues that, in the parity debates of the 1990s, the notion of universalism has been exploited both in favour of and in opposition to women's presence in political life. Recent attempts to bring more women into politics by Giscard d'Estaing, Mitterand and Chirac are charted as distinctive bids by successive presidents to be seen as modernizers of French democracy. Cross analyses the recent exceptional measure of inscribing the notion of political parity between women and men into the text of the Constitution and she questions how parity will be implemented in the near future to ensure an end to discrimination against women in political life.

In Chapter Five, Kate Beeching explores how language and gender are interrelated in French, focusing particularly on recent debates regarding the feminization of job titles and gender asymmetries in references to women and men. She then analyses the relationship between grammatical gender and the assumption and 'playing out' of psycho-social gender identity, with reference to the growing field of empirical studies of language and gender within sociolinguistics. She argues in conclusion that differences in women's and men's speech patterns are related to how they perform gender roles within specific social contexts.

Gill Rye then analyses some key thematics in women's writing in the 1990s in Chapter Six. Focusing on full-length fiction, Rye offers a snapshot of the concerns of both established and new women writers, namely mother–daughter relationships, sexuality, love and memory. In Paule Constant's *La Fille du Gobernator* (1994), set in French Guiana in the 1920s, Rye analyses the mother–daughter dynamic through Constant's exploitation of narrative technique. In Clotilde Escalle's *Pulsion* (1996) and Marie Darieussecq's *Truismes* (1996), Rye focuses on contemporary representations of women's erotic experience and the related problematics of women writers' negotiation of violence and pornography. In recent texts by Hélène Cixous, *Déluge* (1992), *Beethoven à jamais ou l'existence de Dieu* (1993) and *La Fiancée juive de la tentation* (1995), Rye then analyses Cixous's meditations on love and its loss which exploit a variety of narrative forms in which the diverse experiences which make up loving relationships are creatively staged. Finally, issues of memory and selfhood are foregrounded in Christiane Baroche's *La Rage au bois dormant* (1995).

In Chapter Seven, Jane Freedman focuses on the situation of immigrant and ethnic minority women in contemporary France. She highlights some of the difficulties faced by these distinctly heterogeneous groups in French society and discusses some of the strategies that they have adopted to ease their social integration. She then analyses two recent issues, the questions of the *sans-papiers* and the *affaire des foulards* (the question of whether Muslim girls should be permitted to wear the Islamic headscarf at school, thereby challenging the Republican principle of *laïcité* or secularism). Freedman argues that these debates have raised complex issues for immigrant women and for gender relations within ethnic minority communities in France pertaining to identity, visibility and exclusion.

In Chapter Eight, Ursula Tidd analyses recent events in the post-1968 history of French lesbians and surveys contemporary aspects of their situation. Initially situating her discussion in the context of Beauvoir's pioneering analysis of 'la lesbienne' in *Le Deuxième Sexe*, Tidd sketches French lesbians' involvement in second-wave feminism as well as in the post-1968 burgeoning gay movement in France. She then surveys lesbian political and cultural activity in the 1990s before providing a brief critique of the PaCS partnership agreement in terms of how it affects the status of lesbians in contemporary France.

In Chapter Nine, Marion Demossier examines the role of contemporary women in rural France in the light of recent changes in agricultural economy and society. At a time when only 5 per cent of the active population in France are employed in agriculture and differences between rural and urban lifestyles and values are diminishing, Demossier analyses women's changing roles in the evolving rural community. Despite the persistence of traditional gender roles in the context of the division of labour, in rural economic organizations and in family structures and inheritance practices, she argues that more women are playing a major role in rural development in France. Indeed, women are often the key agents of change as they act as mediators between rural life and wider social forces.[5]

Notes

1. Mariette Sineau (1992) seeks to explain the slower access of French women to the right to vote and to civil rights compared with women in the UK in terms of: the earlier industrialization of the UK, which, requiring women to work outside the home, necessitated giving rights to married women independently of their husbands; the effect of the Protestant tradition seeking to protect individual rights and the role of the feminist movement in the UK in fighting for women's emancipation; the impact of different law traditions whereby the Common Law tradition as a regulator of conflicts lends itself less easily to intervention into people's private lives than does the French Code Civil of 1804, which, she argues, intervenes into private lives and, in so doing, seals women's position as subordinate to men, M. Sineau, in G. Duby and M.Perrot (eds) *L'Histoire des femmes en occident, tome V, le XXe siècle*, Paris: Plon, 477.

2. Explanations for the development of childcare facilities in France cannot, however, be reduced to issues of equality alone. France has a long history of childcare out of the home, which is explained in part by the state's desire to take the raising of children out of the hands of the Church and to provide them with a secular education (Lelièvre and Lelièvre, 1991). The number of nursery schools in France was not initially expanded to meet the needs of working mothers because, since the 1950s, a 'political and professional consensus on the social benefits of universal provision for three to six year olds' existed, well before the growth in the number of working mothers occurred (Walters, 1978:10).

3. In 1966 dismissal for pregnancy was prohibited and paid maternity leave for all women was extended to fourteen weeks (six weeks before the birth and eight after). In 1971, a collective agreement on maternity pay was reached, which guaranteed generous maternity pay (see Hantrais, 1990). Since 1988, maternity leave has been counted as a period of employment in estimating length of service and cannot be used as a pretext for reducing service benefits and bonus payments.

When women return to work after maternity leave, they must be reinstated in their previous position and cannot be made redundant during the first four weeks.

4. For a detailed account of these main tendencies of the MLF, see Claire Duchen's definitive study, *Feminism in France, from May '68 to Mitterand*, pp. 27–47.

5. We would like to thank Jennifer Birkett for her helpful comments on an earlier draft of this introduction.

References

Allwood, G. and Wadia, K. (2000 forthcoming) *Women and Politics in the Fifth French Republic*, London: Routledge.

Aubin, C. and Gisserot, H. (1994) *Les femmes en France: 1985–95. Rapport établi par la France en voie de la 4e conférence mondiale sur les femmes*, Paris: La Documentation Française.

Baudelot, C. and Establet, R. (1992), *Allez les filles!*, Paris: Seuil.

Bertrand, F. and Bernadet, R. (1997) 'Agir pour l'égalité de chacun entre filles et garçons', in CEREQ, *Femmes sur le marché du travail. L'autre relation formation-emploi*, no. 70, Marseilles: CEREQ, 23–34.

Bielanski, H. (1994) *New Forms of Work and Activity. Surevy of Experience at Establishment Level in Eight European Countries*, Dublin: European Foundation for the Improvement of Living and Working Conditions.

Bihr, A. and Pfefferkorn, R. (1996) *Hommes/Femmes: l'Introuvable égalité*, Paris: Les Editions de l'Atelier.

Bourdieu, P. (1998) *La Domination masculine*, Paris: Seuil.

Butler, J. (1990) *Gender Trouble, Feminism and the Subversion of Identity*, London: Routledge.

—— (1993) *Bodies That Matter, On the Discursive Limits of Sex*, London: Routledge.

Comité d'Information Féminin (1977) 'Mesures prévues en faveur de la réinsertion professionnelle des mères de famille', November.

Cook, M. and Davie, G. (eds) *Modern France: Society in Transition*, London and New York: Routledge.

Dex, S. Walters, P. and Alden, D.M. (1993) *French and British Mothers at Work*, London: Macmillan.

Duchen, C. (1986) *Feminism in France, from May '68 to Mitterand*, London: Routledge & Kegan Paul.

Fallaize, E. (1993) *French Women's Writing: Recent Fiction*, Basingstoke: Macmillan.

Frischer, D. (1997) *La Revanche des Misogynes. Où en sont les femmes après trente ans de féminisme?,* Paris: Albin Michel.

Frisque, C. (1997) *L'Objet femme*, Ministère de l'Emploi et de la solidarité, Service des droits des femmes, Paris: La Documentation française.

Giroud, F. (1999) *Les Françaises de la Gauloise à la pilule*, Paris: Fayard.

Gregory, A. and Windebank, J. (2000) *Women and Work in Britain and France: Practice, Theory and Policy*, London: Macmillan.

Guigou, E. (1997) *Etre femme en politique*, Paris: Plon.

Halberstam, J. (1998) *Female Masculinity*, Durham and London: Duke University Press.

Halimi, G. (1997) *La nouvelle cause des femmes*, Paris: Seuil.

Hantrais, L. (1990) *Managing professional and family life: a comparative study of British and French women*, Dartmouth Publising, Aldershot.

—— (1995) *Social Policy in the European Union*, London: Macmillan.

—— (1999) 'Paid and unpaid work', in M. Cook and G. Davie (eds) *Modern France: Society in Transition*, London and New York: Routledge, 115–31.

Héritier, F. (1996) *Masculin, Féminin, la pensée de la différence*, Paris, Odile Jacob.

Hirata, H. and Senotier, D. (1996) (eds) *Femmes et partage du travail*, Paris: Syros.

Holmes, D. (1996) *French Women's Writing 1848–1994*, London: Athlone.

Jardine, A. (1979) 'Interview with Simone de Beauvoir' in *Signs: Journal of Women in Culture and Society*, vol. 5, no. 2: 227.

Jenson, J., Hagen, E. and Reddy, C. (1988) (eds) *Feminization of the Labour Force, Paradoxes and Promises*, Cambridge: Polity.

Jenson, J. (1993) 'Représentations des rapports sociaux de sexe dans trois domaines politiques en France', in A. Gautier and J. Heinen (eds) *Le Sexe des politiques sociales*, Paris: Côté-femmes, 25–36.

Jenson, J. and Sineau, M. (1995) *Mitterrand et les Françaises. Un rendez-vous manqué*, Paris: Presses de Sciences Po.

Juter-Loiseau, A. and Guilloux, P. (1979) 'Réflexions sur la formation professionnelle continue des femmes à la recherche d'un travail', *Droit Social*, no. 11, November, 435–46.

La Documentation Française (1993) *L'emploi des femmes, Actes de la journée d'études du 4 mars 1993*, Paris: La Documentation Française.

Lagrave, R.-M. (1992) 'Une émancipation sous tutelle, éducation et travail des femmes au XX siècle', in G. Duby and M. Perrot (eds) *L'Histoire des femmes en occident, vol. 5, le XXe siècle*, Paris: Plon, 431–62.

Lang, J. (1995) *Demain les femmes*, Paris: Grasset.

Lanquetin, M.-T., Laufer, J. and Letablier, M.-T. (1999) 'From Equality to Reconciliation in France?', in L. Hantrais (ed.) *Social Policy in the European Union*, London: Macmillan, 53–65.

Laubier, C. (1990) (ed.) *The Condition of Women in France, 1945 to the Present, a Documentary Anthology*, London, Routledge.

Lelièvre, F. and Lelièvre, C. (1991) *Histoire de la scolarisation des filles*, Nathan: Paris.

Maruani, M. (1998) (ed.) *Les nouvelles frontières de l'inégalité. Hommes et femmes sur le marché du travail*, Paris: Mage/La Découverte.

Maclean, M. (1998) (ed.) *The Mitterrand Years. Legacy and Evaluation*, London: Macmillan.

Ministère du Travail (1978) Note à l'attention des membres de la Commission 'harmonisation vie familiale-vie professionnelle', Comité du Travail Féminin, Note 11-5Cm, 1 September.

Mouchtouris, A. (1994) *Le Féminin Rural. Aspirations sociales et culturelles*, Paris: L'Harmattan.

Pitrou, A. (1996) 'Le Mythe de la famille et du familial', in J-C. Kaufmann (ed.) *Faire ou faire-faire? famille et services*, Rennes: Presses Universitaires de Rennes.

Premier Ministre (1969) 'L'Emploi Féminin et le VIe plan', Secrétariat général du Comité Interministériel de la formation professionnelle et de la promotion sociale, 7 July.

Prost, A. (1984) 'L'Évolution de la politique familiale en France et 1938 à 1981', *Mouvement Social*, no. 129.

Reynolds, S. (1998) 'Women and political representation during the Mitterrand presidence – or the family romance of the Fifth Republic', in M. Maclean (1998) (ed.) *The Mitterrand Years. Legacy and Evaluation*, London: Macmillan, 185–97.

Rodgers, C. (1998) (ed.) *Le Deuxième Sexe de Simone de Beauvoir, un héritage admiré et contesté*, Paris: L'Harmattan.

—— (1999) 'Gender' in M. Cook and G. Davie (eds) *Modern France: Society in Transition*, London and New York: Routledge, 53–72.

Rubery, J. (1988) (ed.) *Women and Recession*, London: Routledge & Kegan Paul.

Sellers, S. (1991) *Language and Sexual Difference: Feminist Writing in France*, London: Macmillan.

Serdjénian, E. (ed.) *Femmes et médias*, Paris: L'Harmattan.

Sineau, M. (1992) in G. Duby and M. Perrot (eds) *L'Histoire des femmes en occident, tome V, le XXe siècle*, Paris: Plon, 477.

Singy, P. (ed.) (1998) *Les Femmes et la langue. L'insécurité linguistique en question*, Lausanne: Delachaux et Niestlé.

Walters, P. (1978) 'Pre-school Care in France', *SSRC Newsletter*, November, 38, 9–11.

Wittig, M. (1992) 'One is not born a Woman' in *The Straight Mind and Other Essays*, Hemel Hempstead: Harvester Wheatsheaf, 9–20.

Yaguello, M. (1991), *En écoutant parler la langue,* Paris: Seuil.

Yaguello, M. (1998), *Petits faits de langue,* Paris: Seuil.

–1–

Women in Paid Work
Abigail Gregory

France is often hailed as a country where women, and particularly mothers, are well-placed in paid work by comparison with many of its European counterparts, a situation that is often attributed to the impact of the state's policies (education, family, employment and labour market regulation). Indeed, a large body of cross-national comparative work, in particular comparing Britain and France, would tend to support this relatively optimistic view (Barrère-Maurisson, Daune-Richard and Letablier, 1989; Beechey, 1989; Blackwell, 1998; Dex, Walters and Aden, 1993; Gregory, 1987, 1989; Hantrais, 1990; Lane, 1993; Rubery, Smith, Fagan and Grimshaw, 1996; Rubery, Smith and Fagan in collaboration with Almond and Parker, 1996a). In this chapter the aim is to explore the situation of women in paid work in France in order to draw attention to areas of progress in recent years and to issues of concern. In so doing an attempt will be made to explain this state of affairs.

A few words should also be said about methodological issues. The chapter focuses on paid work in the formal economy, paid informal work being extremely difficult to chart accurately. National statistics are, in most cases, drawn from the French *Enquête sur L'Emploi* published by INSEE. However, where comparisons are made with other EU member states the Eurostat *Labour Force Survey* is used in order to attempt to reduce problems of comparison. Finally, in describing the contemporary position of French women in paid work this account focuses mainly on trends over the period 1993–8. In addition, where appropriate, an understanding of trends over a longer period is offered.

The chapter begins by describing perhaps the most optimistic feature of recent changes in women's position in paid work – growing activity rates – before moving onto issues of continuing concern: rising unemployment levels, the growth in atypical employment, and ongoing job segregation and pay inequality.

Grounds for Optimism: Women's Increasing Activity Rates

Women's activity rates in France have risen steadily since the late 1960s, even through periods of recession (Hantrais, 1990: 73). This trend corresponds with an increasing salarization of the workforce and, in common with most industrialized countries, a shift in women's employment from agriculture and industry to the services.

By 1997, according to the *Labour Force Survey*, activity rates for women in France, defined as the total number of women in the labour force aged fifteen or over as a percentage of the female population of working age, had reached 48.2 per cent (OOPEC, 1998: Table 003). These levels exceed the average of the EU15 countries (of 45.6 per cent) and place France among the countries with the highest female activity levels in the EU. French levels must be considered to be particularly high given the very significant proportion of women in full-time education in the 15–24 age group (as discussed below). However, these figures relate to all women and do not reflect the considerable diversity in activity levels in France by ethnic group. For example, in 1998 levels in France were below the national average for the female immigrant population as a whole (aged fifteen and over) according to the *Enquête sur L'emploi* (INSEE, 1998: Tables PA01 and PA18): 43.9 per cent compared with 47.6 per cent.

In the 1990s the dominant model in France is one of high levels of participation for women independently of age, family circumstances, social background and region (Letablier, 1995). The French documentation is categorical that women's entry into the labour force is an irreversible fact (Commaille, 1993; Letablier, 1995; Nicole-Drancourt, 1996). Nevertheless, although the overall trend has been of rising activity rates for women, economic activity is strongly influenced by education levels (Coutrot, Fournier, Kieffer and Lelièvre, 1997) and is correlated with whether women are in activity or not: women with few or no educational qualifications are more likely to be out of the labour force, whereas university graduates are more likely to be economically active.[1]

Moreover, activity rates have not risen at the same speed in all age groups (see Table 1.1). Activity rates have fallen significantly for women aged under twenty-five, a trend that shows evidence of continuing (Gissot and Meron, 1996). This reflects in part the growing participation of French women in education between the ages of fifteen and twenty-four (63.1 per cent of women in this age group were in education in France in 1997 compared with 49.4 per cent in the EU15, although differing definitions of 'education' across the EU render comparison hazardous (OOPEC, 1998: Table 002)).

Table 1.1 Activity Rates for Women by Age Group, France, 1993–8 (per cent)

	1993	1998
15–24	29.3	25
25–39	77.8	77.9
40–49	76.8	80
50–59	55.8	63.2
60+	4.6	3.7

Source: INSEE (1998) *Enquête sur l'Emploi,* Paris: INSEE: Table PA01.

On the other hand, for women aged 25–49 activity levels have increased since the early 1980s, reflecting an increasing concentration of paid work and family responsibilities in this age group (Letablier, 1995). Activity rates during the family formation period in France are now among the highest in the EU15 (78.6 per cent) after Denmark, Finland and Sweden (respectively 83.7 per cent, 84.7 per cent and 85.8 per cent) according to the 1997 *Labour Force Survey.*[2] A 1990 Eurobarometer survey of women aged 22–60 (Kempeneers and Lelièvre, 1993) found that French women were more likely to have no interruption in employment (sixty-three per cent) than EU women overall and a significantly smaller proportion stated that they stopped work for good when they had children (16.3 per cent cf 23.8 per cent for the EU12). However there is also evidence, albeit rather dated, that French mothers may be polarized into a group that works fairly continuously and a group that does not work at all (Dex et al., 1993).

Activity levels are particularly high among single mothers, a rapidly expanding household type in France:[3] the majority (70.8 per cent) of single mothers were economically active in 1998 (INSEE, 1998: Table MEN01) and rates of activity have been increasing in the 1990s (Lefaucheur and Martin, 1995, 1997), although so too have their unemployment rates. Activity rates for other groups of single women with no children were much lower in 1998: 62.4 per cent for single women with no children, 57.5 per cent for divorcees and other groups; 7.2 per cent for widowers (INSEE, 1998: MEN 07). Single mothers are not only more likely to be employed than partnered ones – they are also less likely to work part-time: fifteen per cent compared with twenty per cent in 1992 – (Bradshaw, Kennedy, Kilkey, Hutton, Corden, Eardley, Holmes and Neale, 1996: 8).

The increased continuity in mothers' employment across their lives can be attributed to a large extent to the state's efforts to promote women's freedom of choice to have children and to engage in paid work, a policy made explicit in the mid 1970s. Women's ability to reconcile paid work with family responsibilities has been developed through three mutually reinforcing strands of policy: child protection policy leading to the development of state childcare facilities and nurseries (Lanquetin, Laufer and Letablier, 1999); reform in family law to recognize women's dual roles of worker and mother (Lanquetin et al. 1999) and finally, employment law and policies to encourage women's entry into the workforce (Fernandez, 1982) and their continuity in employment (Hantrais, 1990). Most recently, for example, mothers have benefited from employment policy, which has given financial incentives to employers creating 'caring' (cleaning, childcare etc.) jobs through family employment (*emplois familiaux*) and local employment (*emplois de proximité*) (Bailly, 1996; Zilberman, 1995) initiatives. They thus facilitate the continuous employment of their employers, many of whom are women. In addition to the support framework for working mothers described above, single mothers are given financial incentives to engage in paid work by the limitation of the period over which non-contributory benefits are paid and by making subsequent benefits (such as the *Revenu Minimum d'Insertion*) (a 'safety net', financial benefit designed to help the most deprived) dependent on the willingness to actively seek employment (Hantrais, 1993). The availability of extensive public childcare facilities and a culture accepting of paid work for mothers also helps explain the high activity rates of single mothers in France (Millar, 1994).

Despite the rise in activity rates in the longer term, the rate of increase has slowed in recent years, and there is recent evidence that the impact of the extension of the *Congé Parental d'Education* (child-raising leave) to families with two or more children (from those with three or more) has led to a fall in economic activity rates for mothers with two children (Afsa, 1996). The application of this policy has caused some authors (Fagnani, 1998) to accuse the French state of using family policy as an employment policy to incite women to leave the labour market and hence reduce unemployment levels.

Among women aged 50–59 activity rates have increased recently, whereas the rate for women aged sixty and over has fallen considerably (Bosch, Dawkins, and Michon, 1994: Table 6). The 1980s saw the introduction of a series of early retirement measures (*Contrats de Solidarité – Réduction du temps de travail*) and the imposition of a retirement age for men and women of sixty (in 1983), which together had a considerable impact on activity rates in the over sixties (Holcblat, 1998: 78). Activity rates in the 50–64 age group nevertheless remain relatively high in France by EU standards (42.8 per cent compared with 39.4 per cent in 1997), a difference reflecting perhaps the tradition of paid work among French women.

Threats to Women's Position in Paid Work: Rising Unemployment Levels

Women's activity rates have been increasing since the mid 1980s in France, but the proportion of women present in the workforce has been relatively stable. The consequence of this situation has been rising unemployment levels (Gauvin, 1995): they rose substantially in the 1980s, with the rate of increase slowing in recent years. According to the BIT definition of unemployment,[4] 13.8 per cent of economically active French women were unemployed in 1998 (INSEE, 1998: Table DEMO2). In 1997 women's unemployment rates in France were the fifth highest in the EU15 (OOPEC, 1998: Table 009), although it should be borne in mind that unemployment levels are subject to problems of comparison (Hantrais and Letablier, 1996). Once again, the averaged figures mask considerable fluctuation according to women's marital status and ethnic group. According to the *Labour Force Survey*, 25.2 per cent of households with children under fifteen, headed by a woman were unemployed in 1997 compared with 10.2 per cent of all private households (OOPCS, 1998: Table 115). Unemployment rates are also much higher among the ethnic minority population. The 1998 *Enquête Emploi* showed that unemployment rates were 23.5 per cent for ethnic minority women aged fifteen and over but only 13.8 per cent for all women, although the rate for ethnic minority women had fallen somewhat since 1990 (INSEE, 1008:Table DEMO2).

The evidence suggests that it is now harder for women than men to find jobs in France, a situation common to most EU countries, particularly in younger age groups (see Table 1.2). In addition to having higher levels of unemployment French women also remain in unemployment for longer periods than men. Unemployment varies with qualification levels for women (and men), creating a polarization between qualified and unqualified women (see Table 1.3).

Various explanations have been offered for France's high unemployment rates for women: the disproportionate impact of recession in the 1980s on women's employment in textiles (Tomasini, 1994); the growth of part-time jobs, which are relatively unattractive, in the service sector where women's employment is concentrated (Barrère-Maurisson, Daune-Richard and Letablier, 1987); women's direct competition with men for

Table 1.2 Proportion of Women Unemployed
by Age Group, France, 1998

	%
15–24	30
25–49	13.3
50+	9.2

Source: INSEE (1998) *Enquête sur l'Emploi*, Paris:
INSEE: table DEMO3bis.

Table 1.3 Proportion Unemployed by Educational Level, Women aged 15+

Qualification*	Unemployment level (%)
Diplôme supérieur	8.5
Bac plus 2 further years of study	7.8
Bac, brevet professionnel/other qualification at this level	12.8
CAP, BEP/other qualification of this level	14.4
BEPC only	14.3
No qualification	19.3

Source: INSEE (1998) *Enquête sur l'Emploi*, Paris: INSEE: table DEMO3.
* Diplôme supérieur = higher level qualification;
Baccalauréat (bac)/brevet professionnel = 'A' Level standard qualifications (academic or vocational);
CAP/BEP=Diplomas of Vocational Education; BEPC= GCSE level qualification.

qualified full-time jobs (contrasting with countries like the UK, where many women return to work after having children into part-time low-skilled jobs with poor conditions of employment where they no longer compete directly with men); the high proportions of women in education and in early retirement, which close down some alternative routes out of the labour market in times of recession (Gauvin, 1995), and the tendency of women to remain job seekers during recession (whereas previously women – in couples in particular – would be discouraged from job seeking – Gauvin, 1995).

The Growth of 'Atypical' Working

The notion of 'atypical' work, often called precarious work or contingent working, has been the subject of academic and popular debate since the early 1980s, when its growth became marked in Western industrialized countries (De Grip, Hoevenberg and Willems, 1997). As Hantrais and Letablier (1995: 22–4) point out, the contours of precarity vary from country to country as it is an analytical concept whose parameters are defined by national regulation of paid work. In France, however, it is taken to mean paid work outside the norm of full-time permanent employment and refers to part-time working and temporary work in all its guises. I will now examine each of these areas in turn.

The Growth of Part-time Work

Part-time workers in France are currently defined as those working one-fifth shorter hours than the normal working time or the legally allowed maximum of thirty-nine hours or any lesser number of hours specified in collective agreements.[5] The growth of part-time work in France began rather belatedly in the 1970s (this is explained by Garnsey, 1985; Gregory and O'Reilly, 1996 and Barrère-Maurisson et al., 1989). Then part-time rates rose gradually from 1982–7 and, after stabilizing until 1992, rose steeply thereafter (Conseil supérieur de l'emploi, des revenus et des coûts, 1998; Husson, 1996; Le Corre, 1995). According to the *Labour Force Survey* part-time levels had nearly reached the average for the EU15 countries in 1997 (16.8 per cent in France compared with 16.9 per cent in the EU15). This growth in part-time work since the 1980s has been mainly among women (81.8 per cent of all part-time employees in France were women in 1998 according to the *Enquête sur l'emploi* (INSEE, 1998: Table PA03), although levels have risen rapidly for men since the mid 1980s, albeit from low levels (in 1998 5.6 per cent of economically active men worked part time) (see Table 1.4).

In Western economies, including France, the growth in part-time work since the 1970s has been driven by employers' demands for increased flexibility in worktime schedules (Bielanski, 1994) and has been facilitated by technical innovation, increased unemployment and hence weaker union resistance in Western economies since the mid-1970s (Bosch et al., 1994). Some authors also argue that there has been a parallel growth in employees' aspirations for more leisure time (Bielanski, 1994) and greater individual control over working hours or 'time sovereignty', stimulated by the growing diversification in working time schedules (Fagan, 1998).

Table 1.4 Proportion Working Part-time by Sex (%)

	Men	Women	Men and Women
1993	4.1	26.3	13.9
1998	5.6	31.6	17.3

Source: INSEE (1998) *Enquêtes sur l'emploi 1993 and 1998*, Paris: INSEE: Table PA12.

In France, pressures to create part-time jobs, deriving from preoccupations with unemployment and/or worktime flexibility since the 1980s, have led to explicit government measures to encourage the development of this form of work. After moves to collectively reduce working time at the beginning of the 1980s with the aim of reducing unemployment, pressure to improve the competitiveness of French companies in a global market place changed the focus in the mid-1980s to one of improving the flexibility of working time. Rising unemployment levels at the end of the 1980s, however, brought a return to the debate over work sharing, and a series of measures starting with those seeking to increase the use of part-time work, and then measures to link reductions in working time to job creation and flexibility in working time (in the context of *Loi Quinquennale sur L'Emploi* (the 1993 Five Year Employment Law)). Then, the *Loi Robien* of 11 June 1996 was passed, which sought to link job creation or job maintenance in the private sector with collective reductions in working time, through the introduction of multiple forms of working-time flexibility (Girard, 1997). The law of 19 May 1998 introducing the thirty-five hour week has also sought to achieve similar objectives. Recent measures have included an important financial incentive for employers to use part-time workers: firstly through reductions in employers' national insurance contributions for the employment of part timers and secondly through similar reductions for the employment of lower paid workers (for a full description of these measures, see Gregory and Windebank, 2000). A greater decentralization in negotiations over working time, encouraged by the government from the early 1980s, has also played an important role in the process of development of part-time work,[6] as has the growth of *les contrats aidés* (various forms of state-subsidized employment contracts) and particularly the *contrat emploi-solidarité* (a state-aided contract offered to the public sector, which gives a financial incentive for specific groups of the unemployed – young, long-term unemployed – to enter employment on a part-time temporary contract) (Conseil supérieur de l'emploi, des revenus et des coûts, 1998; Gaye and LeCorre, 1998).

In France the rate of part-time working varies over the lifecourse. There has been a substantial increase in part-time working over the period 1993-98 among young people, particularly by women (see Table 1.5) (Conseil Supérieur de l'emploi, des revenus et des coûts, 1998). This has often been the result of the government employment initiatives (Coutrot et al., 1997). Young people take part-time jobs as a means of obtaining their first employment and experience in a labour market that is particularly unwelcoming for them, a feature explained in part by the dominance of

Table 1.5 Proportion of women working part-time by age (%)

Age group	1993	1998
15–24	31.5	42.1
25–39	25.1	31.2
40–49	25.0	30.6
50–59	28.2	29.6
60 +	33.6	38.1

Source: INSEE (1998) *Enquête sur L'Emploi*, Paris: INSEE: Table PA13.

the rules of the internal market for recruitment into French firms (Jeder-Madiot and Ponthieux, 1996; Marsden,1989; Meron and Minni, 1996). In France there has also been an increase in part-time levels for older women (50–64), one explanation for which being the implementation of the early-retirement schemes described earlier (see Table 1.5).

In France part-time rates are relatively low in the years when many women are likely to be carrying their heaviest childcare responsibilities (31.2 per cent), although rates of part-time working are rising in this age group (see Table 1.5). Unlike the situation in the UK, part-time work in France does not seem to be used extensively to return to employment after a break for childbirth (Coutrot et al., 1997).

Nevertheless, French mothers do adapt the extent of part-time working to the age of their youngest child (Dex et al., 1993) (see Table 1.6), but the correlation between the two is weak (Coutrot et al., 1997). Rather, in France, size of family has a greater effect than age of youngest child on levels of part-time work for mothers, with the likelihood of working part-time rather than full time increasing significantly for mothers with three or more children (Coutrot et al., 1997). This is explained in part by the fact that there is a strong financial incentive to work part-time in larger families as non-income-related family allowances are greater for such families, with the benefit rate increasing sharply at the birth of third and subsequent children.

The stage in the life cycle is not the only factor to be related to the recourse to part-time work in France. There is also a correlation between educational levels and the incidence of part-time working. Women who have qualifications higher than the *baccalauréat* (equivalent of the British 'A' Levels) are 1.5 times more likely to work full-time than part-time. By contrast, women with no qualifications are 1.6 times more likely to work part-time than full-time (Coutrot et al., 1997: 149). However, women with higher education are more likely to work part-time than to be out of the

Table 1.6 Full and Part-time Levels by Age of Youngest Child, Mothers, France, 1991

	< 3 years	3–5 years
Full time	36.3	41.6
Part time	13.6	17.9
Percentage part-time/full-time and part-time	27.2	16.8

Source: INSEE (1992) *Les enfants de moins de six ans*, Paris: INSEE: section 3.2.
NB. Full-time employment rates increase when the youngest child reaches the age of three in part because the *Allocation Parentale d'Education* (child-raising allowance) is no longer paid to eligible families after this age.

Table 1.7 Women in Part-time Employment, Groups of Hours usually Worked in Reference Week (Employees), France and EU15, 1997

	%	
Hours	EU15	France
1–10	17.7	10.1
11–20	42.1	39.1
21–24	10.3	9.5
25–30	21.4	22.4
31+	8.4	18.9

Source: OOPEC (1998) *Labour Force Survey*, Luxembourg: OOPEC: Table 078.

labour force in France, whereas the reverse is true for women without higher education (Coutrot et al., 1997).

Women's part-time working hours are longer in France than in the EU15 countries (see Table 1.7). In France there is greater concentration of hours in the longer hours categories (25–30) and particularly thirty-one hours and over, and this trend has been accentuated in recent years (Gaye and Le Corre, 1998; Hoang-Ngoc and Lefresne, 1994).

These longer hours can be attributed to a number of factors: firstly, demand for four-day part-time working (so that mothers can take a Wednesday off to be with their primary and junior school-age children) (Galtier, 1998); secondly, the institutional framework in France, which has historically given an incentive to the development of longer working hours,[6] and finally the specific configuration of local, sectoral and national influences in collective bargaining and in the way in which businesses compete (Gregory and O'Reilly, 1996).

The combination of long part-time hours with low levels of part-time working in France has led to women having a relatively high share of all working hours compared with other EU countries (*Bulletin on Women and Employment in the EU*, 1995). It also contributes to French mothers feeling harried and suffering from 'time famine' (Hantrais, 1990),[8] despite the wide availability of childcare facilities in France. Another contributing factor is the limited flexibility in working hours for French women: national statistics bear witness to the relative lack of flexible working time options in France such as late-morning starts and early afternoon finishes (DARES, 1993), with little improvement over the period 1978–91. It is perhaps unsurprising, then, that there is substantial evidence of a demand for part-time work in France among women, particularly mothers. A 1991 CREDOC survey (Hatchuel, 1991: 36) found that 22 per cent of all women working full-time and 35.7 per cent of women working full-time with a child under six would have preferred to work part time, although the aspiration to work part time is closely related to qualification levels and income (dropping among women with lower qualifications and lower incomes).

In France, discussion about part-time work has been overlaid by the issue of choice over taking this form of work (INSEE-Dares, 1995; Rogerat and Senotier, 1996). The importance of the choice issue in France derives from the fact that women's paid work has traditionally been on a full-time basis and that part-time work has been a recent phenomenon. As such it has been resisted by trades union movements and sociologists (Coutrot et al., 1997). Indeed, the proportion of women stating they were working part-time because they could not find a full-time job were much higher in France than in EU15 (38.8 per cent cf 17.9 per cent) (OOPEC, 1998: Table 059),[9] and this proportion has risen very rapidly in recent years in France (Conseil Supérieur de l'emploi, des revenus et des coûts, 1998; Eydoux, Gauvin, Granie, and Silvera, 1996).

The growth of part-time work in France appears to have developed in three ways (Letablier, 1995). It has to a limited extent been the result of an expansion of 'chosen' or 'voluntary' part-time work, developed primarily in the public sector, by mothers seeking to adapt work to their children, and associated with good conditions of employment (see, for example, its development in banking – O'Reilly, 1994). This tends to be carried out by the higher paid, educated women described earlier who elect to work part-time. Galtier's (1998) recent survey of part-time work in the private sector nevertheless found a number of other groups of women choosing to work part-time, particularly employees in administration in the private sector, employees in retailing, and employees in the intermediary professions in health and the social services. Secondly, its growth derives to a much greater extent from a trend towards greater flexibility in employment emanating from French companies. These part-time jobs are concentrated mainly in the private sector (cleaning, retailing, childcare), and have been associated with poor working conditions and a greater casualization of employment. In France they have been thought to be carried out mainly on an involuntary basis (Belloc, 1986; Coutrot et al., 1997; Galtier, 1998; Maruani and Nicole, 1989), constituting therefore underemployment. Nevertheless, the longitudinal survey of two cohorts of women in the Cote d'Azur region by Bouffartigue, de Coninck and Pendariès (1992) suggested that such part-time work, although not preferable to direct entry into full-time work, represents a halfway house for some women, helping them to exit from unemployment or a discontinuous employment trajectory.

Finally, much of the more recent growth of part-time work, resulting from the French government's programmes to reduce unemployment[10] would seem to be 'non-voluntary' or 'imposed', affecting young women above all. This pattern of development of part-time work in France has led to the view that a polarization is taking place (Conseil Supérieur de l'emploi, des revenus et des coûts, 1998; Letablier, 1995) between women in full-time jobs or permanent part-time jobs with associated good conditions of employment, and those in casual part-time jobs with little chance of integration into the full-time workforce.

There is also evidence in France (Maruani and Decoufle, 1987; Nicole-Drancourt, 1989), as has been the case across Europe (*Bulletin on Women and Employment in the EU*, 1995) that the development of flexibility in working time is a gendered process. Women have been occupying new flexible forms of working time created in the late 1980s – notably part-time work – which have often not been negotiated and have been exempt from payment bonuses whereas the opposite has been true for men (shift work, compressed working weeks etc.). In addition, in France the process of the reduction of working time also appears to be gendered: recent reductions of working time are being achieved partly by the development of part-time contracts, applying particularly to women, rather than by collective reductions in working time (Bloch-London, Bué and Coutrot, 1996). Also, the situation is being aggravated by the delegation of responsibility for the development of working time patterns to collective bargaining, and particularly to company-level bargaining.

This gendered process of change in working hours in France is now leading to concern over the growing disparity between women and men's working hours. Not only are women increasingly working part-time but the proportion of women working short full-time hours (under thirty-four to thirty-eight hours per week) is significantly greater than that of men (see Table 1.8). Furthermore although the disparity between the proportion of men and women working forty-one hours or more a week has fallen slightly between 1993 and 1998, it remains 10.5 per cent. Also, annualized working, permitted by the 1993 *Loi Quinquennale sur L'Emploi*, has led more women taking annualized part-time work with time off during school holidays (Letablier, 1996). These trends are seen to be undermining women's traditionally full-time position in the workforce (de Singly, 1991; Letablier, 1996), and reinforcing their position as carers in the home (Rogerat and Senotier, 1996).

Table 1.8 Proportion of Men and Women in Activity Working Full-time by Usual Working Hours, 1998

	%	
	Men	**Women**
< 34 hours	3.3	8.0
35–38	9.5	13.5
39–40	60.2	61.9
41 or +	27.0	16.5

Source: INSEE (1998) *Enquête sur l'emploi*, Paris: INSEE: Table PA14.

Temporary Work

Women are more likely to be on temporary contracts of one sort or another than men in France, a characteristic of all EU countries (Rubery et al., 1996). However, levels of temporary work are higher for French women than for women in the EU15 (14.2 per cent compared with 13 per cent) and have increased by thirty per cent over the 1993–8 period (see Table 1.9). This growth would seem to have been particularly great among part-time workers (Rubery et al., 1996: Table 2.3.6, p 206).

Temporary work, while remaining a significant, though minority, form of employment, is disproportionately concentrated among the young (under thirty years). The proportion of young women (and men) in temporary work is very high in France (approximately 55 per cent – Rubery et al., 1996a: 209), suggesting that the shortage of permanent jobs for young people is particularly severe.

The rapid growth in temporary work in France reflects in part its attractiveness to employers (the relative cheapness, reliability and flexibility of labour – Belloc and Lagarenne, 1996; Devillechabrolle,

Table 1.9 Proportion of all Women in Activity in Temporary Work, Short-term Contract and in Work Experience and State-Aided Contracts, 1993–8

	%	
	1993	**1998**
Temporary workers	0.5	1.2
Short-term contracts	3.5	4.9
Work experience and state-aided contracts	2.6	2.5
Total	6.6	8.6

Source: INSEE (1998) *Enquête sur l'Emploi*, Paris: INSEE: table PA05.

1998), and in part the French state's job-creation efforts beginning in the early 1980s described above. As part-timers have been given the same protection in law as full timers in France, the distinction between temporary and permanent work has become the main distinction between standard and non-standard forms of employment (Rubery, 1988).

Observers of the French labour market have concluded that the growth of temporary jobs through the state's job creation schemes has had mixed effects (Belloc and Lagarenne, 1996: 129; Letablier, 1996). On the one hand, they have helped women who are in one way or another disadvantaged on the labour market (for example single parents, women aged over fifty or long-term unemployed). On the other hand, they have increased the proportion of women working in jobs which are removed from the 'norm' of full-time permanent work (Belloc and Lagarenne, 1996) and for whom the chance of obtaining stable permanent employment after their completion is low (15–27 per cent a year after completion) and has been falling in the 1990s (Belloc and Lagarenne, 1996).

Occupational Segregation and Pay Inequality

The French state has, during the post-war period, put into a place a legal framework designed to promote equality in employment and to eliminate the inequalities in qualifications between women and men stemming from the education system (as described in the introduction to this book). In addition to the application of the equality principle in this way, the state has also sought to deal with a major perceived source of their inequality: the unequal sharing of responsibility for children and domestic work (Lanquetin et al., 1999).

So to what extent have French women achieved parity with men in terms of their occupational segregation and pay in contemporary France? There is evidence that the growing proportions of women in education and achieving the highest levels of qualifications has led to an increasing proportion of women employed in more highly qualified occupations (see Table 1.10) and a slowing in the increase in the proportion of women employed in traditionally female occupations (Eydoux et al., 1996). However, qualification levels have a greater significance for employment outcomes for women than for men. Young women who have not obtained the *baccalauréat* have much greater difficulties finding a job and are more often located in precarious jobs with poor conditions of employment than young men with the same qualification level (CEREQ, 1997).

Table 1.10 Proportion of Women in Activity by Socio-professional Category (SPC), 1993 and 1998

	%	
SPC*	1993	1998
Artisans, commerçants et chefs d'entreprise	32.7	30.9
Cadres et professions intellectuelles supérieures	31.8	34.2
Professions intermédiaires	44.5	45.9
Employés	76.1	76.0

Source: INSEE, *Enquêtes sur l'Emploi 1993 and 1998*, Paris: INSEE: table PA03.
* *Artisans* etc. includes artisans, small and large business owners. *Cadres* etc. includes executives and managers in the private and public sectors and self-employed lawyers, barristers, accountants, consultants, teachers, scientists and engineers. *Professions intermédiaires* includes middle-ranking employees in administration, primary school teachers, technicians as well as supervisors. *Employés* includes office workers in the public and private sectors, shop workers, personnel of the military and the police, and other service workers (cleaners, nannies, childminders etc.).

Also, despite the progress in recent years, the French labour force, remains markedly sex segregated (Rubery et al., 1996, Table 2.1.2, p 103) as does the type of training followed (CEREQ, 1997). The instruments introduced by Yvette Roudy to address this situation have generally been considered to have produced disappointing results; the blame for this has been attributed to the state, employers and unions (Lanquetin et al., 1999: 59).

Moreover, although the proportion of women who have started a company has risen from eighteen to thirty per cent over the last fifteen years (Majnoni d'Intignano, 1996: 235), women still remain a minority in more senior posts. They only represented 6.3 per cent of company directors in 1997 and these women tended to be concentrated in a narrow range of areas: communication, human resource management, administration and finance, although this depends on the size of the company (Fouquet and Laufer, 1998). Although women's qualifications benefit them more in pay terms at more senior levels than do those of men, women have greater difficulty in reaching these levels than men (Silvera et al., 1995). This difficulty has been attributed to a number of factors: requirements of the job, notably the lack of availability of part-time work at directorship level and the reluctance of many women to sacrifice personal and family commitments to their career (Laufer, 1997); practical difficulties caused by international geographical mobility in dual career couples (with or without children); the complexity of unwritten rules determining access to the ruling élite, masculine organizational cultures and persistent stereotypes about women (Frisher, 1997; Fouquet and Laufer, 1998).

In terms of pay there has been a significant improvement in the degree of pay inequality in relation to men over the last ten years (Service des Droits des Femmes, 1996), and within each socio-professional group the disparity is falling (although this has always been greater at the top of the professional hierarchy than at the bottom). This reduction in inequality has been attributed to factors including the increasing qualification levels of women and the impact of the revaluation of the French minimum wage in recent years, as women are more numerous among the low paid than men. France has one of the best records in terms of pay equality when European and international comparisons are attempted (Silvera et al., 1995), a situation imputed partly to the French minimum wage (Silvera et al., 1995) and partly to the operation of the French industrial relations system where industry agreements structure the system of differentials and methods of payment leading to more homogeneity of pay, status and career prospects in France, with knock-on effects for women (Rubery, 1988: 271).

Despite the improvements in pay equality, there is persistent pay inequality between men and women (see Table 1.12). The reasons for this inequality would seem to be numerous (Laufer, 1986; Silvera et al., 1995): their dissimilar qualifications and concentration in different sectors from men (women are more often concentrated in sectors with low pay) would seem to account for 30–40 per cent of the difference (Thiry, 1985). Mothers are more often found in jobs that allow them to reconcile work and family but that are rarely amongst the highest paid (see for example Crompton and Lefeuvre's findings in relation to pharmacy and accountancy – Crompton and Lefeuvre, 1996).

The remainder would seem to be accounted for by the concentration of women in part-time and temporary work, in smaller companies where pay tends to be lower and in less senior posts, by the way in which jobs are classified and by the pay and bonus system in operation. Indeed, promotional mechanisms often fail to take account of women's employ-

Table 1.11 Net Annual Average Salaries by Socio-professional Category (SPC), Full-time Workers, 1996 (francs)

SPC*	Women	Men	Men's salaries as a proportion of women's
Chefs d'entreprise	153 062	235 243	+53.7%
Cadres et profs intellectuelles supérieures	187 800	245 912	+30.9%
Professions intermédiaires	127 581	144 208	+13.0%
Employés	92 095	100 849	+0.95%
Ouvriers	78 339	94 147	+20.2%
Apprentis et stagiaires	46 767	45 294	−3.2%

N.B. Data provided from the *Déclaration Annuelle des Données Sociales* (DADS), the annual declaration of salaries made by employers.
Source: Friez, A. and Julhès, M. (1998) *Séries longues sur les salaires*, Paris: INSEE, Tables 1–5, p. 54 and 1–3, p. 52.
* For explanation of SPC see Table 1.10. *Ouvriers* include all types of manual workers. *Apprentis et stagiaires* are apprentices and people in work experience.

ment trajectories if they do not conform to the male norm (Laufer, 1997: 81), and penalize breaks in service (for maternity or to follow a partner) (Frisher, 1997). There is also ongoing discrimination against women based on preconceptions about women's traditional roles.

The review of contemporary trends in women's paid work in France reveals support for the conception of French women's employment in terms of integration (rising participation rates of women and gradual desegregation of occupations), differentiation (the continued gap between male and female pay), and polarization in women's employment (between women in more highly qualified professions working full time or who can negotiate part-time work with good working conditions, and less well-qualified women, or younger women in particular, who find themselves more often in part-time work with poor conditions of employment) (Eydoux et al., 1996: 144).

The picture is therefore a mixed one for women on the labour market in France. It is now well-documented that the state can play a very significant role in affecting women's position in paid work (Gregory and Windebank, 2000), and the situation in France is a case in point. On the one hand, French women benefit from state intervention to facilitate the reconciliation of paid work and family, regulation of the labour market and of pay which has until recently limited the growth of part-time working and which has been conducive to reducing levels of pay inequality. On the other, their position is arguably being undermined to a large extent by a range of state policies aimed at increasing the flexibility of the labour market and addressing the country's unemployment (and particularly youth unemployment) problems.

Will changes appearing in the new millennium improve the situation of French women in paid work? We can envisage a number of national and supra-national measures liable to engender change and with mixed effects. Firstly, the reduction of eligibility for government subsidies for the creation of *emplois familiaux* (Cealis and Zilberman, 1998). Secondly, the planned reduction of the working week to thirty-five hours that became law on 19 May 1998 and will be rolled out between the years 2000 and 2002 (Libération Enquête sur le Travail, 1998), but which is being achieved through negotiations between employers and unions primarily at company level. Thirdly, the potential impact of the European Commission's Fourth Equal Opportunities 'mainstreaming' programme leading to a French National Action Plan for employment directed at improving gender equality, and finally the effect of the European Directive on part-time work (Council Directive 97/81 of 15 December 1997) if its recommendations to employers are acted upon. The latter state that more part-time posts should be created at all levels of responsibility and that training should be offered to part-timers to facilitate their professional mobility (*Liaisons Sociales*, 1998). However, the degree to which part-time work will continue to develop in France will depend on the employment creation scenario adopted by the French state. Holcblat (1998) envisages two possible scenarios: in the first place the use by the government of growth initiatives and the blanket reduction of actual weekly working time to thirty-five hours; in the second place, limited growth under the financial constraints imposed by the Euro linked to locally negotiated reductions in working time (and hence an uneven reduction in working time) and a continuation of state initiatives to reduce the cost of employment. While the first scenario bodes well for the division of both paid and unpaid work between men and women (Kergoat and Nicole-Drancourt, 1998), the second is likely to be conducive to the growth of more 'marginal' imposed part-time work, carried out predominantly by women.

In this chapter I have examined women's position in paid work and concluded that the position of French women is relatively strong on the labour market from a European standpoint, but that women's position continues to remain unequal with that of men (location in part-time and temporary work, occupational segregation, pay inequality) and is coming under threat from a number of angles. However, examining women's position in paid work is only half of the story, we need to look at women's paid and unpaid work situation as a whole in order to to fully understand women's working lives in France.

Notes

1. For a full discussion of the variables related to activity levels among French women see Marry, Fournier-Mearelli and Kieffer, 1995 and Villeneuve Gokalp,1994.
2. French women's relatively great continuity in employment across their life cycles can be identified as early as the beginning of this century and was only broken significantly during the immediate post-war period. For an explanation of pre-war and post-war trends see respectively Daric, 1947 and Hantrais, 1990.
3. In 1998, one female households with children under fifteen represented 5.9 per cent of households in France (INSEE, 1998: table MEN01); in the same year the proportion of women living entirely alone reached 18.2 per cent, rising from 17.2 per cent in 1993 (INSEE, 1993 1998: Table MEN 01).
4. To be unemployed, according to this definition, one must be without a waged or unwaged job, be available to work in a waged or unwaged job and to be looking for a job. This definition also includes those who will be resuming a waged or unwaged job at a date following the survey week (INSEE, 1998: 18–19).
5. However, this is likely to change shortly if the green paper on the 35 hour week recently submitted by Martine Aubry for consultation to the social partners becomes law. In article 7 of the green paper the definition of part-time work becomes that of working hours at least one hour less than the legal full-time working week. The green paper also sets out specific conditions for varying part-time hours and for working hours exceeding those stipulated in the part-time contract (Mandraud and Mauduit, 1999).
6. Company-level negotiations (Bangoura, Folques, Le Corre and Mabile, 1995) have been increasing in importance since the introduction of

the Auroux laws in 1982, which imposed annual negotiations over working time at company level and allowed company or sectoral level agreements to derogate from all legislative provisions governing the flexibility in working time.

7. For a full explanation see Gregory and Windebank, 2000: Chapter 2.

8. Hantrais (1990) also suggests that French women suffer from socially imposed time structures (notably the importance of cooked meals) which require them to 'organize more tightly packed time schedules than their British counterparts during the smaller number of hours when they are not at their workplace' (p. 149).

9. The question over the degree to which part-time work is voluntary or involuntary is however a problematical one, for example there is still room for dissatisfaction with working hours even if an individual states that they are working part-time voluntarily (Fagan, 1998).

10. For example those associated with economic restructuring in the public sector, *accompagnement aux restructurations – aide au passage à mi-temps/temps partiel*, the *Contrats Emploi Solidarité*, and more recently the *Emplois Jeunes*. In the private sector there have been incentives through reductions in employers' N.I. contributions (*abattements-temps partiel*) as described above.

References

Afsa, C. (1996) 'L'activité féminine à l'épreuve de l'allocation parentale d'éducation', *Recherches et prévisions*, no. 46: 1–8.

Bailly, J-P. (1996) *Le développement des services de proximité*, Conseil Economique et Social, Paris: La Documentation Française.

Bangoura, S., Folques, D., Le Corre, V., and Mabile, S. (1995) 'Reprise de la négociation d'entreprise en 1994 et au début de l'année 1995', *Premières Synthèses*, no. 120, 15 December: 161–70.

Barrère-Maurisson, M.A., Daune-Richard, A.M., and Letablier, M-T. (1987) 'Activité, emploi et travail des femmes: une comparaison France-Grande-Bretagne', *Actes des Journées Comparisons Internationales en économie sociale*, Ais et CNRS-LEST.

Barrère-Maurisson, M-A., Daune-Richard, A-M., Letablier, M-T., (1989) 'Le travail à temps partiel plus développé au Royaume-Uni qu'en France', *Economie et Statistique*, vol. 220: 47–56.

Beechey, V. (1989) 'Women's Employment in France and Britain: Some Problems of Comparison', *Work, Employment and Society*, vol. 3(3): 369–78.

Belloc, B. (1986) 'De plus en plus de salariés à temps partiel', *Economie et Statistique*, vol. 193–4, November–December: 43–50.

Belloc, B. and Lagarenne, C. (1996) 'Emplois temporaires et emplois aidés', *Données Sociales*, Paris: INSEE.

Bielanski, H. (1994) *New Forms of Work and Activity. Survey of Experience at Establishment Level in Eight European Countries*, Dublin: European Foundation for the Improvement of Living and Working Conditions.

Blackwell, L. (1998) *Occupational Sex Segregation and Part-time Work in Modern Britain*, unpublished Ph.D. Thesis, London: City University.

Bloch-London, C., Bué, J. and Coutrot, T. (1996) 'Politiques de l'emploi: masculin pluriel ou féminin singulier?', in H. Hirata and D. Senotier (eds) *Femmes et partage du travail*, Paris: Syros, pp. 163–76.

Bosch, G., Dawkins, P. and Michon, F. (1994) *Times are changing: working time in fourteen industrialised countries*, Geneva: International Institute for Labour Studies.

Bouffartigue, P., de Coninck, F. and Pendariès, J.-R. (1992) 'Le nouvel âge de l'emploi à temp partiel: un rôle nouveau lors des débuts de vie active des femmes', *Sociologie du Travail*, vol 4: 403–28.

Bradshaw, J., Kennedy, S., Kilkey, M., Hutton, S., Corden, A., Eardley, T., Holmes, H. and Neale, J. (1996) *Policy and the Employment of Lone Parents in 20 Countries*, The EU Report, European Observatory on National Family Policies, Social Policy Research Unit, University of York.

Bulletin on Women and Employment in the EU (1995) no. 7. Commission of the European Communities Directorate-General for Employment, Industrial Relations and Social Affairs.

Cealis, R. and Zilberman, S. (1998) 'Les emplois familiaux et les organismes de services aux personnes en 1997', *Premières informations et premières synthèses*, no. 43.2.

Commaille, J. (1992) *Les stratégies des femmes. Travail, famille et politique*, Paris: La Découverte.

CEREQ (1997) *Femmes sur le marché du travail. L'autre relation formation-emploi*, no. 70, Marseilles: CEREQ.

Coutrot, L., Fournier, I., Kieffer, A. and Lelièvre, E. (1997) 'The Family Cycle and the Growth of Part-Time Employment in France: Boon or Doom?', in H.P. Blossfeld and C. Hakim (eds) *Between Equalization and Marginalization, Women Working Part-Time in Europe and United States of America*, Oxford: OUP.

Conseil supérieur de l'emploi, des revenus et des coûts, (1998) *Durées du travail et emploi*, Paris: Documentation française.

Crompton, R. with Lefeuvre, N. (1996) 'Paid employment and the changing system of gender relations', *Sociology*, 30(3): 427–46.

Dares (Direction de l'Animation, de la Recherche, des Etudes et des Statistiques) (1993) *Dossiers Statistiques du Travail et de l'Emploi*, résultats de l'enquête Conditions de Travail, no. 98–99, Paris: Masson.

Daric, J. (1947) 'L'activité professionnelle des femmes en France. Etude statistique – évolution-comparaisons internationales', *Travaux et documents*, Cahier no. 5, Paris: INED.

Devillechabrolle, V. (1998) *Liaisons sociales/Magazine*, November, 15–15.

De Grip, A., Hoevenberg, J. and Willems, E. (1997) 'L'emploi atypique dans l'Union européenne', *Revue Internationale du Travail*, 136(1): 55–78.

de Singly, F. (1991) 'La création politique des infortunes contemporaines de la femmes mariée salariée', in F. de Singly, and F. Schultheis (eds) *Affaires de famille, Affaires d'Etat: Sociologie de la Famille*, Lille: Editions de l'Est.

Dex, S. Walters, P. and Alden, D.M. (1993) *French and British Mothers at Work*, London: Macmillan.

Eydoux, A., Gauvin, A., Granie, C., and Silvera, R. (1996) *Tendances et perspectives de l'Emploi des Femmes en France au cours des années 1990*, Rapport français du réseau 'Femmes dans l'emploi', Communauté Européenne, DGV, Bureau de l'Egalité des Chances, February.

Fagan, C. (1998) 'Time, Money and the Gender Order: Work Orientations and Working Time Preferences in Britain'. Paper given at the Gender, Work and Organization Conference, UMIST, Manchester, January 8–10.

Fagnani, J. (1998) 'Helping mothers to combine paid and unpaid work – or fighting unemployment? The ambiguities of French family policy', *Community, Work and Family*, 1(3): 297–311.

Fernandez, S. (1982) *Transformation de l'activité féminine: facteurs évolutifs*, Paris: Centre d'Etudes et de l'Emploi.

Fouquet, A. and Laufer, J. (1998) *Effet de plafonnement de carrière des femmes cadres et accès des femmes à la décision dans la sphère économique*, Working paper 98/28, Paris: Centre d'Etudes de l'Emploi.

Frischer, D. (1997) *La revanche des misogynes. Où en sont les femmes après trente ans de féminisme?*, Paris: Albin Michel.

Galtier, B. (1998) *Les salariés à temps partiel dans le secteur privé. Diversité des emplois et des conditions de travail*, document de travail 98-03, Paris: Conseil Supérieur de l'emploi, des revenus et des coûts.

Garnsey, E. (1985)'A comparison of part-time employment in Britain and France'. Paper presented at International Working Group conference on Labour Market Segmentation, Santiago de Compostelle, July.

Gauvin, A. (1995) 'Le sur-chômage féminin à la lumière des comparaisons internationales: chômage, sous emploi et inactivité', *Les Cahiers du Mage*, vols 3–4: 25–36.

Gaye, M. and Le Corre, V. (1998), 'Les incitations financières en faveur du travail à temps partiel', *Premières Informations et Premières synthèses*, no. 41.2.

Girard, D. (1997) '33.000 salariés bénéficiente de la Robien', *La Tribune*, 27 March: 9.

Gissot, C. and Meron, M. (1996) 'Chômage et emploi en mars 1996', *INSEE Première*, no. 427, June.

Gregory, A. (1987) 'Le travail à temps partiel en France et en Grande-Bretagne', *Revue Française des Affaires Sociales*, vol. 3, July-September: 53–60.

Gregory, A. (1989) *A Franco-British comparison of patterns of working hours in large-scale grocery retailing, with specific reference to part-time work*, Ph.D. thesis, Aston University.

Gregory, A. and O'Reilly, J. (1996) 'Checking out and cashing up. The prospects and paradoxes of regulating part-time work in Europe', in Crompton, R., Gallie, D., and Purcell, K. (eds) *Changing Forms of Employment: Organisations, Skills and Gender,* London and New York: Routledge: 207–34.

Gregory, A. and Windebank, J. (1999) *Women and Work in Britain and France: Practice, Theory and Policy*, London: Macmillan.

Hantrais, L. (1990) *Managing Professional and Family Life: a Comparative Study of British and French Women*, Dartmouth Publishing: Aldershot.

Hantrais, L. (1993) 'Women, Work and Welfare in France', in J. Lewis (ed.) *Women and Social Policies in Europe*, Aldershot: Edward Elgar: 116–37.

Hantrais, L. and Letablier, M-T. (1996) *Families and Family Policies in Europe*, London and New York: Longman.

Hantrais, L. and Letablier, M-T. (1995) *Familles, travail et politiques familiales en Europe*, Cahiers du Centre d'Etudes de l'Emploi, no. 35, Paris: Presses Universitaires de France.

Hatchuel, G. (1991) *Activité Féminine et Jeune Enfant*, Collection des Rapports, no. 95, Paris: CREDOC.

Hoang-Ngoc, L. and Lefresne, F. (1994) 'Les règles d'utilisation du temps partiel dans les régimes d'accumulation français et britannique', *Revue de l'IRES*, 14: 144–72.

Holcblat, N. (1998) 'La politique de l'emploi en France', in Barbier, J-C. and Gautié, J. (eds) *Les politiques de l'emploi en Europe et aux Etats-Unis*, Paris: Presses Universitaires de France.

Husson, M. (1996) 'L'emploi des femmes en France. Une comptabilité en temps de travail (1980–1990)', in Hirata, H. and Senotier, D. (eds) *Femmes et partage du travail*, Paris: Syros: 138–47.

INSEE-Dares (1996) *Le travail à temps partiel*, Les Dossiers thématiques, no. 2, Editions Liaisons: Paris.

INSEE (1998) *Enquête sur l'Emploi de 1998 Résultats détaillés*, Paris: INSEE.

Jeder-Madiot, F. and Ponthieux, S. (1996) 'Embauches, métiers et conditions d'emploi des jeunes débutants', *Premières Synthèses*, no. 96-07-29-1, Dares, Ministère du Travail et des Affaires Sociales.

Kempeneers, M. and Lelièvre, E. (1993) 'Women's Work in the EC: Five Career Profiles', *European Journal of Population*, vol. 9: 72–92.

Kergoat, D. and Nicole-Drancourt, C. (1998) *Temps partiel et trajectoires, Itinéraires de salarié(e)s à temps partiel*, Paris: GEDISST-CNRS, GRASS-CNRS.

Lane, C. (1993) 'Gender and the labour market in Europe: Britain, Germany and France compared', *The Sociological Review*, vol. 41(2): 274–301.

Lanquetin, M-T., Laufer, J. and Letablier, M-T. (1999) 'From Equality to Reconciliation in France?', in L. Hantrais (ed.) *Gendered Policies in Europe*, London: Macmillan: 53–65.

Laufer, J. (1986) 'Egalité professionnelle: un atout négligé pour gérer les ressources humaines', *Revue française de gestion*, no. 55: 41–53.

Laufer, J. (1997) 'Accès des femmes à la décision dans la sphère économique', in F. Gaspard (ed.) *Les Femmes dans la prise de décision en France et en Europe*, Paris: L'Harmattan: 75–88.

Le Corre, V. (1995) 'Le recours croissant des entreprises au temps partiel', *Premières synthèses*, no. 97, DARES, 4 July.

Lefaucheur, N. and Martin, C. (1995), *Qui doit nourrir l'enfant dont le père est 'absent'*. Rapport de recherche sur les fondements des politiques familiales européennes (Angleterre-France-Italie-Portugal), Travaux de Recherche et d'Analyse du Social et de la Sociabilité, Paris.

Lefaucheur, N. and Martin, C. (1997) 'Single Mothers in France: Supported Mothers and Workers', in S. Duncan and R. Edwards (eds) *Single Mothers in an International Context: Mothers or Workers?*, London: UCL Press.

Letablier, M-T. (1995) 'Women's Labour Force Participation in France: the paradoxes of the 1990s', *Journal of Area Studies Special Issue, Women in Eastern and Western Europe – in Transition and Recession*, 6: 108–16.

Liaisons Sociales (1998) 'Travail à temps partiel. Directive européenne', no. 7807, 21 February.

Libération, Enquête sur le travail (1998) 'Les principales dispositions du projet de loi. Le 19 mai 1998', http://www.liberation.fr/travail/index.html.

Majnoni d'Intagnano, B. (1996) *Femmes, si vous saviez . . .*, Paris: Editions de Fallois.

Mandraud, I. and Mauduit, L. (1999) 'Ce que prévoit l'avant-projet de loi de Mme Aubry sur les 35 heures', *Le Monde*, 26 June: 8.

Marry, C., Fournier-Mearelli, I. and Kieffer, A. (1995) 'Activité des jeunes femmes: héritages et transmissions', *Economie et Statistique*, vol. 3(4): 67–79.

Marsden, D. (1989) 'Institutions and Labour Mobility: Occupational and internal labour markets in Britain, France, Italy and West Germany', in R. Brunetta and C. Dell Aringa (eds), *Markets, Institutions and Cooperation*, London: Macmillan.

Maruani, M. and Decoufle, A.-C. (1987) 'Pour une sociologie de l'emploi', *Revue française des affaires sociales*, 41(3): 7–29.

Maruani, M. and Nicole, C. (1989) *La flexibilité à temps partiel – conditions d'emploi dans le commerce*, Collection Droits des femmes, Paris: La Documentation française.

Meron, M. and Minni, C. (1996) 'L'emploi des jeunes: plus tardif et plus instable qu'il y a vingt ans', *Données Sociales*, Paris: INSEE.

Millar, J. (1994) 'Defining lone parents: family structures and social relations', in Hantrais, L. and Letablier, M.-T. (eds) *Conceptualising the Family*, Cross-National Research Papers, Fourth Series: Concepts and Contexts in International Comparisons of Family Policies in Europe, no. 1, Loughborough Univeristy: the Cross-National Research Group.

Nicole-Drancourt, C. (1996) 'Rapport à l'activité et insertion professionnelle', *Les Cahiers du Mage*, no. 1, Egalité, discrimination: hommes et femmes sur le marché du travail: 37–8.

Niel, X. (1998) 'Six femmes au foyer sur dix aimeraient travailler', *Premières informations et premières synthèses*, no. 09.1

OOPEC (1998) *European Labour Force Survey*, Brussels: OOPEC.

O'Reilly, J. (1994) *Banking on Flexibility*, Aldershot: Avebury.

Rogerat, C. and Senotier, D. (1996) 'De l'usage du temps de chômage', in H. Hirata and D. Senotier (eds) *Femmes et partage du travail*, Paris: Syros: 138–47.

Rubery, J. (1988) *Women and Recession*, London: Routledge & Kegan Paul.

Rubery, J., Smith, M., Fagan, C., and Grimshaw, D. (1996) *Les femmes et le taux d'emploi en Europe*, European Network on the Situation of Women in the Labour Market. Report for the Equal Opportunities Unit, DGV, of the European Commission, Manchester School of Management, August.

Rubery, J. Smith, M. and Fagan, C. in collaboration with Almond, P. and Parker, J. (1996a) *Trends and Prospects for Women's Employment in the 1990s*, European Network of Experts on the Situation of Women in the Labour Market, Report for the Equal Opportunities Unit, DGV, of the European Commission, Manchester School of Management, UMIST, November.

Service des Droits des Femmes (1996) *6e bilan d'application de la loi sur l'égalité professionnelle*. Compte rendu de la séance du 19 décembre 1996, Paris: Ministère de l'emploi et de la solidarité.

Silvera, R. in collaboration with Sonnac, N., Anxo, D. and Johansson, M. (1995) *Le salaire des femmes: toutes choses inégales . . . les discriminations salariales en France et à l'étranger*, Paris: La Documentation française.

Thiry, B. (1985) 'La discrimination salariale entre hommes et femmes sur le marché du travail en France', *Annales de l'INSEE*, no. 58.

Tomasini, M. (1994) 'Hommes et femmes sur le marché du travail 1973-1993', *INSEE Première*, no. 324, June.

Villeneuve-Gokalp, C. (1994) 'Garder son emploi, garder ses enfants: une analyse par catégorie sociale', in H. Léridon and C. Villeneuve-Gokalp (eds) *Constance et inconstances de la famille*, INED/PUF: Paris, 233–341.

Zilberman, S. (1995) 'L'évolution des emplois familiaux de 1992 à 1994', *Premières Synthèses*, 17 August, pp. 197–203.

–2–

Women's Unpaid Work and Leisure
Jan Windebank

The aim of this chapter is to examine the relationship between women's unpaid work and their leisure. The finding that women have far less leisure time relative to men in contemporary France is explained in terms of the fact that, despite their extensive participation in the labour force, they still shoulder the burden of responsibility for domestic work and child rearing and continue to undertake much of the caring work in the kinship group and community.

To commence, therefore, this chapter first outlines how to measure women's unpaid work and leisure in contemporary French society. Following this, a sketch is provided of the poverty of leisure time confronting women. This is then explained through an in-depth analysis of both unpaid domestic work and community work. This reveals that women's entry into employment, far from being liberatory, has actually led to a 'triple burden' on women of increasing responsibility for employment but little or no reduction in their unpaid domestic and community work commitments. Indeed, where women do escape such a 'triple burden', it is shown to nearly always be at the expense of other women who are employed on low wages to care for their ascendants or descendants or who are paid to do their housework. Therefore, the liberation of some French women from some of their unpaid work relies on the exploitation of other women's low-status and poorly paid labour because there has been little gender renegotiation of this work within the household. In other words, French women's entry onto the formal labour market has been made possible by a redistribution of unpaid work between women. Men are not taking on a greater share of the workload, with the effect that although men's leisure time is increasing, the relative time available for leisure for women is witnessing a drastic reduction, whatever their employment status.

Measuring Women's Unpaid Work and Leisure

Unlike employment where regular national evaluations of its magnitude and character take place, the measurement of other forms of work has not until recently been considered a serious topic for investigation, reflecting the dominance of the ideology that employment is the principal form of work in contemporary society. However, since the 1960s, there has been an international feminist campaign to recognize unpaid work grounded in the view that the ways in which such work is measured and valued have significant implications for women and impact heavily on social policy-making (Chadeau and Fouquet, 1981; Luxton, 1997). Arguing that the national accounts are systematically skewed because they ignore the value of women's unpaid work, they have sought to change the ways in which international bodies and national governments measure economic activity. Indeed, this campaign has met with considerable success.

Of potential long-term significance to the revaluing of unpaid work is a recommendation, made in 1993 by the UN after a review of the UN System of National Accounts, that 'satellite national accounts' be developed that incorporate the value of unpaid work. This became an obligation for France under the terms of the Final Act of the 1995 UN Fourth World Conference on Women in Beijing (United Nations, 1995: Section 209: f, g). These computations will be an adjunct to the standard national accounts that were roundly criticized for their silence on women's unpaid work. Although such accounts remain subsidiary, it is clear that they represent a step in the right direction. In more recent years, moreover, the French government has accepted this decision and sought to develop 'satellite' accounts of the value of unpaid work as part of wider redefinition of the relationship between the state, the market and the family.

The way in which they will take on board such recommendations is by using time-budget studies (Roy, 1991). A time-budget study is a technique for data collection where respondents complete diaries chronicling the number of minutes spent on a range of activities. From these, it is possible to calculate the time spent on unpaid work and, for that matter, leisure. Indeed, it is now widely accepted that measuring time use is as useful and accurate in assessing unpaid work as money is in measuring paid employment.

In France, time-budget studies conducted in 1975 (Chadeau and Fouquet, 1981) and 1985 (Roy, 1991) by the INSEE, as well as a nationwide survey on 'domestic production' undertaken in the late 1980s, all provide quantitative data on the gender division of unpaid work. The overwhelming finding of these studies is that the French population spends more time engaged in unpaid work than in employment. The importance of these large-scale surveys, therefore, is that they provide solid statistical evidence that the family has not lost its productive functions under capitalism. For example, the 1975 French time-budget study revealed that unpaid work occupied an average of thirty-one hours per person per week whereas professional work occupied only twenty-eight. In other words, unpaid work occupied 52 per cent of total work time for that year (Chadeau and Fouquet, 1981). By 1986, moreover, unpaid work had risen to occupy 55 per cent of total working time, suggesting that in terms of its role in production, the household was becoming more important rather than less (Roy, 1991). There is no reason to think that this pattern has undergone any significant change in the 1990s. Unpaid work, therefore, appears to be increasing rather than decreasing in importance relative to paid work in France, leading some analysts to discuss the advent of a post-employ-ment or 'post-formalization' society (Williams and Windebank, 2000).

Nevertheless, many of these time-budget studies may well be under-estimating the time spent on unpaid work compared with employment. On the one hand, this is because the time spent in employment may be overestimated since the total time engaged in employment is usually counted when much of this time may include meal and coffee breaks, associated travel, as well as socializing. On the other hand, this is because the time spent in unpaid work may be underestimated. First, time-budget studies only measure an individual's commitment in time to a concrete activity. They do not capture the time and effort involved in planning and managing one's own and others' activities which may often occur when one is watching television, lying in bed or undertaking some other supposedly leisure pursuit or indeed when one is engaged in one's employment (Haicault, 1984). Second, there is much evidence that unlike an employee's relationship to his or her company, women must be permanently available to their families so that time not actually spent in the service of the family may still be constrained time (Chabaud, Fougeyrollas and Sonthonnax, 1985). Third and finally, there is the argument that much of women's work burden within the household and family derives from their caring duties for other household members. Whilst time-budget studies can capture the practical aspects of this care-giving work, they cannot capture its emotional and affective side, which is either ignored completely, or indeed, can be portrayed as leisure and socializing.

For these reasons, many have argued that if women's relationship to unpaid work and leisure is to be more fully understood, there is a need to combine the results of such time-budget studies with other survey techniques that assess issues such as responsibility for managing and organizing unpaid work and emotional commitment (see, for example, Luxton, 1997). These other techniques include survey questions and in-depth interviews. They also include participant observation where researchers spend lengthy periods in households helping out and observing the labour process so as to compare what people say they do with what is actually done as well as understanding the configuration of the emotional work involved in the unpaid sphere (Luxton, 1986). Indeed, some have argued that the ideal is to combine all four methods – survey questions, time use, in-depth interviews and participant observation if unpaid work and leisure are to be more fully understood (Peters, 1997).

Leisure Time

As Table 2.1 shows, the national-level time-budget study conducted in the mid-1980s in France reveals that men had significantly more leisure time than women of an equivalent employment status. Full-time employed men, for instance, had 28.8 per cent more leisure time than full-time employed women. Part-time employed men, meanwhile, had 47.4 per cent more leisure time than part-time employed women and non-employed men had 32.2 per cent more leisure time than non-employed women. This finding that women had less free time than men, whatever their employment status, echoes previous findings on men's and women's leisure time (Hantrais, 1985; Hantrais, Clark and Samuel, 1984).

To explain this lack of leisure time of women relative to men, whatever their employment status, one must examine their unpaid work commitments in greater detail. As Table 2.1 shows, more full-time employment for women means more work overall. In other words, women employed full-time are working the longest total hours of any group. On the basis of this time-budget data, we can calculate that a shift from no employment to 40 hours of employment per week resulted in a reduction in domestic work time of only 12.3 hours. That is, for each extra hour of paid employment, full-time employed women were doing about 18 minutes less domestic work. Getting a job thus meant a substantial rise in their total (paid plus unpaid) work time and a substantial reduction in their leisure time. To explain why this is the case, first the gender division of unpaid domestic work will be examined and then the gender divisions of unpaid community work.

Table 2.1 Structure of Time in France: by Employment Status, 1986

Hours per Week	Men	Women
Full-time employed:		
Personal time	71.0	72.5
Employment	44.9	40.1
Unpaid work	16.5	27.7
Total work time	61.4	67.8
Free time	35.6	27.7
Part-time employed:		
Personal time	74.0	74.1
Employment	33.3	25.8
Unpaid work	13.4	36.0
Total work time	46.7	61.8
Free time	47.3	32.1
Non-employed:		
Personal time	80.2	79.7
Employment	1.4	0.8
Unpaid work	23.6	40.0
Total work time	25.0	40.8
Free time	62.8	47.5

Source: derived from Roy (1991: Figure 1).

Unpaid Domestic Work

'Domestic work' refers to the unpaid work carried out by household members for themselves and each other. This can include routine house-work (for example, cooking, cleaning, washing and shopping); non-routine work (such as gardening, do-it-yourself and car maintenance); and childcare, which is often considered to be the most onerous of women's contemporary domestic duties. The activities usually associated with domestic work are to be found in all societies with women being assigned to similar types of tasks in all contexts. However, although in pre-capitalist societies a strict gender division of tasks may have existed, productive and reproductive tasks were not separated in time and space. Consequently, women's domestic activities counted as work alongside subsistence agriculture and production for the market. It is only in industrial societies, such as France, where the employment place became separated from the household temporally and spatially, and where women's household activities became detached from the notion of work. Indeed, the concept of 'domestic work/labour' was originally developed within women's studies research and the feminist movement in the 1960s and 1970s in North America and Europe as part of a strategy to emphasize both the practical importance of women's work in the home to the functioning of society and the economy and, more importantly, the theoretical importance of women's responsibility for this labour in explaining their oppression. Indeed, one of the major contributions to the study of 'work' that feminist academics and theorists and women's studies researchers have made since the 1970s is to challenge the dominant ideology that views work as synonymous with employment. An analysis of women's participation in domestic labour must therefore be central to any understanding of women's lives in France.

Here, therefore, we examine the extent and nature of domestic labour in couple-based households, the subject upon which most of the emphasis has been placed in the research on this form of work (for a discussion of such work in single-person households, see Gregory and Windebank 2000). In the 1960s and 1970s, it was assumed by some that the rise in the number of working wives would be accompanied by a corresponding increase in the husband's input into domestic work. Young and Wilmott (1975), for example, argued that the middle classes in particular were leading the way towards more egalitarian, 'symmetrical' marriage relationships in which the husband and wife shared the tasks of both wage earning and domestic labour. This was part of a much wider debate at a time when society was becoming more middle class, and it was assumed that what the middle classes were currently doing would be replicated later by the working class. Here, with the fortune of historical hindsight, we examine whether such a shift towards more egalitarian marriage relationships has indeed taken place in France. To do this, we examine first the amount of domestic work undertaken by men and women in France and, second, the types of domestic tasks that they perform and third, the division of responsibilities for such work.

Volume of Domestic Work Conducted by French Men and Women

As Table 2.1 illustrated, more full-time employment for women means more work overall. These data, nevertheless, are a snapshot of one particular period. They provide no clue as to whether there is an increasingly symmetrical egalitarian arrangement emerging over time. The only known data on this, from earlier time-budget studies, reveal that although husbands have increased the proportion of all unpaid work that they undertake from the 1960s to the 1980s (to about a third of all unpaid domestic work), their share of the total (paid and unpaid) work undertaken has decreased. The overall outcome, in other words, has been that wives' share of the total work time increased with their entry into employment due to the fact that the renegotiation of the division of domestic labour did not keep pace with their entry into employment (Gershuny, Godwin and Jones, 1994).

Gender Differences in the Types of Domestic Work Conducted

The overall finding, similar to other nations, is that French women are primarily responsible for conducting the routine domestic tasks (such as washing and ironing, preparation of the evening meal, household cleaning) and much of the rise in men's contribution to domestic work can be attributed to their increased engagement in non-routine domestic work (such as DIY activities). Indeed, according to men's testimonies, and as Table 2.2 reveals, of those French men who said that they contributed to the domestic work, only between a quarter and a half said that they did various routine tasks. The important point of this data is perhaps the fact that so few French men claim to engage in domestic work of a routine nature.

On the basis of this evidence, therefore, it would seem that routine domestic work is predominantly undertaken by women, even in dual-earner households. Men's contribution to the domestic workload in contrast, tends to be much more in the realm of non-routine domestic work. It appears, in consequence, that any notion of a shift towards a more 'egalitarian' and 'symmetrical' division of domestic labour is far from the reality, given the ways in which individual domestic tasks remain

Table 2.2 Nature of the Tasks Undertaken by French Men 'Who do Something' According to their Own and their Partners' Testimonies

	According to men's partners	According to men
Shopping	48	54
Washing up	48	44
Transporting children	49	49
Dressing children	38	31
Cooking	37	27
Household cleaning	35	24

Source: Eurobarometer, *Enquete Famille et Emploi dans L'Europe des Douze*, 1990 (cited in INSEE, 1995: Table 7.3.2)

highly segregated. Who, therefore, retains overall responsibility for domestic work and who helps out?

The Gender Division of Responsibility for Domestic Work

So far, we have seen that the increase in married women's employment has been accompanied to some extent by an increase in men's domestic involvement, albeit insufficient to compensate for women's increased involvement in paid work and, on the whole, this increased participation is in a limited range of tasks. To find out whether men are taking the responsibility for domestic work, such as by managing, planning, organizing and supervising the housework, or whether they are merely helping out, we have to look to more qualitative studies. All of these studies indicate that women retain the responsibility (Chabaud et al., 1985; Fougeyrollas, 1994; Haicault, 1984; Nicole-Drancourt, 1989) and men's role is simply one of 'assistant' rather than 'equal partner'. The idea that it is a woman's responsibility to ensure that the domestic work gets done, which usually means doing it herself, especially the routine domestic work, thus appears to be firmly embedded in everyday life.

This fact that men generally tend to 'help out' rather than take responsibility for the domestic workload is well portrayed in a survey of dual-earner couples with children in France conducted by the author (Windebank, 1999). When discussing the gender division of domestic work, women commonly made comments such as 'he helps out where he can' and 'he does a lot but it's more helping out than anything else'. As another respondent put it: 'My husband helps me out when I cannot manage everything and that's how it is.' Indeed, many of the women in this study did not have high aspirations of what they expected from their husbands. As one respondent asserted, 'I have an indispensable husband. He does everything around the house. When I need him to, he will step in and replace me. If I am ill, he'll do things like the laundry. He isn't against doing such things. He'll do it.' Indeed, a key finding of this research is that the division of the domestic workload is often closely associated with men tending to do things either which are closed- rather than open-ended in nature (such as cooking a meal) or engaging in pleasurable non-routine tasks rather than what they see as unpleasurable routine work.

Two further issues need to be considered here. The first is that there is a perception that women should be permanently available to their partners and children and the second is that if any emotional caring work is required then it is women's responsibility. These two features extend the concept of responsibility to the wider realm of social support, an activity that is often a major component of women's investment within the household. Whatever women do in terms of hours of domestic work, and even if they do not carry out particular tasks themselves, the argument here is that it is always they who are responsible for the management of family life. For example, on the basis of fieldwork in France, Haicault (1984) developed the concept of the *charge mentale* (mental burden) to describe the way in which employed women must constantly balance two sets of responsibilities – for their homes and families and for their jobs – and that they carry these two sets of responsibilities in their heads wherever they are physically, that is, at work or home. Similarly, Chabaud et al. (1985) describe the relationship of women to their household tasks and families as one of 'permanent availability' because even when they are physically doing nothing, or engaging in a so-called leisure activity such as watching television at home, for many women this time is still constrained because they have to be 'on-call' to respond to the needs of their husbands and/or offspring. In a study of mothers with careers, Nicole-Drancourt (1989) arrived at much the same conclusion, stressing that women in her study managed their family and work lives in spite of their male partners rather than because of them.

Indeed, Bryson (1996: 217) argues that to see how women remain responsible for domestic work, one needs look no further than the fact that despite men sometimes sharing the domestic labour, or even in extremely rare cases taking major responsibility for it (though usually only temporarily), there has been no transfer to women of a cultural acceptability to 'keep' a househusband, unlike men for whom it remains culturally acceptable so far as a housewife is concerned. As she puts it: 'The capacity to expropriate domestic labour is gender specific and the rights to it lie with men.' The way forward is not, of course, to extend this right to some or all women but to revalue the two forms of work and to ensure equal participation of men in such work. Nevertheless, how to achieve both of these things is a vexing question in a world where there is a dominant emphasis on paid work and little or no increase in men's contribution to unpaid domestic work.

Here, therefore, it has been shown that women engage to a far greater extent than men in domestic work whatever their employment status, especially the routine domestic tasks, and take overall responsibility for planning and arranging the domestic workload as well as for the emotional and managerial aspects of such work. As such, it is little surprise that French women have so much less leisure time than French men. Is it the same, however, when we consider unpaid community work? Does this further reinforce the leisure famine of French women relative to men, or does it reduce the inequalities in leisure time?

Unpaid Community Work

'Unpaid community work' refers to unpaid work undertaken by household members for members of households other than their own such as kin, friends and neighbours. This is a form of economic activity that up until now has been mostly ignored in mainstream discussions of women's work, but is important if a rounded picture of women's overall workload and their caring responsibilities is to be obtained. In order to examine this activity, two principal forms of community work are distinguished: kinship work and neighbourhood activity. This is because each is based on different principles of exchange. Kinship work is chiefly based on 'kinship obligation' whereas neighbourhood inter-household transfers are primarily based on 'reciprocal exchange' (Short, 1996).

Taking each form of community work in turn, we first examine the amount undertaken by men and women and second, the gender divisions in the character of this work. This reveals that, like the situation with domestic work, community work, whether based on kinship obligation or reciprocity, is conducted more by women than men and displays deep gender divisions. In consequence, community work will be shown to act as an additional load on women, resulting in many having a 'triple burden' of paid work, domestic labour and community work. Furthermore, we will show that full-time employment for women in France has made as little impact on their share of community work as it has on domestic labour. Obviously, this has important implications for 'progress in gender relations'.

To review the magnitude and character of community work, an immediate problem to be confronted is that there is limited evidence based on little more than scattered one-off studies. Here, therefore, we have to piece together individual studies that frequently use different definitions of the phenomenon under investigation, and widely contrasting methods, and have often been conducted at very different times.

Exchanges of Labour within the Kinship Network

There is a popular conception in France that kinship groups have broken down as sources of support and constraint for individuals and nuclear families (see Dechaux, 1996; Enjolras, 1995; Martin, 1996; Pitrou, 1996). However, although fewer families now live together in intergenerational households and groupings, this does not mean that family solidarities have totally disintegrated. As Colvez (1989) finds, despite elderly people living independently of their descendants, they still receive assistance from them. Of the 589 individuals needing assistance with small house-work tasks in this study, 21 per cent were most often assisted by family of the same generation, 29 per cent by younger family, 5 per cent by friends and neighbours, 41 per cent by professionals and 4 per cent by others. Of the 1009 individuals who needed assistance with their shopping, moreover, 27 per cent were assisted by family of the same age, 44 per cent by younger members of the family, 5 per cent by friends or neigh-bours, 11 per cent by professionals and 3 per cent by others. It appears from this evidence, therefore, that 'kinship economies' (Short, 1996) are still prevalent and their breakdown is perhaps not so widespread as many have assumed. Indeed, it is often the case that the exchanges and transfers of money, goods and services within kinship economies are crucial for the maintenance of a decent standard of living for many households. The issue throughout this section, however, is one of who provides this kinship support. In other words, on whose shoulders does the work fall? To answer this question, we examine first the amount of kinship support provided by men and women and second, the character of the activity men and women undertake.

Amount of Kinship Work Undertaken by Men and Women

In France, the principal source of data on the magnitude and character of kinship support is provided by a statistical survey on 'family assistance and relationships' conducted by the INSEE (Chabaud-Rychter and Fougeyrollas-Schwebel, 1989; Fougeyrollas, 1994). The results highlight the position that kinship occupies in everyday exchanges as well as the disparities in the practices of men and women. So far as the volume of such work is concerned, this survey examines kinship support within the context of men's and women's overall workload. This reveals that of all the activities that they undertake, men conduct 39 per cent for themselves (20 per cent in the case of women), 16 per cent for the household (25 per cent for women), 4 per cent for kin living outside the household (4 per cent for women) and 5 per cent for other people (4 per cent for women). The remaining percentages consist of meaningless responses and indi-viduals from whom no response was received. Besides the fact that French women are less oriented towards doing activities for themselves and more oriented towards doing activities for the household, the important point here is that the proportion of all work which is undertaken for kin living outside the household is approximately equal for French men and women. That is, of all activities performed during the course of a week, 4 per cent of both men's and women's work is specifically aimed at benefiting relatives (or one activity in every 25 undertaken). Some activities, nevertheless, are more likely to be undertaken for kin than others. For example, 18 per cent of all the 'odd jobs' performed in France are conducted for relatives living in another household. Likewise, 10 per cent of sociable activities (especially conversations) are conducted for and with relatives, 9 per cent of all gardening activities, 8 per cent of shopping trips, 6 per cent of cooking activities, 5 per cent of sewing, 4 per cent of housework activities and 3 per cent of meals (Chabaud-Rychter and Fougeyrollas-Schwebel, 1989).

The fact that both women and men perform the same proportion of their total workload for kin living in another household, however, does not mean that men and women perform the same amount of kinship work. Women perform, on average, many more activities for kin in a normal week than men, simply because they conduct many more activities in total per week than men. As Chabaud-Rychter and Fougeyrollas-Schwebel (1989) find, women perform on average four activities per week for their parents and parents-in-law, four for their children living outside the household and one activity per week for their brothers and sisters. Men, in contrast, conduct just two activities per week for their ascendants, three for their descendants and one per fortnight for their brothers and sisters. The result, as Fougeyrollas (1994) shows in a later analysis of the same data set, is that of all services provided to kin, 42 per cent are conducted by women, 31 per cent by men and 25 per cent by the two together, whereas 2 per cent are realized by other people in the household such as children or older people.

In total, therefore, women are involved in a greater proportion of the total workload for kin than men. When this finding is thus coupled with women's insertion into employment and their contribution to the domestic workload, the result is that a 'triple burden' is widespread and intensely felt by French women. Nevertheless, it is not solely the amount of kinship support that is provided that is important if we are to understand the gendering of kinship economies. There is also a need to explore the gender variations in the nature of the work undertaken.

Gender Variations in the Nature of Kinship Exchange

In France, the types of activities that men and women perform for relatives are gendered in much the same way as domestic work. That is, men tend to perform tasks that are viewed as 'masculine', that are non-routine and have closed-ended time frames. Women, on the other hand, conduct tasks that are viewed as 'feminine' in nature, that are often routine and are frequently open-ended in character. For example, Fougeyrollas (1994) finds that 96 per cent of DIY tasks undertaken for kin are conducted by men, as is 77 per cent of household maintenance, whereas women conduct 97 per cent of the sewing and knitting carried out for kin, 81 per cent of the housework, 71 per cent of the caring activity, 54 per cent of the child care and 54 per cent of the shopping. Such a gendering of kinship exchange is reinforced by many other studies (for example, Dechaux, 1990; Delbes 1983; Duriez 1996; Favrot-Laurens, 1996; Gokalp and David, 1982; Lefaucheur and Martin, 1997; Lemel, 1996; Le Gall, 1996; Marpsat, 1991; Pitrou, 1990; de Singly and Maunaye, 1996).

Hence, so far as kinship economies are concerned, the evidence displays that women not only undertake more kinship work than men but that there is a gender division of kinship activity that mirrors the gender divisions prevalent in domestic work. Furthermore, by examining kinship activities, it becomes clear that when women require help to carry out the routine domestic and caring work in their own household, they often rely on their women ascendants and descendants rather than on their male partners. Indeed, almost all women find themselves in an interdependent circuit of exchanges with other women with whom they have kinship ties whereby they fill in for them by doing a part of these other women's domestic and caring work. As such, there exists a relative interchange-ability of women at the service of each matrimonial family, such as where the mother intervenes to permit the daughter to deliver her household responsibilities whilst also taking on employment (Chabaud-Rychter and Fougeyrollas-Schwebel, 1989; Dechaux, 1990). This interdependence of women, however, merely serves to perpetuate the cleavage in men's and women's roles as it reduces the need for a renegotiation of the gender division of domestic labour even when the woman in the household is unable or unwilling to carry out the traditional duties of the 'woman at home'.

Non-kinship Exchanges of Labour

Community work, however, does not only cover kinship economies. There is also non-kinship exchange that is undertaken by household members for friends and acquaintances living in other households. On the whole, this activity occurs within the neighbourhood. The degree to which such material and non-material assistance is provided, nevertheless, is in major part dependent upon the nature and extent of the social networks in which individuals are embedded. Here, therefore, we examine both the magnitude and character of non-kin exchange undertaken by men and women.

Amount of Non-kin Exchange Undertaken by Men and Women

In examining the extent to which men and women engage in neighbourhood exchange with friends and neighbours, the primary issue is that there is very little research that directly focuses on this issue. The vast majority of the evidence available tends to be a by-product of investigations into either other forms of work or the way in which care is provided for specific social groups. As such, the evidence available on non-kinship exchange is the most limited of all the forms of work examined in this chapter. Nevertheless, some clear trends can be identified.

Women undertake the majority of non-kinship work. Chabaud-Rychter and Fougeyrollas-Schwebel (1989) find that some 4 per cent of all activities undertaken by men and women are conducted for non-kinship acquaintances living outside their household. Given that women conduct a larger number of activities on average than men, the result is that women undertake a greater volume of non-kinship based community work than men. This is reinforced by a further study of support given by relatives and friends to single parents conducted in 1990 among 336 mothers living in Normandy who were divorced or separated for more than four years and received, or had previously received, benefits from the Family Allowance Fund (Martin, 1996). The vast majority of support from friends given to these single mothers came from women rather than men.

Gender Variations in the Character of Non-kin Exchange

When the character of non-kin exchange is examined, the gender divisions identified in domestic work and kinship economies are mirrored yet again. As Chabaud-Rychter and Fougeyrollas-Schwebel (1989) identify in France, the gender division of non-kin exchange is very similar to the gender divisions of kinship economies with women conducting much of the 'female'-oriented, routine and open-ended work such as housework, caring and emotional support, whereas men tend to engage in more 'masculine'-oriented, non-routine and closed-ended activities such as DIY projects and odd jobs such as car repair and gardening, often working with the friend or acquaintance in order to complete the task.

In this realm, moreover, it was emotional rather than material support that dominated such exchanges and this was overwhelmingly provided by women. Perhaps this is also the reason why in similar studies conducted in France, very little support from friends and neighbours was identified. Both Foudi, Stankiewicz and Vanecloo (1982) and Barthe (1988) examined whether friends and neighbours undertook a range of tasks but omitted to consider the issue of emotional support, which many participants do not consider to be the provision of 'work' to households. What is certain, however, is that in France, the higher participation of women in full-time employment, longer working hours and more continuous employment will mean that there is a smaller and smaller pool of women available in the community to help out as friends (or family). The result is that French women will have less and less access to informal support networks of other women upon whom to call.

In sum, this chapter has revealed that women's increased entry into paid work in France has not been matched by a similar renegotiation of the gender division of domestic labour and community work. The result is that women are increasingly suffering a 'triple burden' of paid work and responsibility for unpaid domestic and community work. Unsurprisingly, the outcome is that women are becoming harried (see Chapter 1) in that they have much less leisure time than men, whatever their employment status.

This raises a number of issues. Much research on women's working lives has assumed that more paid work for women is the key to women's liberation and gender equality. In this chapter, however, it has been shown that equating progress in gender relations with women's position in the labour force alone is to only look at part of the story: it ignores women's position in unpaid work and their access to leisure time. It is women rather than men who carry out the majority of domestic and (both kinship and non-kinship based) community work. Women tend to undertake the tasks considered 'feminine' and those that are routine and open-ended whilst men conduct tasks that are perceived as 'masculine' and that are non-routine and closed-ended in character. Contrary to popular expectations, therefore, French women's increased entry in the labour force has not been matched by a renegotiation of domestic and community work. This, moreover, is likely to worsen over the coming years with demographic changes. The relative growth of older people without sufficient pension provision to enable them to pay for formal care is likely to lead to even greater caring responsibilities falling on women's shoulders.

This raises fundamental questions about what constitutes progress in gender relations. If women are not present in the formal labour force, then there are major implications for women's citizenship rights, as these entitlements are increasingly linked to employment. However, the adoption of a 'male' employment model (full-time continuous employment) for women is likely to represent a backward step for gender relations in general while prevailing cultural, and arguably out-dated, mores regarding men's and women's roles persist. For further progress in gender relations, therefore, there is perhaps a need to pay much less attention to women's access to employment and much greater attention to the gender division of unpaid work. Indeed, unless men's participation in unpaid work can be encouraged, then French women will continue to suffer not only from the triple burden of employment, domestic labour and community responsibilities but will find themselves relatively starved of leisure time.

References

Barthe, M.A. (1988), *L'Economie Cachée*, Paris: Syros Alternatives.

Bryson, L. (1996), 'Revaluing the household economy', *Women's Studies International Forum*, vol. 19: 207–19.

Chabaud, D., Fougeyrollas, D. and Sonthonnax, F. (1985), *Espace et Temps du Travail Domestique*, Paris: Méridiens.

Chabaud-Rychter, D. and Fougeyrollas-Schwebel, D. (1989), 'Exchanges of services in the extended family', Paper presented to the XXVth *CFR International seminar on Family, Informal Networks and Social Policy*, Belgrade 7–11 October.

Chadeau, A. and Fouquet, A. (1981), 'Peut-on mesurer le travail domestique?', *Economie et Statistique*, vol. 136: 29–42.

Colvez, A. (1989), '*Aide à domicile, nouveaux dispositifs, nouvelles pratiques*', paper presented to the UNIOPSS conference, 7 November, Paris.

Dechaux, J.-H. (1990), 'Les echanges economiques au sein de la parentale', *Sociologie du Travail*, vol. 1: 73–94.

Dechaux, J.-H. (1996), Les services dans la parente: fonctions, regulation, effets, in J-C. Kaufmann (ed.), *Faire ou faire-faire? famille et services*, Rennes: Presses Universitaires de Rennes.

Delbes, C. (1983), 'Les familles des salaries du secteur prive a la veille de la retraite, 2. Les relations familiales', *Population*, vol. 6: 22–41.

Duriez, B. (1996), 'L'aide familiale a domicile', in J-C. Kaufmann (ed.*), Faire ou faire-faire? Famille et services*, Rennes: Presses Universitaires de Rennes.

Enjolras, B. (1995), *Le Marché Providence: aide à domicile, politique sociale et création d'emploi*, Paris: Desclée de Brower.

Favrot-Laurens, G. (1996), 'Soins familiaux ou soins professionnels? La construction des catégories dans la prise en charge des personnes agées dépendantes', in J.-C. Kaufmann (ed.), *Faire ou faire-faire? Famille et services*, Rennes: Presses Universitaires de Rennes.

Foudi, R., Stankiewicz, F. and Vanecloo, N. (1982), 'Chomeurs et economie informelle', *Cahiers de l'observation du changement social et culturel*, no.17, Paris: CNRS.

Fougeyrollas, D. (1994), 'Entraide familiale: de l'universel au particulier', *Société Contemporaine*, vol. 17: 51–73.

Gershuny, J, Godwin, M and Jones, S (1994), 'The domestic labour revolution: a process of lagged adaptation', in M. Anderson, F. Bechhofer and J. Gershuny (eds), *The Social and Political Economy of the Household*, Oxford: Oxford University Press.

Gokalp, C. and David, M.G. (1982), 'La garde de jeunes enfants', *Population et Societe*, vol. 161: 22–32.

Gregory, A. and Windebank, J. (2000), *Women's Work in Britain and France: practice, theory and policy*, Basingstoke: Macmillan.

Haicault, M. (1984), 'La gestion ordinaire de la vie en deux', *Sociologie du Travail*, vol. 3: 268–77.

Hantrais, L. (1999) 'Paid and unpaid work', in M. Cook and G. Davie (eds) *Modern France*, Routledge, London, 115–31.

Hantrais, L. (1985), 'Leisure lifestyles and the synchronisation of family schedules: a Franco-British perspective', *World Leisure and Recreation*, vol. 3: 18–24.

Hantrais, L., Clark, P.A. and Samuel, N. (1984), 'Time-space dimensions of work, family and leisure in France and Britain', *Leisure Studies*, vol. 3: 301–17.

INSEE (1995), *Les Femmes: contours et caractères*, Paris: INSEE.

Le Gall, D. (1996), 'Faire garder les enfants dans les familles à beau-parent', in J.-C. Kaufmann (ed.), *Faire ou faire-faire? famille et services*, Rennes: Presses Universitaires de Rennes.

Lefaucheur, N. and Martin, C. (1997), 'Single mothers in France: supported mothers and workers', in S. Duncan and R. Edwards (eds), *Single Mothers in an International Context: mothers or workers?*, London: UCL Press.

Lemel, Y. (1996), 'La rarete relative des aides à la production domestique', in J.-C. Kaufmann (ed.), *Faire ou faire-faire? Famille et services*, Rennes: Presses Universitaires de Rennes.

Luxton, M. (1997), 'The UN, women and household labour: measuring and valuing unpaid work', *Women's Studies International Forum*, vol. 20: 431–39.

Martin, C. (1996), *L'après-divorce. Rupture du lien familial et vulnerabilité*, Rennes: Presses Universitaires de Rennes.

Marpsat, M. (1991), 'Les échanges au sein de la famille: l'héritage, aides financières, garde des enfants et visites aux grands parents', *Economie et Statistique*, vol. 239: 59–66.

Nicole-Drancourt, C. (1989), 'Stratégies professionnelles et organisation des familles', *Revue Française de Sociologie*, vol. 30: 57–80.

Peters, S. (1997), 'Feminist strategies for policy and research – the economic and social dynamics of families', in M. Luxton (ed.), *Feminism and Families: Changing Policies and Critical Practices*, Halifax: Fernwood Books.

Pitrou, A. (1990), 'Des carrières de femmes 'solidaires', *Femmes Info*, vol. 75/76: 18–20.

Pitrou, A. (1996), 'Le mythe de la famille et du familial', in J-C. Kaufmann (ed.), *Faire ou faire-faire? famille et services*, Rennes: Presses Universitaires de Rennes.

Roy, C. (1991), 'Les emplois du temps dans quelques pays occidentaux', *Données Sociales*, vol. 3: 223–5.

Short, P. (1996), 'Kinship, reciprocity and vulnerability', *Australian Journal of Social Issues*, vol. 31: 127–45.

Singly de, F. and Maunaye, E. (1996), 'Le rôle et sa délégation', in J-C. Kaufmann (ed.), *Faire ou faire-faire? Famille et services*, Rennes: Presses Universitaires de Rennes.

United Nations Development Programme (1995), *Human Development Report 1995*, Oxford: Oxford University Press.

Williams, C.C. and Windebank, J. (1999), 'The formalisation thesis: a critical evaluation', *Futures*, vol. 31(6): 547–58.

Windebank, J. (1999), 'Political motherhood and the everyday experience of mothering: a comparison of the child care strategies of French and British working mothers', *Journal of Social Policy*, 28(1): 1–25.

Young, M. and Wilmott, P. (1975), *The Symmetrical Family: a Study of Work and Leisure in the London Region*, Harmondsworth: Penguin.

−3−

Women and the Media
Maggie Allison

The role of the media in purveying perceptions of myths, realities, information, desires and values has never before been so influential, with the development of new media technologies and generalized public access to them and their products. Thus any concerns as to the power and pervasiveness of the media in relation to gender (im)balances and issues must now be heightened. France is not exempt from these developments and it is within this context that one must approach the relationship between women and the media in France, whilst also concentrating on French specificities. At the same time it is relevant to take into account political and social shifts affecting ways in which society is constructed and organized. This is particularly so with the developing awareness in politics, industry and public life that the hitherto macho/male-dominant mode must become more flexible, pragmatically in order for political parties to appeal to the female voter, but also in keeping with the growing body of opinion that believes more 'feminine' characteristics are changing the tenor of public discourse and practice.

Against this background, while also noting the backlash against women in the 1990s, this chapter will assess aspects of present-day French media in relation to women, their in/visibility and their active/passive roles. It will begin by looking at the evolving gender context and will subsequently address representations in advertising and in relation to sexual harassment; it will contrast feminine press with feminist press and will indicate some of the media influences on women in politics. The chapter will then proceed to discuss women as media professionals in terms of their numbers and role in the workforce, women as media stars, and new developments in media provision for women. It will conclude with an assessment of the role of the Association des Femmes Journalistes (AFJ) (Association of French Women Journalists).

Introduction: Regendering the Context

Gender roles and attitudes are embedded in historical change and societal development, with women framed in terms of the 'male-as-norm' syndrome and within patriarchal frameworks. Classic or stereotypical images of women have evolved in relation to a male-dominated society entailing major wars, industrial and technological development, economic crises, the tertiarization and informatization of society, and new working patterns. Despite women's movements throughout this century achieving some major advances, the overall societal construct and prevailing discourse has remained male. The effects that this has had on media representations of women, and also on their participation in the media professions within an evolving gender distribution among the workforce at large, cannot be ignored. Nevertheless, in the final decades of the millennium there is an awareness that these values need to change, not necessarily in recognition of women's value(s) *per se*, but because masculine values no longer achieve the desired result. The premise is that we are progressively witnessing a foregrounding of feminine values over masculine values at a period in history when there has been no major world war for over fifty years, and the key word is 'collaboration' rather than 'confrontation'.

Anne Beaufumé notes that a two-pronged feminization of French society is developing: on the one hand the increasingly influential role of women in French society, and on the other the rise in so-called feminine values, particularly in relation to consumerism and the world of work (Beaufumé, 1998). Her views were presaged by those of Claude Fischler whose article *Une féminisation des mœurs?* ('A feminization of behaviour patterns?') demonstrates how, in the Western world, women are demographically in the majority and increasingly present in the workplace, two phenomena that contribute to a feminization both of social structures and, ultimately, of mores (Fischler, 1993).

Mike Burke in *Valeurs féminines, le pouvoir de demain?* (Burke, 1998) and Bernard Cathelat in *L'Alternative des valeurs féminines* (Cathelat, 1998) pursue this change of emphasis in a range of spheres from politics to management and advertising. Both stress the need to adopt feminine values, but certainly do not equate this with a qualitative advance for women themselves for, as Cathelat says, it is less to do with the sex of the individual than with the principles on which society functions.

The issue here is to see if and to what extent this 'feminizing' trend impacts upon media portrayals of women and their role within the profession.

Women as they Appear in the Media: Women's In/visibility

Writing in 1980 Margaret Gallagher already highlighted the male agenda of media content thus: 'the mass media's role is primarily to reinforce definitions and identities set in a framework constructed for and by men' (Gallagher, 1980). Her article draws on material gathered for two UNESCO reports, later to be updated in a 1995 report on gender patterns in media employment (Gallagher, 1995). Gallagher's work, spanning two decades, has recently, and more specifically, interacted with research as to the visibility of women in the French media conducted in collaboration with a working group – 'Femmes dans les médias' (Women in the Media) – set up by the AFJ. The commission, headed by Monique Trancart, operating in conjunction with 'Mediawatch', a Canadian feminist organization concerned with eliminating sexism in the media, conducted a survey of twenty French media as part of a worldwide study on 18 January 1995, and a survey of seven media on one day per month from September 1995 to August 1996 (Trancart 1998).

The year-long research showed that of people interviewed by the media only 17.25 per cent were women; those whose professions were mentioned were more likely to be men, with 42 per cent of the 'no noted profession' category being women, far higher than the proportion of women to men interviewed. Equally, women were more likely to be presented as victims – one woman in six, for one man in fourteen: in reality men are just as likely to be victims of certain events or attacks as women, but displaying women as more vulnerable perpetuates this common belief, with a concomitant effect on their own feeling of freedom and security. Women were also more readily left anonymous, one in three for one in seven men, with one in thirteen being referred to only by her first name, compared to one in fifty for men. If one adds to this list the proportion of men occurring in the predominating topics of defence, international affairs, politics, wars, terrorism etc. which automatically call upon male authority figures, we can see that Trancart's conclusion: 'Nous dirons que l'abondance de ces sujets dans l'information contribue donc à écarter les femmes' ('It is our view that the preponderance of these topics in the news contributes to the exclusion of women') regrettably confirms the observation of Margaret Gallagher two decades earlier (Trancart, 1998: 9). The study also showed that in spite of an increase in the number of card-carrying women journalists, they were not proportionally represented in the sample analysed. The conclusion of the Mediawatch survey was that women appear far less frequently than men in proportion to the reality, as expressed by INSEE (*Institut National des Études Statistiques et*

Économiques) (National Institute for Statistics and Economic Surveys): for example 40 per cent of French executives are women compared with 60 per cent men, but according to Mediawatch their visibility was 15 per cent to 85 per cent of men.

Such sidelining of women figuring in the media may imply lack of visibility, but this contrasts with paradoxical physical prominence in certain contexts, as will be demonstrated in the next section.

Gender and Sexual Visibility: Advertising and Sexual Harassment

Legislation since the 1960s has given women increased control over their own bodies, increased rights in the workplace, and protection against sexual harassment. Nonetheless at both physical and professional levels women are still subjected to sexist stereotyping and to the 'esprit gaulois' phenomenon, which condones male ribaldry and denigration of women: paradoxically some French women are ambivalent towards or unconcerned by the tradition of the French male seducer of which this plays a part. This section will assess to what extent the 'French seduction' syndrome inhibits positive and empowering representations of women both in advertising and as regards sexual harassment.

The European Advertising Standards Alliance in its 1997 handbook sets out guidelines for self-discipline in the advertising industry and liaises with corresponding bodies in the member states, the BVP (Bureau de Vérification de la Publicité) (equivalent of the Advertising Standards Authority in Britain) being the French body.[1] The European Council's resolution of 5 October 1995 as to the image of women and men in advertising and in the media, committed itself to promoting better images of women and their role in major institutions of society, and to combating traditional clichés in the belief that: (a) sexual stereotypes in media and advertising are gender inequality factors; (b) media and advertising have the potential to change gender attitudes.

The BVP in its 1998 *Règles déontologiques* (code of ethics) regarding the image of women states that advertising must respect women's dignity, its images of women must not be seen as provocative, nor should they be used gratuitously as a lure, and advertising should not imply an inferior status for women. Whereas its role is to guide advertisers as to the legality or appropriacy of their material, it operates primarily as a consultative body, only taking legal action where a sufficient number of complaints are made, preferably by organizations or competitors. It has been criticized, particularly by Marie-Victoire Louis, in the course of an anti-sexist advertising campaign organized from 1992–5 by the AVFT (Association Européenne contre les violences faites aux femmes au travail) (European Association against violence committed against women at work).[2] Her 1997 article in *Nouvelles Questions Féministes* analyses several advertising campaigns in terms of the code of ethics outlined above (Louis 1997). She describes the 1992 advertisement for the *Monoprix* store as follows: 'La publicité montrait une jeune femme assise, à moitié nue, les jambes entrouvertes, les seins à demi découverts, sous la photo de laquelle on pouvait lire le texte suivant: "C'est quand on n'a presque rien sur soi qu'ils découvrent que l'on a plein de choses en nous".'[3] The BVP denied that this contravened their code whereas Louis's analysis both demonstrates the reverse, and points out the inadequacies of the BVP's own terminology for dealing with the wide range of portrayals that occur.

A more recent controversial advertising campaign was that for Wonderbra, which in 1997 made headlines not just in France but also in Britain. Its narrative depended upon the nightmare scenario in which someone – here a woman – could be taken short at any time and find oneself virtually undressed, but have 'dignity' saved thanks to Wonderbra, all summed up in the slogan: 'on ne sait jamais' ('you never know'). The impact of the series of three 'retro' advertisements was created by the voyeuristic element: in one case a woman (larger than life) in a launderette is putting on a jumper that has shrunk in the machine, before the admiring gaze of a young boy. The *Figaro Économique* (16 September 1997) quotes Mercedes Erra, head of the advertising agency Euro RSCG, as saying: 'On a voulu être loin de la business woman qui assure' ('We wanted to get away from the competent business woman'), preferring to employ a discourse 'which does away with all the complexes resulting from past militancy and removes the last traces of the superwoman of the 90s.' We are witnessing here an aspect of the post-feminist, or simply anti-feminist, backlash, summed up by the title of the *Figaro Économique* article: 'Le retour de la femme-objet: Wonderbra [. . .] s'adresse aux femmes dont la préoccupation est de plaire quitte à choquer certaines féministes' ('Woman as object is back: Wonderbra [. . .] appeals to women who want to be attractive, at the risk of shocking some feminists'). Although provocative, this series is relatively mild compared with the nudity and truncated female bodies mounted by Lilliputian males featured in the Kookaï underwear campaign of autumn 1998 (one 'mowing' a woman's pubic hair at the bikini line), giving rise to a rash of press attention.

The advertiser's assumption that women wish to please and are available is also integral to the phenomenon of sexual harassment and

Louis makes the link between the two, insisting that there should be legislation to penalize representations that incite sexual harassment, prostitution, violence and rape (Louis, 1997: 105). In spite of the many serious articles on the subject, much media coverage of the public and parliamentary debates during the processing of the sexual harassment legislation in 1991 and 1992[4] drew on heterosexist and male chauvinist traditions: stereotypes of the 'unlovely' female, unappreciative of male attentions abounded, with the cover of the *Événement du Jeudi* (30 April 1992) depicting an angry woman hurling a bucket of water towards a rapidly disappearing male, and *Libération* (30 April 1992) carrying a two-page spread cartoon of a male whose extended member pointed, in parallel with his smoking cigar, into the ribs of a grim-faced woman, hands in the air hold-up fashion. Indeed *Libération's* front cover of the same day took sexual aggression into the realms of sadism, with a photomontage representing quite literally the *droit de cuissage* (seigneurial rights) tradition, with a high-heeled female leg being eaten from a tray by a male diner.

The traditional male tactic, to put a humorous gloss on the issue, parallels the 'women can't take a joke' approach and seeks to undermine the seriousness of the problem, as illustrated by the journalist J.-M. Leulliot asking Mme Véronique Neiertz, Minister for Women's Rights at that time, if inviting her to dinner would constitute sexual harassment. Such flippancy was mirrored by the heckling Mme Yvette Roudy received in the Assemblée Nationale during the second reading of the Bill (2 December 1991) from right wing deputies: 'Elle nous harcèle. Continuellement.' ('She's harassing us. Constantly.') TF1 hedged its bets as to its position: the company was co-producer of a much-acclaimed comedy of the moment, *Promotion Canapé* (Casting Couch Syndrome), with TF1 news items ending : 'We must do away with the casting couch syndrome', thereby indirectly promoting their own product. By contrast, however, they screened an excellent documentary, *Le Droit de cuissage* (Seigneurial Rights) (14 January 1989), including references to the work of the AVFT.[5] In sum, one can say that the media treatment was ambivalent to say the least and in many cases belittling and aggressive. The sexual harassment legislation created far fewer genuine ripples than did anti-smoking legislation which was passed at approximately the same period.

Mainstream Women's Press

Magazines aimed at a female reading public have been in existence since the last quarter of the nineteenth century, for example *L'Écho de la mode*

Table 3.1 Circulation of Feminine and Family Press, 1997

Launch date	Titles	Publishing Group	Circulation
Weeklies			
1945	Elle	Hachette-Filipacchi	339 000
1984	Femme actuelle	Prisma Presse	1 893 000
1947	Bonne soirée	Bayard Presse	273 000
1986	Maxi	Bauer	706 000
1980	Madame Figaro	Hersant	527 000
Monthlies			
1954	Marie-Claire	Marie-Claire	531 000
1944–1945	Marie-France	Marie-Claire	228 000
1973	Cosmopolitan	Marie-Claire	251 000
1988	Avantages	Marie-Claire	615 000
1980	Biba	Excelsior	211 000
1982	Prima	Prisma Presse	
1919	Modes et Travaux	EMAP	724 000
1997	Questions de Femmes	Ayache	300 000
1921	Vogue	Condé-Nast	93 000
1921	L'Officiel de la couture	Jalou	103 000
1976	Dépêche mode		89 000
1933	Votre Beauté	Nijdam	98 000
1960	20 ans	Excelsior	150 000
1987	Jeune et jolie	Filipacchi	198 000
1969	Parents	Hachette	404 000
1976	Enfants magazine	Bayard	202 000

Source: Albert, P. (1998), *La Presse Française*, Paris: Documentation Française, p. 149.

(*Fashion Echo*) was founded in 1878. In the twentieth century, and in particular since the end of World War Two, women have increasingly been targets for consumer spending and have become the 'willing victims' of capitalism, with much of the mainstream women's press providing a vehicle for advertising of consumer goods and copy regularly geared to advertising features. Pierre Albert in *La Presse française* (1998) points out that the seventy-five titles of women's and 'women's interest' magazines sell overall 2.9 billion copies per year, representing the biggest magazine advertising outlet in France. *Elle* magazine, launched in 1945, will be referred to in particular in this section.

Interestingly in Table 3.1 (Albert 1998: 149) women's magazines are classified along with 'family' publications such as *Parents* (Parenting) and *Enfants magazine* (Children's Magazine) rather than under a more general category, showing that in spite of changes in women's status in society, the parenting and homemaking responsibilities are still seen to be their domain. Until the 1970s this sector situated women firmly in these societal roles, consistent with the needs of an evolving postwar nation. The events of May 1968, however, did not totally bypass the idealized world of the 'glossies' and at the beginning of the crisis *Elle* produced a much-reduced edition with, uncharacteristically, a front cover devoted to a picture of demonstrating students. If the magazine oriented itself during the 1970s to a somewhat younger audience, it nonetheless maintained its homely touch with regular *fiches tricot* (knitting patterns) on its back cover. By 1982 the latter had given way to full page glossy advertisements, reflecting not only what Albert sees as shifts in mores and fashions, but also the increased competition in the magazine market, and in consumer society in general, leading to new launches, such as *Prima* in 1982. Hence, whereas the 1970s, according to Dardigna, experienced the need for the feminine press to capitalize on feminism, with such publications as *Marie-Claire* providing guidance as to how to become 'liberated' (Dardigna, 1978), Bonvoisin and Maignien point out that the *Prima* venture coincided with a new mood among women who had emerged from the militancy of the seventies and could combine feminism and femininity, and become 'real' women once more, independent women combining career and home, but still remain attractive to men. Nevertheless the imbalance of domestic responsibility prevailed (Bonvoisin and Maignien, 1996).

The French feminine press of the 1990s is taking its reflection of societal shifts and changes in women's lives a step further. The ever-present didactic element is developing in tune not just with women's emancipation and more varied life patterns but also with the globalization of practical and political concerns. This produces an overlapping of content with both news press and non-mainstream women's press and is reflected in articles concerning such topics as immigration, world poverty, human and political rights, with certain personalities and causes recurring, as with the case, for instance, of Taslima Nasreen, the exiled Bangladeshi writer. Even though a large proportion of the copy is still geared to how women look, there is increasing awareness that they should also be able to think, express opinions and read, as evidenced in the annual *Elle* book prize. There is a sense then, although this should not be overstated, that in some of the French feminine press there is a 'mainstreaming' of women's concerns and a drawing of women out of their own more restricted world into a more public forum.

A typical issue of *Elle* might carry some seven or eight pages, out of 150 or more, devoted to public and women's development topics. This is the case with the March 1999 number, whose one-page tongue-in-cheek editorial: 'Chic, papa est enceint!' ('Great, Daddy's pregnant!') (p. 7), is supported by a three-page feature on the Kurds including an interview with Danielle Mitterrand (pp. 14–16), and a three-page article on male/ female salary levels: 'Salaires: dis, c'est encore loin l'égalité?' (Salaries: tell me, how long before equal pay?) (pp. 73, 74, 76). This last, however, is immediately followed by an article entitled: 'Nicole Kidman se dévoile' (Nicole Kidman reveals all) (pp. 78–83), sporting a two-page portrait of the actress reclining in provocative lingerie on a satin chaise longue. To confirm the impact, this in turn is succeeded by a four-page dossier on reawakening male desire: 'Urgent! Comment rendre le désir aux hommes?' ('Help! How can we restore men's libido?') (pp. 88–91). The editors, then, know full well how to achieve the right dosage of 'mainstream' issues versus 'traditional features' to maintain their readership, their sales figures, their advertising revenue and women's place.

Finally, while the domestic role is still evident in French women's magazines, there is a further tendency for overlap with general readership magazines such as *Cosmopolitan* and also an adaptation to new press geared to men. *Elle* occasionally provides a supplement entitled *iL*, whose fifth issue (21 April 1997) was complemented in the main magazine by an eight-page article asking: 'L'homme est-il en danger?' ('Is man/are men at risk?'), thereby undermining positive imaging of women and their developing public role. Hachette are in 1999 comtemplating transforming *iL* into a regular, independent publication at a time when France is responding increasingly to an Americanized market with the launch of *Men's Health* in April 1999 (*Libération,* 17 April 1999). March 1999 also saw the first edition of a new monthly, *Perso* (Personal), aimed at young women interested in fashion and star personalities: its cover depicts the film star Emma de Caunes, reclining, legs spread wide with a tiny doll similarly seated in the angle of her genital area. The effect of the *mise en abyme* and the objectifying of the young woman is all too clear.

In this sector, then, market forces and a male-led view of the economy are, predictably, maintaining the ethos of masculine values and again counteracting women's rightful and dignified visibility in the media.

Alternative Women's Press

The main thrust of this section is to examine the role of press publications produced not *for* women, but *by* women: it will provide a historical contextualization to an overview of the present position.

There has been a long history of women's journalism in France with the most notable example being *La Fronde*, founded and directed by

Marguerite Durand[6] from 1897 to 1903, whose content and production were entirely in the hands of women. One of its journalists, Caroline Rémy, under the pseudonym of Séverine, in 1914 became only the second woman to obtain a journalist's licence in France (Martin, 1997: 124). Today her name lives on in the *Prix Séverine* (Séverine Prize) awarded by the AFJ for the book of the year which contibutes best to a new assessment of women's role. In common with *La Fronde*, Hubertine Auclert's *La Citoyenne* (*Woman Citizen*) , which ran from 1881 to 1891, promoted human rights, women's rights, and campaigned for women's suffrage in addition to addressing itself to all issues of the day: these were newspapers written from a women's perspective but not confined to 'feminine' topics, much to the surprise and perplexity of male fellow journalists.[7]

Approximately a century later in the wake of May 1968, the 1970s were to witness a burgeoning of feminist press (weekly, monthly, intermittent, short-term) produced by women for women and usually aimed at specific readerships. Myriame El Yamini in *Médias et féminismes* (*Media and Feminisms*) lists, together with their tendencies and readerships, 142 such publications founded between 1970 and 1990 (El Yamani 1998, 73–8). She distinguishes between three categories of publication: those that reflect feminist activism; those that are concerned with more theoretical aspects of feminism; and those of a more institutional nature, emanating from the Ministry of/Secretariat for Women's Rights, for example.

Two contrasting titles that will be briefly examined here are *Le Torchon Brûle* (literally: *The Teacloth is on Fire*) and *Femmes en Mouvements Hebdo* (literally: *Women in Movements Weekly*). The first of these two corresponds to El Yamani's first category, being the first publication produced by the *Mouvement de Libération des Femmes* (*Women's Liberation Mouvement*). Appearing only six times between May 1971 and mid-1973 it claimed on its cover to be *menstruel*, a play on words between the French word *mensuel* (monthly) and 'menstrual', indicating a subversion of traditional media discourse and in keeping with the whole style of this tabloid size publication on rough newsprint. Most of the content was provided by *MLF* members from Paris and the provinces and concerned the major issues of the time such as contraception (legalized in 1967) and abortion (not legalized until 1975), taking wickedly humorous but cutting swipes at patriarchal society, its institutions and repressions, while mobilizing and providing practical survival information for readers.

By contrast, *Femmes en Mouvements Hebdo* falls into El Yamani's second category, that of reflective, theoretical feminism and emerged from the women's group *Psychépo* (*Psychoanalysis and Politics*) headed up by Antoinette Fouque.[8] Appearing first as a monthly from 1978–9, it existed as a weekly from October 1979 to July 1982, aspiring to free women from patriarchal control in all domains, in particular those of politics, information and artistic creation. With semi-gloss paper and considerable photographic content, its copy focused, in addition to women's issues as such, on cultural activities and writers destined to become part of the feminist literary canon.

A publication that predates both of these and still in existence is *Clara Magazine*. Coming into being at the Liberation, it sprang out of *Femmes Solidaires* (*Solidarity Women*), itself an offshoot of the *Union des Femmes Françaises* (*Union of French Women*) which had resisted Nazism. Acting as the women's wing of the French Communist Party, it has a global remit and is associated with the *Fédération Démocratique Internationale des Femmes* (*Women's International Democratic Federation*). The magazine, relying largely on subscription sales and with a recently updated, more glossy image, cross references with the 'feminine press' category discussed above, in that many key women figures such as Gisèle Halimi and Geneviève Fraisse appear here as they do in *Elle*, and similar topics, such as the parity debate and the use of RU 486, the so-called 'morning-after' pill, also feature. The editor, Ernestine Ronai, describes the stance of the magazine as projecting positive images of women and their achievements, reporting on women's hardships, struggles and oppression, while at the same time avoiding endorsement of the victim culture associated with women. The message here is of empowerment, as evidenced in the magazine's sub-title: *Elles font avancer leur temps* (They move the world along).[9]

El Yamani deplores the loss of the wealth of women's press and asks if some future turning point will reawaken it. A range of magazines do still exist and persist, such as *Cahiers du Féminisme* (*Feminist Notebook*), a quarterly dating from 1975 whose emphasis is class struggle, its affiliation the Communist Revolutionary League and its content as to women's issues and relevant legislation extremely well-researched; the quarterly *La Griffe: rapports sociaux de sexe* (*Claws: gender relations*), based in Lyon, with a reflective, sociocultural content; the monthly *Lesbia Magazine*, in existence since 1982, covering issues both of particular interest to lesbian and feminist women; and the more recent *Marie Pas Claire* (a pastiche title contrasting with the mainstream *Marie Claire*), with an activist informational bias and a touch of *Le Torchon Brûle* style. More academic and theoretical publications include the two journals *Nouvelles questions féministes* (*New Feminist Questions*) and the more recent quarterly, *Lunes*.

Mainstream Media: Women and the Body Politic

It is against a whole range of mediatized assumptions as to women's roles
in society, as discussed above, that groups and individual women struggle
to gain recognition for their capacities and potential in the public arena
and to become visible figures of influence. The mainstream media still,
for the most part, see women public and political figures as predominantly
sexual beings within a heterosexual framework, hampering their representation in both senses of the word. This section will look at such
representations of women in the political sphere during the 1995 French
presidential election and the 1997 French general election.

The political arena is *par excellence* an area where women's invisiblilty
is the most marked and where finding one's identity and space is perhaps
at its most acute: all the prejudices concerning women's private and public
roles are at their most pronounced here, confirming the career-woman/
responsible-wife-and-mother dilemma exploited in the women's press.
Women politicians interviewed on those pages and elsewhere, find
themselves facing inappropriate questions of a nature that would not be
put to their male counterparts, for women are seen here as the exception
to the (male) rule, and their achievement as exceptional rather than natural.
Moreover if they do not display the marks of being a 'standard' woman,
they are seen as problematic, if not deviant. Such was the case of Arlette
Laguiller, of Lutte Ouvrière (Workers Combat Party), one of the two
women candidates in the 1995 Presidential election: with no evident
partner, no children and an unfussy mode of dress, she was 'feminized'
by the interviewer on the France 2 channel's *Heure de vérité* (*Moment of
Truth*) programme by his asking if she would keep on the studio make-
up, it being the first time in her life she had worn any. Similarly *Elle* said
of her : 'Arlette est une vedette qui n'aime pas les paillettes [. . .] À 54
ans Arlette n'a ni enfant ni mari' (Arlette is a star who doesn't like sparkle
. . . At 54 she has neither child nor husband) (*Elle,* 8 March 1995).

The lack of these attributes, then, renders a woman incomplete and
insubstantial, but in reverse she is also the agent to consolidate the male
authority figure, being a part of his trappings but not his total identity. It
is this female support role that was foregrounded in relation to the male
candidates with their spouses being given increased space in the media,
giving women *and* politics a higher profile, but not necessarily benefiting
women *in* politics. The effect is to emphasize not just traditional values
per se but the heterosexual base on which political authority is posited,
incorporating the assumption of male seduction. *Elle* picked up on this,
by running an article entitled *Laquelle Elysée-vous* (Which one – ie,

candidate's wife – will you 'Elyselect'? – elect to the Élysée Palace?), and a second one in the form of a test: 'Êtes-vous plutôt Sylviane ou Bernadette? [. . .] Pour être sure de faire le bon CHOIX, mettez-vous à la place de sa femme. Notre test [. . .] vous révélera si vous auriez pu séduire LIONEL JOSPIN ou JACQUES CHIRAC' [10] (*Elle*, 7 May 1995). The more sinister consequence of this was that legitimate women politicians were similarly lined up alongside male candidates, with a Harris poll tipping Simone Veil as a prime ministerial mate for Balladur, and Martine Aubry for Jospin (*Elle*, 6 March 1995). This, despite its positive aspects, reinforces the commonplace that women's turn is not now but always next, that they are on trial and, importantly, that they have a consort role.

The media subsequently had a field day when, following Jacques Chirac's election to the presidency, Prime Minister Juppé included twelve women in his cabinet (only four of whom survived more than six months): this gave rise to the famous *'Juppettes'* ('Bits of skirt') epithet and a front-page montage of the *Nouvel Observateur* featuring a benign Chirac with the smaller scale twelve women set against his tweedy chest, and the headline: 'LES FEMMES DE CHIRAC' (Chirac's women) – or should this read 'wives', given the ambiguity in French? (*Nouvel Observateur*, 20 July 1995). Either way, these women were under the tutelage of the two male authority figures.

If women politicians were in the wings during the presidential election, they were out in force for the general election that Chirac called three years early in 1997. However, like all parties and candidates they were taken by surprise by the 21 April announcement and, in the manner of reporting of prestige events, were much less visible than were the male spokespersons and leaders in the ensuing media stampede. The only female party leader was Dominique Voynet, of the Green Party. A review of *Libération* and *Le Figaro* for the period leading up to the two rounds of elections of 25 May 1997 and 1 June 1997, showed there was no feature article concerning a woman politician for nearly four weeks until that in *Libération* (19 May 1997): 'Martine Aubry sème ses graines de l'aubrisme' (Martine Aubry sows the seeds of Aubryism), whereas articles and interviews with male candidates proliferated. In *Libération*'s and *Le Figaro*'s daily chronicles *Ils ont dit* ('What they said') very rarely did women figure, but a high proportion of reports stressed women's lack of control of the situation, referring to them as *bousculées* (pressured) and *parachutées* (catapulted) into unfamiliar contexts and constituencies, whereas these terms were virtually never applied to men. Women were, indeed, often *parachutées* by virtue of the male-dominated party system, which designated them as candidates for unwinnable seats and/or against high-profile members of the opposition. Moreover, when a woman was selected for a (safe) seat in preference to a male rival, it was the latter's good grace in ceding the place that caused comment, as in the case of André Vauchez who gave way for Dominique Voynet, now Minister for the Environment.

When women candidates *were* consulted, there emerged a trend that would confirm the premise in the introduction to this chapter, such that more feminine values and approaches are sought among the electorate: after the dissolution of the Assemblée Nationale Catherine Trautmann is quoted as saying that the French want 'qu'on s'occupe de leur vie quotidienne' (that we should attend to what affects their daily lives) (*Le Figaro*, 26 May 1999); Isabelle Hubert says that her potential constituents talk to her of their lives, their jobs and their fears for the future (*Le Figaro*, 22 May 1999); and Martine Aubry that there is a need for: 'une vraie moralité des valeurs [. . .] une autre façon de faire la politique [. . .] changer la façon de vivre entre nous' (a real set of moral values; a different way of conducting politics; change the way we live together) (*Libération*, 19 May 1999).

With sixty-three women elected, increasing the proportion from 5.9 per cent to 10.7 per cent, with fourteen women in government, their visibility and audibility is increasing, and, they are certainly no longer 'token women'. Nevertheless, media foregrounding of a small number of high-profile women ministers, Martine Aubry (Employment), Élizabeth Guigou (Justice), Catherine Trautmann (Culture and Communications), and Dominique Voynet (Environment), runs the risk of substituting for the proportional coverage one might expect to be accorded to the remaining fifty-nine 'junior' women deputies. In accordance with the findings of Mediawatch, this has the metonymical effect of 'the gang of four' representing the whole cohort, and their resulting visibility, by virtue of their 'otherness', obscures the fact that women ministers are still in a definite minority.

Women in the Media Professions: In/visibility and Women's Place

Statistically there are now more women working in the media sector that ever before, but this does not mean that proportionally they are represented equally at all levels and in positions of influence, as Table 3.2 shows.

These statistics, the latest available from the CCIJP (Commission de la Carte d'Identité des Journalistes Professionnels) (Authorizing Body for the Attribution of Identity Cards to Professional Journalists), confirm

Table 3.2 Cards Authorised: Statistics at 31 December 1997

	Men	Women	Total
CARDHOLDERS			
Salaried journalists	13,771	7,716	21, 478
comprising			
Press photographers	647	39	
Sketch artists	18	2	
Photo journalists	416	46	
Shorthand editors	11	140	
Proof editors	51	83	
Translation editors	20	33	
Freelance journalists paid per copy	**2, 611**	**1,931**	**4,542**
Comprising			
Press photographers	510	64	
Sketch artists	28	2	
Photo journalists	238	37	
Shorthand editors	0	5	
Proof editors	6	23	
Translation editors	0	4	
Job seekers	**678**	**575**	**1,253**
Directors	**448**	**73**	**521**
TRAINEES			
Salaried journalists	**732**	**690**	**1,422**
Freelance journalists	**376**	**402**	**778**
Paid per copy			
	18,606	**11,387**	**30,003**

Source: CCIJP (1997).

the data in their own survey *Les journalistes français en 1990* (French Journalists in 1990) (CCIJP 1991), which shows that from 1974 to 1979 between 19.5 per cent and 23.4 per cent of accredited journalists were women, and by 1990 they constituted 34 per cent: the 1997 figure is 38 per cent and rising. Significantly, women are less likely to be in contract employment, but are more evident among the *pigistes* (freelance workers). If the survey evaluates the profession as being 'younger, more feminized, more qualified' (CCIJP 1991, 21–35), with rather more than 50 per cent trainee journalists women, a range of indicators shows that women have more qualifications than their male counterparts and the gap is widening, but they are not correspondingly rewarded professionally. In particular they have difficulty gaining access to the technical side of the media, with many men having had the advantage of prior training in the army film and photography corps during national service. They are also paid consistently worse than men: Florence Beaugé puts the average monthly difference currently at 2,800FF (Beaugé 1999, 42).

Paradoxically the media themselves over the past two decades have highlighted increased visibility of women who do reach prominence, with a clear evolution from the 'sois belle ou tais-toi' ('be beautiful or keep quiet') article in an early 1980s TV magazine (*Télé 7 Jours*, 27 August 1983) to more up-beat features announcing: 'Les femmes prennent l'antenne' (Women take over the air waves) in both *Madame Figaro* (30 November 1991) and *Pèlerin Magazine* (21 August 1992). There is, however, some ambivalence in *TVSD*'s (26 November 1992) account of the feminization of the media, declaring that when it comes to audience ratings women presenters do just as well if not better than men, but under the headline: 'La télé en jupons' ('Petticoat TV'). Such articles became more frequent in the early 1990s as a result of the Gulf War: as Patricia Allémonière, head of the foreign affairs desk at TF1, explained, the Iraqi invasion of Kuweit on 2 August 1990 took place when many male colleagues were on holiday *en famille,* and all media required mass coverage, providing a golden opportunity for women to move into territory a hitherto predominantly male preserve.[11] Although a handful of women were already notable exceptions, as the *Télérama* article (11 January 1989) 'Les femmes montent au front' ('Women enter the front line') indicates, the public grew increasingly used to seeing women journalists in danger zones, with a correspondingly positive effect on audience ratings. A France 2 reporter puts it thus: 'On était devenues des produits de marketing, un peu comme des savonnettes, mais [. . .] on a joué le jeu [. . .] et profité d'eux de la même façon qu'ils profitaient de nous' (Beaugé, 1999: 43).[12]

But this does not mean that the battle is won for women journalists: these *baroudeuses de l'info* (women news warriors), as they are termed in the press, may be chided by a male superior on their return from the front for having abandoned their family for too long, and for every *grand(e) reporter* (female senior correspondent) there are many more who are assigned to traditional areas such as health and education. The 'women's page' will often be referred to by male colleagues as *la rubrique des connasses* (the silly bitches' column), and women freelancers, whose high proportion reflects the need for flexible working hours, find their paper spiked or drastically revised more often than do their male counterparts. Women news readers in both radio and television will be assigned weekend or early morning slots before making the peak audience times.

Most, however, are in agreement that their presence in journalism contributes positively to perceptions of women in society: while not concentrating on women's issues, women reporters strive to give a more gender-balanced account of the news and take the trouble to locate female authority figures to interview whenever possible.

Women media stars, however, as with prominent women politicians, tread a fine line between putting the case for women and operating as gender neutral professionals: again their high visibility camouflages the proportional invisibility of others. Among these are Anne Sinclair, who for many years hosted the weekly *7 sur 7* (7 days in 7) high profile interview programme, Claire Chazal, currently fronting weekend news on TFI, and someone whose success is legendary, Christine Ockrent, famous for becoming in October 1981 the first anchor woman and chief editor of the French Channel 2 evening news, nick-named *La Messe de Vingt Heures* (the 8.00 pm Mass). Respected for her professionalism, having begun her career as a researcher for CBS News, she incarnated an Americanization, allied to her famous smile of confidence, an air of mischief and, as her women colleagues testify, an androgynous seductive-ness: 'le style Ockrent, volontairement ambigu, cette beauté asexuée, charmeuse, cérébrale et dominatrice. Les années 80 vouaient un culte à "l'androgénéité"'[13] (Rambert and Maquelle, 1991: 137).

Androgynous or not, *la reine Christine* (Queen Christine) as she came to be known, recognized her impact: 'J'ai été bien involontairement l'un des symboles, d'une certaine manière l'une des vitrines, de cette féminisa-tion de la société en France'[14] (Rambert and Maquelle, 1991: 137). This feminine visibility did not necessarily reflect feminine values in media circles. Okcrent, too, was subjected to sexist prejudice, saying that in addition to women continually having to prove themselves, they are reproached for not conforming to the stereotype of a woman 'conditioned to seduce', and resented by men, and even some women, for being a woman boss (Ockrent, 1997: 193–4).

Effecting Change

Earlier in this chapter differences between mainstream and feminist press were addressed. Whereas the latter provide a clear platform for alternative perceptions, trying to achieve this from within the mainstream environ-ment is more complex, particularly in the audiovisual media. Two strands will be dealt with here: women's proactivity and women-oriented pro-gramming; and the work of the Association des Femmes Journalistes.[16]

New Moods, New Modes

Le Monde Diplomatique is not renowned for positive attitudes towards women, but Florence Beaugé, a salaried journalist with the paper, constantly strives to foreground women's perspectives and in March 1999 co-edited a comprehensive issue of *Manière de Voir* compiling some thirty articles on gender and women's issues published in the paper between 1993 and 1999. A woman copy editor working for Bayard Press on *Enfants magazine*, revises all material that systematically prioritizes the male over the female and makes suggestions for copy that reflects girls' interests: needless to say, she meets resistance.[17] Until approximately five years ago there was also resistance towards women in certain aspects of radio. A news presenter with Radio France Internationale (the equivalent of BBC World Service) confirms this, but is aware as she speaks to a francophone audience, largely in Africa, that she can bring a woman's empathy to women, treatment of the excision debate (February 1999) being a case in point.

In addition to the positive action by such mainstream presenters as Brigitte Patient of Radio France Inter whose talk show has included a series of features by Florence Montreynaud (an active member of the AFJ) on 'the first woman to . . .', private radio allows for a more direct approach, as with the programme Femmes Libres (Free women) hosted by Nelly since 1981 on the anarchist radio station Radio Libertaire (Libertarian Radio): overtly militant feminist, her weekly two-hour programme is run by women for women but interviews men, too, reaching an audience of 40,000.[17] Ventures such as these respond in some measure to the dissatisfactions expressed in research conducted by Sylvie Debras at regional level: findings showed that neither mainstream news media nor the feminine press corresponded to their needs (Debras 1998). Thanks to cable and satellite there is now a television channel, Téva, which claims to do precisely that, under the slogan: 'Téva, les femmes aussi ont une chaîne qui pense à elles!' (Téva, women too have a channel which thinks about them!), drawing an estimated two million viewers, of whom 68 per cent are women.

Networking Women Journalists

Underpinning much of the proactive work of women journalists is the Association des Femmes Journalistes. Founded in 1981 and with approximately 400 members of wide-ranging expertise, it has two main objectives: to achieve equality with male journalist colleagues, and to research and improve the image of women in the media, in which Mediawatch plays a part. Their permanent campaigning for non-sexist language means that members react swiftly to insulting incidents such as the heckler at the 1999 Paris Agricultural Show who invited Dominique Voynet to: 'Enlève ta culotte, salope!' ('Get your knickers off, slut!'). A protest petition was immediately organized, as in the case of women modelling scanty underwear live, brothel style, in the windows of the Galeries Lafayette in spring 1999. Other dimensions of their remit include raising awareness of new media and their influence on the journalist profession, solidarity with women journalists in other parts of the world, and a federation with those in Cameroon and Benin, all of which are maintained by strong networking and informed by a monthly newsletter.

The AFJ raises its profile by awarding four prizes, Le Prix Séverine, for the most gender-aware book or essay of the year, Le prix AFJ du Documentaire, normally selected at the annual Women's Film Festival in Créteil, Le Prix AFJ de la Presse for the best article on women's role, and the Prix Pub (Advertising Prize) for the least sexist advertisement of the year. This last was awarded in April 1999 for the Sida Info Service (Aids Information Service) series of posters promoting use of condoms and reworking fairytale mythology under the campaign headline: 'Make sure your love story remains a fairytale'. The fact that Catherine Trautmann, Minister for Culture and Communications, presented the award bears testimony to the increasing authority of the AFJ whose members are regularly included in discussions at ministerial level. The title of their current collective volume in conjunction with a Paris school of journalism sums up the AFJ mission: *Dites-le avec les femmes: le sexisme ordinaire dans les medias* (*Say it with Women: everyday Sexism in the Media*) (Barré et al., 1999).

It is fitting to end this chapter with the above account of the work of French women journalists and the AFJ because they epitomize both the successes and the ongoing struggles of women in relation to the media not just in recent times but spanning the twentieth century. On the one hand there are more visible women in the media professions, yet on the other there are very few in top executive positions. The twelve-strong board of directors at TF1 boasts only one woman, the employees' representative, in a presumably non-executive role (TF1 publicity dossier 1998), whereas the president and director general of Téva are both women. More generally, however, the overall superior qualifications of younger women entering the profession is beginning to take effect. Of females in the 26–30 age group, 86.9 per cent have qualifications of Bac + N, compared with 72.3 of males, and 7.5 per cent of females in the 36–45 age group are in executive positions compared with 5.2 per cent of males (CCIJP: 1991). Nonetheless, as Table 3.2 shows, the vast majority in the prestigious field of photo journalism are male, bearing out the gender imbalance in technical expertise, and notwithstanding the increased number of women journalists working in frontline locations. Women still have to show, in a patriarchal environment, that they can be taken seriously, but they are increasingly proving to be highly competitive in the media professions, particularly those without children and who are therefore more mobile. This development is resented by their male counterparts, as the following statement from a woman television journalist confirms, 'On est vécues comme dangereusement compétitives. On a du mal a être reconnues', ('We are perceived as dangerous rivals. It's hard to be accepted') (CCIJP, 1991). High-profile women have given added authority to their sex and gender, but even they still need to prove themselves and they risk reprisals if they 'overplay' their capabilities.

At another level, the technological explosion providing greater access to pornography contributes to the perpetuation of the stereotyping of women as available and exploitable sexual beings, as recent advertising campaigns have shown. Nonetheless, although the massive feminist movements of the 1970s are a thing of the past, action is increasingly taking place in a more 'mainstream' way, as evidenced by the AFJ, that is to say, within professional life where women increasingly play a part. By launching anti-sexist campaigns, by harnessing the experience of feminists of long standing such as Benoîte Groult and Gisèle Halimi, by engaging with political figures and combining the powerful domains of media and politics, the AFJ is becoming a respected and influential force.

These developments are occurring at the same time as the parity debate has captured the attention of the whole nation, with a range of significant outcomes: male politicians, anxious not to appear old hat and out of touch with women voters, are paying lip service at least to the notion of parity, while a newspaper such as *Libération* uncharacteristically published an apology: 'Avis à nos lectrices' ('Notice to our female readers'), to all women primary school teachers for not having included a single woman in their focus group on this sector, saying:

En plein débat sur la parité, cette absence était d'autant plus inadmissible que les enseignantes sont majoritaires dans l'Education nationale. Nous n'avons aucune excuse. Tout juste cette piteuse explication: autour de la table ronde, nous avons cherché un équilibre entre partisans et adversaires de la réforme, syndiqués et non syndiqués. Obnubilés par ces subtils dosages, nous n'avons constaté qu'après que tout nos invités étaient des hommes. (*Libération*, 19 February 1999).[18]

This perfect illustration of the data provided by Mediawatch, and the contrition of *Libération* in the current gender-political climate show some of the shifts suggested by Burke and Cathalat and provide grounds for cautious optimism in the task of redressing imbalances in media representations of women and the role of women in the media. But one wonders how long it will be before such apologies become redundant.

Notes

1. Bureau de Vérification de la Publicité, 11, rue St Florentin, 75008 Paris; Tel: 00 33 1 40 15 15 40.
2. AVFT (Association Européenne contre les Violences faites aux Femmes au Travail), 71 rue St Jacques, 75005; Tel: 00 33 1 44 24 81 35.
3. 'The advertisement showed the photograph of a young woman seated, half naked, breasts barely covered, beneath which was written: "It's when we have virtually nothing on that they discover how much we have within".'
4. Article 222–33 of the French penal code (*Code Pénal*) stipulates that whosoever abuses his/her authority and uses orders, threats or pressure to obtain sexual favours is liable to a year's imprisonment and a 100.000FF fine. This is backed up by articles 122-46, 47 and 48 of the French Work Code (*Code du Travail*), which authorize sanctions to be taken in the workplace.
5. Documented case studies are to be found in: AVFT (1990).
6. For further information on Marguerite Durand as a feminist journalist consult Rabaut (1996).
7. See Taïeb (1982 and 1999).
8. For a fuller account of the development of women's movements and publications of this period, see Duchen (1986).
9. Personal interview with Ernestine Ronai in January 1999.
10. 'Are you Sylviane or Bernadette? [. . .] to be sure of making the right CHOICE put yourself in his wife's shoes. Our test [. . .] will show if you could have seduced Lionel Jospin or Jacques Chirac.'
11. Personal interview with Patricia Allémonière in January 1999.
12. 'We had become consumer products, rather like bars of soap, but [. . .] we played the game [. . .] we cashed in on them just as they cashed in on us'.

13. 'The deliberately ambiguous Ockrent style, that asexual beauty, intellectual and dominating. The 80s were a time for the cult of androgyny' (Rambert and Maquelle 1991: 137).
14. 'Unwittingly I was one of the symbols, in a way one of the showcases, for the feminization of French society' (Rambert and Maquelle 1991: 137).
15. My very warm thanks go to Natacha Henry and many other members of the AFJ for their time and support in the preparation of this paper: their networking greatly facilitated the interviews conducted with a wide range of women journalists. Association des Femmes Journalistes, Maison de l'Europe, 35 rue des Francs-Bourgeois, 75004 Paris; Tel: 00 33 6 08 03 26 94.
16. Some women preferred to remain anonymous due to lack of sympathy for their views in their place of work.
17. Radio Libertaire, wavelength: MF 89.4, is obtainable in Paris/Île de France.
18. 'In the midst of the parity debate, this omission was all the more unforgivable since women predominate in state education. There is no excuse. We [. . .] just offer this pitiful explanation: for the round table we had sought equal numbers for either side of the debate on reforms, trade unionists and non trade unionists. Mesmerized by these subtleties, we only noticed afterwards that all our guests were male.'

References

Albert, P. (1998), *La Presse française,* Paris: La Documentation Française.
AVFT (1990), *De l'Abus de pouvoir sexuel: le Harcèlement sexuel au travail*, Paris: Éditions La Découverte.
Barré,V., Debras, S., Henry, N. and Trancart, M. (1999), *Dites-le avec des femmes: le sexisme ordinaire dans les médias*, Paris: CFD-AFJ.
Beaufumé, A. 1998), 'Les Femmes et les sensibilités féminines', *Lunes*, no. 3 (April): 6–14.
Beaugé, F. (1999), 'Le 'deuxième sexe' du journalisme', *Manière de voir*, vol. 44, Paris: *Le Monde Diplomatique*, 42–5.
Bonvoisin, S.-M. and Maignien, M. (1996), *La Presse féminine*, Paris: Presses Universitaires de France, (First publ. 1986).
Burke, M. (1998), *Valeurs féminines, le pouvoir de demain*, Paris: Éditions Village Mondial.

Cathelat, B. (1998), *L'Alternative des valeurs féminines*, Paris: Éditions Denoël.

CCIJP, (1991), *Les Journalistes français en 1990: Radiographie d'une profession*, Paris: La Documentation Française.

Dardigna, M. (1978), *La Presse 'féminine': fonction idéologique*, Paris: Maspéro.

Debras, S. (1998), 'La Voix des femmes au chapitre: Presse quotidienne régionale, presse féminine, perception et profils de lectrice', *Médias Pouvoirs*, no. 4: 30–42.

Duchen, C, (1986), *Feminism in France: From May '68 to Mitterrand*, London: Routledge & Kegan Paul.

El Yamani, M. (1988), *Médias et féminismes: Minoritaires sans paroles*, Paris: L'Harmattan.

Fischler, C. (1993), 'Une Féminisation des moeurs?', *Esprit*, November: 9–23.

Gallagher, M. (1980), 'Male chauvinism in the mass media', *The Unesco Courrier*, July: 20–25.

An Unfinished Story: Gender Patterns in Media Employment (1995), Reports and Papers on Mass Communication 110, Paris: Unesco Publishing.

Guide Alliance de l'Autodiscipline (1997), Brussels: European Advertising Standards Alliance.

Louis, M.-V. (1997), 'Les Campagnes de l'AVFT contre les publicités sexistes en France: 1992–1995', *Nouvelles Questions Féministes*, vol. 18: 3–4: 79–115.

Martin, M. (1997), *Médias et journalistes de la République*, Paris: Éditions Odile Jacob.

Ockrent, C. (1997), *La Mémoire du cœur*, Paris: Fayard.

Rabaut, J. (1996), *'La Fronde' féministe ou 'Le Temps' en jupons*, Paris: L'Harmattan.

Rambert, C. and Maquelle, S. (1991), *Des Femmes d'influence: Pouvoirs et télévision*, Paris: Hachette Carrère.

Taïeb, E. (1982), *Hubertine Auclert: La Citoyenne 1848–1914*, Paris: Syros.

—— (1999), 'Penser la Parité avec Hubertine Auclert', *Lunes*, no. 7 (April): 34–41.

Trancart, M. (1998), *Portrait des femmes dans l'information*, Paris: Association des Femmes Journalistes.

—4—

Women and Politics
Máire Fedelma Cross

Une assemblée législative composée entièrement d'hommes est aussi incompétente pour faire les lois qui régissent une société composée d'hommes et de femmes, que le serait une assemblée composée de privilégiés pour discuter les intérêts des travailleurs, ou une assemblée de capitalistes pour soutenir l'honneur du pays. (Jeanne Deroin, editor of the newspaper *L'Opinion des femmes*, Campaign poster '*Aux Electeurs de la Seine*', April 1849).

The French political system is both rich and complex. Much has been written in English about the evolution of France's five different republics from an institutional and ideological perspective: their constitutions, parliament, presidency and political parties (Cole, 1998; Hayward, 1973; Hazareesingh, 1994; Hewlett, 1998; Stevens, 1992; Thompson, 1969; Wright, 1989). However, in this complex evolution as in these studies, women seem to be incidental. Among the French studies of politics (Avril, 1990; Borella, 1990; Duverger, 1974) women are just as conspicuous by their absence or invisibility in the part they played in the historical shaping of French politics.

This does not mean that women have been absent from politics: far from it. As citizens, French women are present in as many of the vast number of political parties and associations as are men. But for women the relationship with politics is different from that of men (Faure, 1987: 135). It is determined primarily by the fact that in France the relationship of women and politics is essentially one of an historical marginalization purely on grounds of gender. Their formal exclusion from the democratic process no longer exists, but in reality their equal sharing of political power is as inaccessible as ever. Opposition to women in politics has been most persistent in political parties and the government, which consists of the *conseil des ministres* led by the Prime Minister and the head of the executive, who is also head of state, the President, elected by universal suffrage. Like the political process, the relationship of women and men in politics today is also a very complex one. Firstly, not all women have accepted the status quo of the patriarchal political establishment. There is a long tradition of campaigns for civic and civil rights for women going back to before 1789, as any study of the history of feminism can demonstrate (Albistur and Armogathe, 1977; Bard, 1995; Hause, 1984; Riot-Sarcey, 1994). Secondly, the state has always had a vested interest in women as citizens, albeit unenfranchized ones. In particular, ever since the expansion of the public sector at the end of the nineteenth century, women have been prominent as salaried workers and as instruments of implementing state policy, most often in health and education. Ever since legislation has been passed regulating men's and women's lives (Accampano, Fuchs and Stewart, 1995), women have been the subject of political debate, particularly in matters of working hours for women, maternity benefits and matters of child raising. As economic and social actors therefore, women have been the subjects of politics. Thirdly, and most importantly, women have always been just as interested in politics, or for that matter, as indifferent to politics as have men. The majority of women who have engaged in politics however, have not taken up a feminist stance. Although women were excluded from voting or standing for election until 1945, this did not deter many from taking part in the founding and running of political parties they were barred from electing under the Third Republic (Klejman and Rochefort, 1989; Reynolds, 1996; Smith, 1996). Fourthly, although no longer barred from politics since 1945, women politicians are still a rarity. By 1987, there had only ever been nine women government ministers (De Cordon, 1987: 36). The subject of women and politics is just as complex as is the political system and relations between men and women in politics. As a category, women are the subjects of politics. Yet it is as individual citizens that women choose to act politically. They are not a natural political family on the Right or the Left. They are one half of the human race. They cannot be categorized by social class, religious belief, racial origin or economic activity, although some sectors of employment are heavily feminized. Therefore, it is exceedingly difficult to qualify the term 'women and politics'. While few mainstream political theorists have conceded any contribution by women to France's rich political tradition, any rectification of this scant attention in the past is usually confined to the bounds of the feminist movement as a pressure group or the success of 'women's demands' (Hall, 1994: 89; Stevens, 1992: 267–70). As Reynolds has indicated (1995: 2), not even Rosanvallon, who is one of the few who looks at the definition of universal suffrage as gender exclusive for over a century (1992: 130–45), can explain why so few women succeed in politics in contemporary France.

Gender Inequality in French Politics

Why does the French political system produce so few women politicians? It has been acknowledged officially in a parliamentary report and elsewhere (Martin, 1998: 3; Mossuz-Lavau, 1998: 21) that France is the *lanterne rouge* for Europe in political gender inequalities:

> Malgré les termes de l'ordonnance du 21 avril 1944, selon lesquels 'les femmes sont électrices et éligibles dans les mêmes conditions que les hommes' et en dépit d'une évolution enregistrée lors des dernières consultations électorales, force est de constater que le taux de présence des femmes dans les assemblées parlementaires et locales, inférieur, comme dans tous les pays du monde, à leur importance numérique dans le corps électoral, l'est davantage en France que dans la plupart des pays démocratiques. (Cabanel, 1999: 4)[2]

The Assemblée nationale elected in June 1997 increased its female members by 80 per cent to sixty-three out of 577. The Senate report stressed that this increase happened without any institutional positive discrimination or alterations to the electoral system, but accepted that the percentage had remained consistently low for fifty years (5.6 per cent in 1945, 6 per cent in 1993). With nineteen women *sénateurs* out of 321, the two houses have a 9.18 per cent female presence (82 women and 893 men). For *conseils municipaux,* the rate went up from 14 per cent in 1983 to 17.7 per cent in 1989 and 21.7 per cent in 1995 (110,986 women councillors) The rate is rather better for regional councils, at 24.16 per cent up from 10.5 per cent in 1992, the number of women candidates having increased from 27 per cent to 36.9 per cent. Only one woman is president of a *conseil général*, there are two women presidents of regional councils, nine women out of twenty-eight are government ministers in Jospin's government.

France's political system functions with too few women elected representatives in its many democratic institutions, and too few women appointed to high office or in highly paid state functions (Courtois, 1999b). From where does the resistance to women politicians stem? How can one rectify the glaring anomaly? These questions have dominated the public perception of women in politics to the detriment almost of those actively and fully engaged in public roles as *deputés* and, more recently, as Ministers in the socialist governments as evident from their books (Bredin, 1997, Cresson, 1998, Royal, 1996, Roudy, 1995). Democracy has not yet come of age, according to Edith Cresson, until it can accept mistakes from a woman politician as readily as it does those from a man politician (Interview with Anne Sinclair on programme 'Sept sur sept', France 2, on her appointment in April 1990).

According to the Senate report there is a constitutional obstacle:

> L'égal accès à l'éligibilité étant établi en droit, il reste à déterminer comment sa mise en oeuvre peut se traduire par un nombre d'élues en rapport avec le nombre des citoyennes sans remettre en cause les principes constitutionnels de la souveraineté nationale, de l'égalité et de la liberté de l'électeur. (Cabanel 1999: 7)[3]

Opportunities in French Politics to End Exclusion

For a definition of women and politics, there are two aspects of interest to this chapter. Firstly, as long as women remain a very small minority in elected bodies, there is an unresolved contradiction in French politics. Secondly, it is only by their gendered under-representation and by nothing else that French women are a political category. Since women do not form an interest group in this author's opinion, it is futile or even dangerous to generalize about how women behave in politics (Adler, 1993: 190–203; De Cordon, 1987: 229–59). Women as individuals are active in political organizations according to their ideological choices and sociological circumstances, be they professional, family, cultural or religious. As women are to be found in every section of society, they cannot be represented in politics simply as a pressure-group movement. The feminist groups who have had some influence on contemporary politics and have sought to alter the system in the name of all women are a very small minority with whom other women have rarely experienced a strong sense of identity and solidarity. Only in the case of a specific demand, such as the campaign for the right to abortion in the early 1970s, have feminists succeeded in attracting broader support or any attention in politics. Even then, the resulting reform of the law passed in 1975 was a very watered-down version of feminist demands. A similar situation has arisen with the 1990s *parité* campaign, which shall be discussed later in this chapter. Although the proposed reform of the constitution falls very short of feminist demands, the *parité* campaign of the 1990s has elicited broad support and a focus that was lacking in recent years for women in politics. Indeed the symbolic importance far outstretches the actual changes envisaged by recent reform. It remains to be seen how the recently accepted principle of *parité* will be enacted beyond good constitutional intentions (Gaspard, 1998b: 26).

Therefore, the question of ending exclusion is the focal point of our study of women and politics. For the purpose of this chapter, and at the cost of omitting many other fascinating aspects of the term, women and politics must be restricted considerably to one aspect: the conditions surrounding the recent attempt to break the glass ceiling inherent in the French political structure (Comte and Lipietz, 1999: 14). Our study is narrowed, but the most recent challenge to exclusion demands a wider debate on the French political system as a whole. This brings out the paradox for women: either the spotlight is on them because of their exclusion and, for a moment, they are right at the heart of politics, or else they are almost invisible as politicians devote their time to other affairs of state.

The manner in which the French régime has been able unfairly to exclude women from power sharing leads us to ask how the system itself functions as an excluding system. In order to understand why women have been excluded from political power it is vital to discuss the power structures of the French Republic.

The nineteenth-century scientific socialist Karl Marx saw the political system as part of the superstructure holding a society together and the means whereby the élite could maintain and reproduce its hold on power. Theories of power and the continued privileged access to power by the ruling classes have abounded in twentieth-century France, notably among intellectuals such as Jean-Paul Sartre, Louis Althusser, Michel Foucault and Pierre Bourdieu. Looking at French politics through the lens of women's involvement with the system gives an insight into the success or failure of that system's ability to function to the satisfaction of all its citizens.

Women and the Historical Exception

Jules Ferry, a founding father of the Third Republic, is reputed to have said that the First Republic gave peasants land, the Second, the vote and the Third, education. French women could say the First, Second and Third Republics excluded women from liberty, fraternity and equality. It was only during the period leading up to the *Libération,* at the end of World War Two in the transition from Third to Fourth Republic in 1944, that a decree was issued by a provisional government in exile in Algeria to grant women eligibility to vote and stand for election under the same terms as men in the next parliament. In 1998, forty years after the founding of the Fifth Republic, the subject of women and political inequality returned to the parliamentary agenda at an exceptional moment and as an indication that the political system is deficient.

Cohabitation: Dilemma for Politicians, Golden Opportunity for Women

When the Fifth Republic constitution was devised in 1958, the founders assumed that the two executive positions of President and Prime Minister would normally come from the same political majority (Duverger, 1974, Wright, 1989). The first exception to this occurred from 1986 until 1988, the second between 1993 and 1995. On both of these occasions, the socialist President Mitterrand was coming to the end of his seven-year mandate and did not resign even though a majority government of the Right was in power, both in March 1986 and in March 1993. Since 1997 France has been run by a third period of political *cohabitation*, which is likely to be more lengthy, since President Chirac from the Gaullist party the RPR, (Rassemblement pour la République) is not due to stand for re-election until May 2002 and the next legislative elections are not due either until June 2002. Prime Minister Lionel Jospin, leader of the PS (Parti socialiste) came to power in June 1997 as a result of an early parliamentary election. President Chirac who, as leader of the executive, was empowered to dissolve the parliament in anticipation of the due date of March 1998 did so in the hope of outmanoeuvring the Left, which had suffered a landslide defeat in 1993. Instead the Right suffered such a defeat in 1997. As a result of his political miscalculation, President Chirac's position has been one of isolation (Massot, 1999: 14). Although (at the time of writing) the RPR is still the largest party of the Right, it is currently in opposition in the Assemblée nationale with the PS the leading party of the parliamentary majority known as *la gauche plurielle*, a combination of left-wing groups, the PS, the PCF (Parti communiste français), the Mouvement des citoyens, and the ecologists (les Verts). Elected shortly after Tony Blair's Labour party brought 120 women MPs to the House of Commons, the Socialist Party also fielded a larger number of female candidates who were successful, although only half as many those of the 'New' Labour party. Nevertheless, the Jospin government was to contain more women ministers than there were in total in the previous forty years of the Fifth Republic. This in itself was hailed as a great victory for Jospin. However, what is more important is the effect of the power struggle within this executive cohabitation, which could last as long as five years, ending with both men in the race for the presidency (Courtois, 1999a: 6). The competitive relationship between Jospin and Chirac to retain their high popularity ratings in anticipation of a tough presidential campaign in 2002 has had a significant impact on the success of institutional political reform. For once, the present leaders are falling over themselves to climb on to the *parité* bandwagon. There is momentum for reform coming from men in power, the vital allies for women to enter political power (De Montvalon, 1999: 8). Added to that, the positive responses from opinion polls over the desirability of increased responsibilities for women in politics (Sineau in Martin, 1998: 69–74) and the increase in the number of women in power in key ministries, such as employment, (Martine Aubry) justice, (Elizabeth Guigou) and education, (Ségolène Royal), has in turn increased pressure for change from within government (Royal, 1999: 5) to alter the law in favour of women.

Although there has been an increase in the numbers of women in government and in positions of responsibility, elsewhere the change is still negligible (Jenson and Sineau, 1995). Those who argued that women would progressively gain access to power with their right to vote and stand for election have been defeated by reality (Mossuz-Lavau, 1999: 17). Gender inequality in politics has been so persistent that demands from women for an equal share in power have shamed political leaders into making a gesture of exceptional intervention to change the political system by this particular form of positive discrimination which has come to be known as *parité*. After years of political neglect, it is no coincidence therefore that it is during an exceptional moment of political conflict in French politics that women have been able to challenge successfully the political impasse. The question was brought out into the open and the public could judge the indifference or hostility of the men politicians when put directly to *deputés* and *senateurs* in a parliamentary debate in March 1998 and during the debate on the Bill to alter the constitution in favour of *parité* in 1998 and 1999. A look at the historical evolution of the French political system is necessary to understand the neglect, why women have been the exception in politics and why exceptional steps have been necessary to alter the French political system to end this neglect.

Universalism: the French Exception

The modern French political system is reputed to date from the Revolution of 1789. Hailed as the greatest single event in French political history, the results are still cited today as the *raison d'être* of the present political regime, the Republic. The revolutionary process overthrew the *ancien régime* and ushered in a system which founded its legitimacy in national sovereignty embodied in representative government and the belief in principles of equal rights of the citizen and liberty of expression and property ownership, to be guaranteed by an ordered modernized state apparatus, which would provide national and international security. The first important feature of French politics is the long period of instability that followed the revolution. It took over 100 years before the Republic was finally secure and parliamentary democratic stability settled. Even since the founding of the Third Republic, France went through further institutional upsets in 1940 and 1958. Another feature of the French political system is that male suffrage was not extended gradually as in Britain but was associated with the overthrow of another regime (Rosanvallon, 1992: 333). The manner in which all men were granted the vote was revolutionary in 1848. The year 1789 is a shorthand term for a process of whole revolutionary transformation, which lasted well beyond the arrival in power of Napoleon in 1799. This founding moment is significant for our story of women and politics although only recently has the revolutionary period been examined from the aspect of women and politics (Hufton, 1992; Hunt, 1992; Landes, 1988). What is considered a crucial moment of modernization in politics (Cole, 1998: 5; Hazareesingh, 1994: 68–75) is critical for the construction of the political relationship of men and women, namely one of imbalance. Did women play a greater part in politics as a result of the Revolution? At first sight, not at all. The universal principle of citizenship became sacrosanct to political legitimacy. By failing to qualify exactly what *homme* meant, the founding text, the *Déclaration des droits de l'homme et du citoyen,* excluded women from the public sphere. Philosophical justifications for this exclusion were found later. Whether or not it was deliberate, the result was the same. This initial oversight then was transformed into specific exclusion from public life throughout the nineteenth century. The dominant discourse and ideology expressed by writers and philosophers, such as Rousseau and Proudhon, argued to maintain women in the domestic private sphere while men should proceed to shape future political institutions in the public sphere distinct and separate from the domestic sphere in a new way (Landes, 1988: 93–200). Women in politics during the volatile revolutionary situation of 1795 and subsequent moments of crisis such as 1848 were seen as a potentially subversive threat to the regime (Barry, 1996: 77–104; Gordon and Cross, 1996: 59–141; Landes, 1988: 140–6). As well as the chronic inherent political instability and intransigence over electoral reform, an important consequence of the revolutionary modernization process was a formalization of relations between citizens in a highly theoretical way. By the terms of the *code Napoléon* of 1803, written to modernize the French legal system, women were granted as much autonomy as criminals, lunatics and children, condemned to submit to either father or husband for legal decisions about property, work outside the home, or children. By this same formal procedure women were constructed as political nonentities. The only way of undoing this exclusion it seemed was to recognize the weakness of the original process.

In 1998 and 1999 the opponents of parity referred to the sanctity of universalism as their strongest argument against change, whether it be the constitution, the electoral system or the role of political parties; altering these would go against the founding Republican principle of universalism (Badinter, 1999: 86–9). Those in favour of *parité* issued a formal challenge to accept a different interpretation of 1789 (Gaspard, 1995: 13). Such was the institutional opposition that it would take another highly formalized process of the political system to achieve any alteration in favour of women.

Women's exclusion from the political system was fundamental yet incomplete; powerless citizens, they still posed a threat but were of no electoral interest to political parties seeking power. This powerlessness did not disqualify them from an interest in politics. Although never more than a minority movement in the nineteenth and twentieth centuries, individuals and women's organizations challenged the political system in the name of universalism (Albistur and Armogathe, 1977; Bard, 1995; McMillan, 1981). If all citizens were equal, they demanded, why distinguish between men and women? The opportunities to voice this argument were few. The patriarchal structure was impregnable it seemed but for this inherent instability mentioned above. Women protested against their political exclusion at another important defining moment for French democracy in 1848, when the founders of the Second Republic decreed in February 1848 that political suffrage should be universal. By this they meant masculine. Jeanne Deroin gained notoriety when she and a small group of women challenged this gendered definition of universal, all the while reiterating their loyalty to the new Republican ideals. When put to the vote in the constitutional assembly 899 voted against women's suffrage and one voted in favour in the name of universality (Gordon and Cross, 1996: 66). This challenge revealed the double think of politicians and the fundamental, but deeply inherent, contradiction of French Republicanism with which women have had to battle constantly (Roudy, 1995: 164). The strong philosophical tradition of French politics provided other outlets for women. In contrast to the lack of opportunity in politics, many women found opportunities to write to express their views elsewhere and indeed French feminism contains a strong body of philosophical and literary thought based on the notion of difference, but this only exacerbated women's marginalization (Cross, 1997a: 170–5). For our study of women and politics, it is important to note that the reasoning behind the power structure created an illogical intransigence over gender equality. The argument emerged that *homme* was a neutral, abstract term, but it meant men. Women were naturally unsuited to politics. They were naturally different because of their biological functions. This double think prevailed, even though it had been decreed by the principles of liberty, equality and fraternity that political power is neutral. The Republic was founded on the notion that one cannot subdivide citizens into different categories who are equal before the law, without distinction of race or religion. Once male suffrage was declared as universal in 1848, women were without allies in politics unlike the suffrage campaign in the United Kingdom (of Great Britain and Ireland as it was then) at the end of the nineteenth century, where working-class men were without the franchise and could act as political allies for the suffragettes.

In France, for the suffrage question to appear on the agenda required a massive effort on the part of women to get political parties to act on their behalf (Smith, 1996: 63–103). Party tactics guided the reasoning behind their exclusion as much as misogyny. The radicals who considered themselves to be on the Left and the true inheritors of the Republican ideal were obsessed with the clerical threat to the Republic. They exploited the fear of instability to turn down the demand for women's suffrage. A powerful lobby of women socialists furiously opposed any alliance with bourgeois women. Party politics were very fragmented and ideologically bitterly divided during the Third and Fourth Republic. The institutional power of the Senate which could block any law passed by the lower house meant their reticence to grant women the vote delayed women's suffrage considerably.

The Relevance of Republican Values to Gender Inequality and Equality

This intransigence on the part of men in total control of political power was upheld by the peculiarity of the original founding principles but whose contradiction was to prove its Achilles heel. According to Hazareesingh (1994: 68–9), the Republican tradition has the following parameters inherited from the 1789 Revolution. It promotes the notion of popular sovereignty linked to the exercise of critical reason, affirms the possibility and desirability of creating a rational political order, emphasizes the universality of the principles and values created by the new political order, projects a new concept of patriotism and nationalism and highlights the notion that political structures can be used to promote greater equality and social justice. Participationism, perfectionism, universalism, nationalism and revolutionism can therefore define Republicanism. Although Hazaree-singh does not discuss it, four out of these five are of direct relevance to changing the political system to include women.

This Republican agenda in its patriarchal form is incomplete as long as it marginalizes women. It is possible to use these parameters to legitimize the inclusion of women in the Republic. They indicate where the Republican values can be renewed and, similarly, they qualify where the men politicians find it harder to adjust than in others, in the context of French party politics at the end of the twentieth century. Of course, feminists have been insisting since 1789 that unless there is an equal place granted to women to participate in politics the Republic is a dead letter (Gordon and Cross, 1996). *Paritaires* are saying today that this will not occur naturally (Agacinski, 1999: 1). Some form of positive discrimination to alter the current system is imperative. Universality is a key term used both to support and oppose *parité*. The desirability and necessity of perfectibility of the system using rational logic in order to renew and preserve its vitality is also used by the *paritaires*. Finally, the voluntarist notion that the permanent revolution is a right of the outcasts in order to bring about change in their favour pertains equally. Women fighting for equality of power sharing are shaming the politicians into admitting that the system is in need of a change in order to remain loyal to its 1789 inheritance and Republican credibility.

From being political pariahs to enfranchised citizens, it took fifty years for women's absence from power to become noteworthy. Feminist groups which formed in the 1970s and successfully campaigned for changes in the law were more successful in the domain of personal and civil rights (Duchen, 1986: 103–24). In politics they were not taken seriously and they returned the derision by dismissing political activity as useless and irrelevant, Antoinette Fouque being a prime example (Cross, 1997a: 173). Hayward claims that French feminists and ecologists were late in developing in France and so followed foreign models, the American one in the case of feminism (Hayward, 1994: 296). Whether or not they were militant because of outside influences is debatable but there was the equally influential French revolutionary tradition to spur French women into action. Since the early days of the 'new wave' feminist movement in the 1970s, a new generation of women, the beneficiaries of greater access to education and employment, became seriously involved in mainstream politics in the 1980s. Intellectual theoretical debates that rendered feminism obscure for many no longer held as much sway (Cross, 1997a: 165). Fouque herself became a European MP in the PS group in 1994.

Since the 1990s, there has been greater media interest in the question of the lives of 'ordinary' women and politics with articles in *Le Monde, Le Nouvel Observateur, L'Evénement du jeudi, Le Nouvel Economiste* and even some television programmes. The higher profile of the new career paths of individual women politicians who have become Secretary of State or ministers, such as Françoise Giroud, Simone Veil, Yvette Roudy, Edith Cresson, Catherine Trautmann, Martine Aubry, Elizabeth Guigou, Ségolene Royal, has had a knock-on effect providing a focus for campaigning for gender equality in power which, hitherto, had been considered worthy of interest only among feminist intellectuals and pressure groups (Duchen, 1986: 143; Cross, 1997a: 164). It had become obvious that the addition of twelve million new voters since 1945 did not fundamentally recast the political system (Martin, 1997: 57). Indeed, women's voting patterns are now almost identical to those of men although women voted briefly more for the Right than for the Left (Mossuz-Lavau et Sineau, 1983). Women's suffrage is no longer considered as potentially damaging to any particular group as it had been by the radicals throughout the life of the Third Republic (McMillan, 1981; Smith, 1996). It also became clear that the gendered vote began to matter. During the very closely run presidential election campaign of 1974 between the Socialist Mitterrand and the first non-Gaullist President Valéry Giscard d'Estaing, women were the greatest part of the floating electorate that had to be wooed by the Right and by the Left. Giscard realized that women could be targeted as subjects of political reform and as potential supporters once in power. He broke new ground when he gave women a higher profile in government through his Health Minister, Simone Veil, and Françoise Giroud, appointed to the newly created Secrétaire d'Etat à la condition féminine. Mitterrand followed suit in 1981 by upgrading the former post to a Cabinet Minister's post for 'les droits des femmes' giving that post to Yvette Roudy and bringing in other women ministers to posts which were considered non-traditional appointments for women politicians (Edith Cresson served as Minister for Agriculture).

These moves were symbolic, the result of an initiative from above to attempt to remove obstacles to women politicians elsewhere in the system. Yet there was no improvement in representation of women in parliament, not because there were no votes for women candidates, but because there were too few women in positions of power in political parties both on the Right and on the Left (De Cordon, 1987: 85).

Reform from Above

May 1974 marked a new awareness of the lack of women politicians. When Giscard realized he had to make an impact to win women away from Gaullism and the Left, he discovered very few women in the pool of senior politicians from where appointable Ministers are to be found. Simone Veil was in a senior administrative post outside elected political bodies (Adler, 1993: 170). Despite women's absence from the *états-majors* and the élites of political parties, Mitterrand resorted to the same tactic. This appointment of senior women from outside political parties to positions of power is known as *le fait du prince*. Mitterrand even went as far as appointing Edith Cresson as France's first woman Prime Minister. This appointment backfired on him when Cresson proved to be rather unpopular but her experience was a salutary one for women. It showed how intransigent men in political parties were about allowing women to share power (Schlemla, 1993).

Against the Glass Ceiling

The few women who did gain access to power after May 1974 both witnessed at first hand and publicized the effect of the system of party politics on the relationship between men and women in politics. Because party politics is such a combative process, those in power refuse to give anything to those out of power without a struggle, hence the misogyny of men in politics and the closed circle of political parties controlled by men (Mossuz-Lavau, 1998: 25). Determined to fight for greater access to political organizations for women, Yvette Roudy was one who refused to give up (Roudy, 1995: 31). In 1982 she tried to introduce a Bill to impose quotas on political parties to ensure a minimum number of women were chosen as electoral candidates. This was rejected as unconstitutional by the supreme authority in French politics, the *conseil constitutionnel* on the grounds that it would discriminate in favour of one group in French society. Her failed experience gave rise to the move by women to ask for the constitution to be changed (Roudy, 1985: 20–1). Activists such as Françoise Gaspard, France Le Gall, Claude Servan-Schreiber and others decided that the greatest hurdle to women in politics is the conservative refusal to acknowledge that the 1789 definition of universalism in the constitution is flawed. Therefore the first step was to remove the constitutional impediment.

Pawns in Party Politics

The exceptional constitutional attention given to women and politics occurred at a critical moment for French party politics. Various hypotheses are offered for loss of electoral support: electoral fatigue (France votes frequently), the electoral system itself, the shift to the Centre by the mainstream parties and the decline of ideological differences; all this makes it harder for the electorate to distinguish between the main government parties. The ideological shifts since the Left came to power in 1981 and the wear-and-tear effect of an ageing Fifth Republic have brought the French exception to an end (Cross, 1997b: 54–6; Cole, 1998: 147; Hewlett, 1998: 60–91) Some parties (such as the RPR, the PCF and the UDF (Union pour la démocratie française)) are having trouble maintaining the vitality necessary to win seats, such as during the European 1999 elections. Others are breaking up and forming new groups by splitting away from the parent party (for example, Alain Madelin, Démocratie liberale, Bruno Mégret, Mouvement national and Charles Pasqua, Rassemblement pour la France). The Right parties are bitterly divided over Europe, economic policies and the Front national's presence in local politics. Both Chirac and Jospin are competing to renew the political system (Robert-Diard, 1998: 6) There is a move to increase citizen participation in public debate and movements (Chevallier, 1999: 10) The need to open the door to women has been included along with a proposal to end the *cumul des mandats* (the simultaneous holding of more than one elected office) and introduce electoral reform as a possible means to renew the involvement and interest by the public in politics and arrest the decline of votes or members in political parties. The campaign for *parité* begun by feminist pressure has proved to be a political boon for the same politicians in power in the cohabitation period since 1997, who had previously found it so difficult to admit that the stumbling blocks to women in politics from within political parties must be removed. In the latest *parité* campaign, exceptional measures have been considered acceptable to break the glass ceiling.

Parité and the Constitution

In December 1998, a majority of deputés in the Assemblée nationale approved a Bill to amend Article 3 of the constitution of the Fifth Republic adopted in 1958. This Bill was to insert the principle of *parité* into the constitution. One political commentator remarked how little public enthusiasm was expressed about this significant political act (De Rudder,

1999: 40). The same author expected women to make a fuss about the victory of finally getting something done to remove the glaring inequality of women's representation in political institutions in France. However, it remains to be seen whether the alteration of the wording of the constitution will have any binding power to impose *parité* on political parties. Inserting a clause into the constitution was the option chosen by the government as the most acceptable way to implement equality of representation of men and women in all decision-making bodies of the democratic process. It was not the choice of the fervent campaigners for *parité* (Gaspard, 1998a: 216) who consider it a red herring and prefer to see more drastic action taken through electoral reform. The Prime Minister assured the sénateurs that *parité* reform would not be a way of imposing reform of the electoral system, something the sénateurs fear most and something that the *paritaires* see as the next inevitable change if the principle is to be put into practice (Grudzielski, 1999: 16).

As it happens, any rejoicing in December 1998 would have been premature. In January the Senate voted overwhelmingly to reject the proposed Bill much to the embarrassment of President Chirac and Prime Minister Jospin, who had both separately pledged to try to reverse the political gender inequality when elected to office in 1995 and 1997 respectively. They had done so to endorse the increasingly successful campaign for *parité* that had begun in the early 1990s. Eventually the Senate did pass the Bill and, at the time of writing, it is due to go before a special constitutional meeting of both houses in June 1999, which meets for formal approval of changes to the constitution.

The final wording of the Bill is simply to add one sentence to Article 3. After:

> La souveraineté nationale appartient au peuple qui l'exerce par ses repré-sentants et par la voie du référendum. Aucune section du peuple ni aucun individu ne peut s'en attribuer l'exercice. Le suffrage peut être direct ou indirect dans les conditions prévues par la Constitution. Il est toujours universel, égal et secret. Sont électeurs, dans les conditions déterminées par la loi, tous les nationaux français majeurs des deux sexes, jouissant de leurs droits civils et politiques.[4]

is added:

> La loi favorise les conditions dans lesquelles est organisé l'égal accès des femmes et des hommes aux mandats électoraux et fonctions électives.[5]

The first version favoured by Chirac was 'la loi favorise', whereas the second version favoured by the Assemblée Nationale was 'la loi détermine'. Chirac's version was accepted by the Assemblée Nationale in the second reading as a compromise to accommodate the good relations between Jospin and Chirac and to shame the conservative Right in the Senate into going back on their first outright rejection of the lower house's proposal to alter Article 3. The *antiparitaires* in the Senate had argued that it was up to the political parties to implement *parité* at the level of the choice of candidates for election. After the Senate's second reading of the Bill they accepted the alteration to Article 3 but insisted on retaining their original suggestion to alter Article 4. After:

> Les partis et groupements politiques concourent à l'expression du suffrage. Ils se forment et exercent leur activité librement. Ils doivent respecter les principes de la souveraineté nationale et de la démocratie.[6]

a further sentence was added to Article 4:

> Ils contribuent à la mise en oeuvre du principe énoncé au dernier aliéna de l'article 3 dans les conditions déterminées par la loi.[7]

Respect for Democratic Decisions, Weakness of the System, or Prevarication?

Reform to end gender inequality in politics has occurred very slowly involving laborious decision-making processes in both houses of Parliament, which is in fact the essence of democracy. Yet momentous decisions are also taken via other circuits which are far from democratic. Following the introduction of the *parité* Bill in the autumn of 1998, the shadow of war hung over Europe. As a member country of NATO, France was involved in weeks of military intervention and destruction in the former Yugoslavia in March 1999. No consultation of the French electorate took place before NATO began bombing the Serbs in March 1999. An executive decision was made independently of the *deputés* in the Assemblée nationale and of the Senate. The only voices of dissent to be heard were from the leader of the PCF, Robert Hue and Daniel Cohn Bendit, leader of the ecologists, Les Verts, for the European elections in June 1999. The elected members were not given the chance to express their opinions about the war involvement. Why are some processes of decision making adopted rather than others? In the past nothing in the constitutions of the Third or Fourth or Fifth Republic prevented the executive from issuing a decree to implement equal political rights for women as occurred in Algeria in 1944. In 1974, it was enough for the newly-elected President Giscard d'Estaing to decide to lower the voting age to eighteen years and this was done in a trice. Yet the whole democratic process, which consists of an overwhelming majority of men, has been paralysed for nearly a century with regard to women in politics over the procedure to adopt to create a space for women in the political process. This time the Right-wing groups in the Senate, which is a much weaker institution than the Third Republic upper house, were shamed into co-operation with Chirac. Normally one to remain aloof from the parliamentary organizations of the political parties, he exercized enormous pressure on the party whips in the Senate between the first reading of the 26 January and the 4 March 1999 (Bacque, 1999: 6). Amid cries of '*ringards!*' the intrepid right-wing opponents of *parité* led by Robert Badinter from the PS, were forced into accepting the reform to avoid damaging their President's chances of regaining power in the presidential election (Aphatie and Bacque, 1999: 6). Threatened with humiliation and a referendum on the question or, worse again, reform of the electoral system of the Senate itself, not to mention the re-introduction of proportional representation the senators had no choice but to relent. The Bill was voted with 289 for and eight against. The immediate impact has been a sigh of relief that France will no longer be 'behind' other countries. Indeed parties have had a chance to implement *parité* on a voluntary basis: it is significant that the UDF led by François Bayrou, keen to be seen as the new 'third way', left of the RPR and a viable alternative to the PS, chose to have as many women as men figure on its list of candidates for the European elections of June 1999.

What is unclear is how this *parité* is to be implemented. In order to get the Bill through Jospin had to promise the Senate that *parité* would not be the fig leaf to cover electoral reform. Just exactly how women will gain a space in power remains to be seen.

In 1998 and 1999 *parité* became an issue for the wider political community beyond the question of an equal relationship between men and women in politics. No longer confined to a specific female emancipa-tion issue it had a greater chance of success. Through *parité* women have challenged the fabric of the French regime. Although it has been for a relatively brief moment the debate around women and politics has had institutional repercussions on the many powerful players who go to make up the regime:

le projet de parité va très au-delà du seul accroissement du nombre de femmes élues: son enjeu est la construction d'une société dans laquelle les décisions politiques, mais aussi administratives, économiques, associatives, culturelles, seront prises par des femmes et des hommes ensemble, une société cogérée par les deux sexes pesant d'un même poids. (Gaspard et Servan-Schreiber, 1995: 13)[8]

In sum, this chapter has outlined some of the recent issues surrounding women and politics in France. The debate about women's contribution to politics hinges around a wider issue of the quality of representative democracy. Is democracy in crisis? Are political parties in crisis? The Right needs to renew itself in France just as it does in Great Britain. In order to recover from electoral defeat, leaders of parties are prepared to try anything that might renew the membership, increase funding from contributions and sway the electorate back in their direction. Men politicians are less willing. *Parité* finally got to the statute book in 1999 because of three factors: feminists and women's groups were united in using a simple concept as a tactic to break the glass ceiling because it challenged the founding principles of the Republic; competition is intense among leaders of political parties to be seen as modernizers of democracy; the exceptional cohabitation circumstances which has skewed the power struggle between Left and Right have weakened the potential opponents to change.

The introduction of the modernizing theme of the political system has been an opportunity for President Chirac to reassert his moral authority in domestic politics, resume control over the divided Gaullist movement and shake up the weakened Right. Opposition to *parité* from within political parties has nowhere to hide. *Le fait du prince* has been used to put pressure on political parties to change. The vested interest of one group is strangling the essential lifeblood of the Republic.

The success of the *parité* campaign is due largely to recognition by a large enough consensus of men politicians that women will not gradually become more numerous in French political bodies without some intervention. It is now recognized that whereas formerly France was behind other countries in levels of women in political power, there have been few cases where specific positive discrimination has been introduced to increase the number of women politicians (Cabanel 1999: 5) and nowhere has anything like *parité* been tried. True to its exceptional past, France can boast of taking a courageous step of political exceptionalism and can now turn its shameful position of gender inequality on its head and be the first country to initiate a move for *parité*.

Notes

1. 'A legislative assembly entirely composed of men is just as incompetent to pass laws which govern a society that includes men and women as an assembly composed of the privileged would be to discuss the interests of workers, or an assembly of capitalists to uphold the honour of the country.'
2. Although the decree of 21 April 1944 granted women the same rights as men to vote and stand for election, and notwithstanding the improvement after the 1997 legislative elections, it has to be said that the proportion of women in parliamentary and local assemblies is much lower than their electoral weight as is the case for most countries but that that this is much lower in France compared to any other democratic country.
3. 'It remains to be seen how the right of equality of eligibility can be put into effect so as to produce the same proportion of elected women as women citizens without putting into jeopardy the constitutional principles of national sovereignty, of equality and freedom of the voter.'
4. 'National sovereignty belongs to the people who exercise it through their elected representatives or referendum. No one section of the people or one individual can usurp this right. Suffrage can be direct or indirect in conditions decided by the constitution. It is always universal, equal and secret. All French nationals, men and women, in possession of all their civil and political rights are entitled to vote.'
5. 'The law is in favour of promoting conditions in which men and women have equal access to electoral mandates.'
6. 'Parties and political groups compete for votes. They are free to form and organize. They must respect the principles of national sovereignty and democracy.'
7. 'They contribute to the putting into practice the principle outlined in the last section of Article 3 in conditions set out by the law.'
8. 'The *parité* campaign wants much more than the numerical increase of elected women: what is at stake is the construction of a society in which decisions whether they be in politics, economics, civil service, cultural or other associations, are taken by women and men together, a society run with the same input from both sexes.'

References

Accampo, E.A., Fuchs, R.G. and Stewart, M. L. (1995), *Gender and the Politics of Social Reform in France, 1870–1914,* Baltimore and London: The John Hopkins University Press.

Adler, L. (1993), *Les femmes politiques*, Paris: Seuil.

Agacinski, S. (1999), 'Contre l'effacement des sexes', *Le Monde*, 6 February: 1.

Albistur, M. and Armogathe, D. (1977), *Histoire du féminisme français*, Paris: Des femmes.

Aphatie, J.-M. and Bacque, R. (1999), 'Face aux projets de modernisation de la vie publique, les sénateurs doivent choisir entre l'isolement et le compromis', *Le Monde*, 3 March: 6.

Avril, P. (1990), *Essais sur les partis politiques*, Paris: Editions Payot.

Bacque, R. (1998), 'Mme Aubry avocate tardive du féminisme', *Le Monde*, 16 December: 7.

Bacque, R. (1999), 'La droite sénatoriale accepte la parité approuvée par Jacques Chirac', *Le Monde,* 5 March: 6.

Badinter, E. (1999), 'La parité est une régression', *L'Evénement*, 744, 4–10 February: 86–9.

Bard, C. (1995), *Les filles de Marianne. Histoire des féminismes 1914–1940*, Paris: Fayard.

Barry, D. (1996), *Women and Political Insurgency: France in the Mid-Nineteenth Century,* Basingstoke and London: Macmillan.

Borella, F. (1990), *Les partis politiques dans la France d'aujourd'hui*, (cinquième édition entièrement nouvelle), Paris: Editions du Seuil.

Bredin, F. (1997), *Députée. Journal de bord*, Paris: Fayard.

Cabanel, G. (1999), 'Projet de loi consitutionnel relatif à l'égalité entre les femmes et les hommes', *Rapport 156* (98–99), commission des lois du Sénat, 20 January, 52pp.

Chevallier, J. (1999), 'Les transformations de la citoyenneté', *Regards sur l'actualité*, April, pp.3–18.

Cole, A. (1998), *French Politics and Society*, London: Prentice Hall, Europe.

Comte, F. and Lipietz, A. (1999), 'Briser le plafond de verre!', *Le Monde*, 17 February: 14.

Courtois, G. (1999a), 'Chirac-Jospin: l'enjeu de la parité', *Le Monde*, 15 February: 1,6.

Courtois, G. (1999b), 'Majoritaires dans la fonction publique, les femmes deviennent rares aux postes de responsabilité', *Le Monde*, 18 February: 6.

Cresson, E. (1998), *Innover ou subir*, Paris: Flammarion.

Cross, M. (1997a), 'Feminism' in C. Flood and L Bell. (eds), *Political Ideologies in Contemporary France*, London and Washington: Pinter, 162-79.

Cross, M. (1997b), 'Party politics', in S. Perry, *Aspects of Contemporary France*, London and New York: Routledge, 44–62.

De Cordon, V. (1987), *Vivement des femmes. Enquête sur leur place dans la vie politique*, Paris: Editions Ballard.

De Montvalon, J.-B. (1999), 'La droite cherche une position commune sur l'égalité hommes femmes en politique' *Le Monde*, 12 February: 8.

De Rudder, C. (1999), 'Vers la République des quotas? Parité, la révolution qui divise', *Le Nouvel Observateur*, no. 1784, 14–20 January: 40–4.

Duchen, C. (1986), *Feminism in France From May '68 to Mitterrand*, London, Boston and Henley: Routledge and Keegan Paul.

Duchen, C. (1994), *Women's Rights and Women's Lives in France 1944–1968*, London and New York: Routledge.

Duverger, M. (1974), *La monarchie présidentielle*, Paris: Editions Robert Laffont.

Faure, C. (1985), *Democracy without Women. Feminism and the Rise of Liberal Individualism in France,* Bloomington and Indianapolis: Indiana University Press.

Fédier, M. (1990), *Femmes. La grande mutation*, Paris: L'âge du verseau.

Gaspard, F. (1998a), in J. Martin, (ed.), *La parité. Enjeux et mise en oeuvre*, Toulouse: Presses universitaires du Mirail: 205–17.

Gaspard, F. (1998b), 'La parité, principe de stratégie', *Le Monde diplomatique*, November: 26.

Gaspard, F. and Servan-Schreiber, C. (1995), 'La parité, condition nécessaire de l'universel', *Le Monde*, 8 March: 13.

Gaspard, F., Servan-Schreiber C., Le Gall A. (1992), *Au pouvoir citoyennes! Liberté, égalité, parité*, Paris: Seuil.

Gordon, F. and Cross, M. (1996), *Early French Feminisms 1830–1940: A Passion for Liberty,* Cheltenham: Edward Elgar.

Grudzielski, S. (1999), 'La parité républicaine par le double vote', *Le Monde,* 25 February: 16.

Hall, P., (1994), 'Pluralism and pressure Politics' in Hall, P., Hayward, J. and Machin, H., *Developments in French Politics,* London, Macmillan and New York: St. Martin's Press, 77–92.

Hall, P., Hayward, J. and Machin, H. (1994), *Developments in French Politics,* London, Macmillan and New York: St. Martin's Press.

Hause, S. (1984), *Women's Suffrage and Social Politics in the Third Republic*, Guilford: Princeton University Press.

Hayward, J. (1994), 'Conclusion: Political Science, the State and Modernisation' in Hall, P., Hayward, J. and Machin, H., *Developments in French Politics,* London: Macmillan and New York: St. Martin's Press, 282–97.

Hayward, J. (1973), *The One and Indivisible Republic,* London: Wiedenfield & Nicholson.

Hazareesingh, S. (1994), *Political Traditions in Modern France*, Oxford: Oxford University Press.

Hewlett, N. (1998), *Modern French Politics. Analysing Conflict and Consensus since 1945*, Cambridge: Polity Press.

Huard, R. (1996), *La naissance du parti politique en France*, Paris: Presses de Sciences Po.

Hufton, O. (1992), *Women and the Limits of Citizenship in the French Revolution*, London and Toronto: University of Toronto Press.

Hunt, L. (1992), *The Family Romance of the French Revolution*, Berkeley: University of California Press.

Jenson, J. and Sineau, M. (1995), *Mitterrand et les Françaises. Un rendez-vous manqué*, Paris: Presses de la fondation nationale des sciences politiques.

Klejman, L. et Rochefort, F. (1989), *L'égalité en marche. Le féminisme sous la Troisième République*, Paris: Presses de la fondation nationale des sciences politiques, des femmes.

Laguillier, A. (1996), *C'est toute ma vie. Une femme dans le camp des travailleurs*, Paris: Plon.

Landes, J. B. (1988), *Women and the Public Sphere in the Age of the French Revolution,* Ithaca and London: Cornell University Press.

Le Bras-Chopard, A. and Mossuz-Lavau, J. (1997), *Les femmes et la politique*, Paris: L'Harmattan.

Martin, J. (ed.), (1998), *La parité. Enjeux et mise en oeuvre*, Toulouse: Presses universitaires du Mirail.

Martin, V. (1997), 'Les premiers votes des femmes. Vécus et schèmas de représentations 1944–1946', in A. Le Bras-Chopard and J. Mossuz-Lavau, *Les femmes et la politique*, Paris: L'Harmattan: 57–79.

Massot, J. (1999), 'Le présidentialisme majoritaire à rude épreuve', *Le Monde*, 9 January:14.

McMillan, J. (1981), *Housewife or Harlot. The Place of Women in French Society 1870–1914*, New York: St. Martin's Press.

Mossuz-Lavau (1999) 'Les antiparitaires se trompent', *Le Monde*, 25 February: 17.

Mossuz-Lavau, J. and Sineau, M. (1983), *Enqûete sur les femmes en politique en France*, Paris: Presses universitaires de France.

Mossuz-Lavau, J. (1998), *Femmes/Hommes, pour la parité*, Paris: Presses de Sciences Po.

Reynolds, S. (1995), 'Le sacre de la citoyenne? Pierre Rosanvallon and the Significant Other', *Modern and Contemporary France*, vol. 1(2), April: 218–22.

Reynolds, S. (1996), *France between the Wars: Gender and Politics*, London and New York: Routledge.

Reynolds, S. (ed.), (1986), *Women, State and Revolution. Essays on Power and Gender in Europe since 1789*, Brighton: Harvester Wheatsheaf.

Riot-Sarcey, M. (1994), *La démocratie à l'épreuve des femmes. Trois figures critiques du pouvoir 1830–1848*, Paris: Bibliothèque Albin Michel Histoire.

Robert-Diard, P. (1998), 'Jacques Chirac se pose en modernisateur de la démocratie', *Le Monde*, 5 December: 6.

Rosanvallon, P. (1992), *Le sacre du citoyen. Histoire du suffrage universel en France*, Paris: Editions Gallimard.

Roudy, Y. (1995), *Mais de quoi ont-ils peur ? Un vent de misogynie souffle sur la politique*, Paris: Albin Michel.

Roudy, Y. (1985), *A cause d'elles*, Paris: Albin Michel.

Royal, S. (1996), *La vérité d'une femme*, Paris: Editions Stock.

Royal, S. (1999), 'La parité par l'éducation', *Le Monde*, 13 March: 5.

Schlemla, E. (1993), *Edith Cresson: la femme piégée*, Paris: Flammarion.

Sineau, M. (1998), 'La féminisation du pouvoir vue par les Français(es) et par les hommes politiques' in Martin, J. (réd.), *La parité. Enjeux et mise en oeuvre*, Toulouse: Presses universitaires du Mirail, 61–81.

Sineau, M. (1988), *Des femmes en politique*, Paris: Editions Economica.

Smith, P. (1996), *Feminism and the Third Republic. Women's Political and Civil Rights in France 1918–1945*, Oxford: Clarendon Press.

Stevens, A. (1992), *The Government and Politics of France,* London: Macmillan and New York: St Martin's Press.

Thompson, D. (1969), *Democracy in France since 1870*, London, Oxford and New York: Oxford University Press.

Wright V. (1989), *The Government and Politics of France,* 3rd edn, London: Unwin Hyman.

Women and Language
Kate Beeching

It will be the business of this chapter to explore the manner in which language and gender are interrelated in French in a society in which women play an increasingly important role in the public and political arena whilst largely retaining their traditional (unpaid) roles in the family and larger community. One of the concerns of linguists and, in particular of sociolinguists, is to investigate the relationship between language and society and to attempt to describe it in a scientific and objective manner. The interrelationship between language and society may be perceived in three ways: either language reflects the status quo, or language creates or helps perpetuate the status quo, or both of these are the case. Whilst most academic linguists do not enter into debates about what should or should not be done (indeed governments rarely invite linguists to help in their policy making), it would be churlish not to point out the manner in which language usage may perpetuate inequalities in society or anomalies that arise where language does not appear to reflect social realities.

In 1984, faced with resistance from the Académie Française with regard to the recommendations of the Roudy Commission regarding the feminization of job titles, the commission's chair Benoîte Groult remarked that 'toute langue, pour rester vivante, doit s'adapter aux réalités nouvelles' ('in order to remain alive, all languages must adapt to new conditions') and 'la présence de femmes de plus en plus nombreuses dans des métiers de plus en plus divers est une de ces réalités' ('the presence of more and more women in more and more different professions is one of these conditions'). In the US genuine attempts to introduce non-sexist language were undermined by some risibly precious and linguistically dubious formulations (such as replacing *men*struate with *fem*struate or *his*tory with *her*story). Such forms are derided as being 'politically correct', a term that is then extended to all changes, including those which are perfectly reasonable ones (and recognized as such by the next generation, which is accustomed to them) such as the use of the word 'chair' for chairman or 'la ministre' instead of 'le ministre' for a female minister.

The reactionary nature of the derogatory term 'politically correct' reflects a resistance or anxiety before a change that may feel uncomfortable to both sexes – men must renounce some of their power and women their dependence. This resistance to change is compounded in France by a strong sense that the language must be defended (from anglicisms, for example) and by the national pride that is invested in the rigour and solidity and rule-bound nature of the French language, with bodies and manuals to maintain 'bon usage' (correct usage) (see Fleischman, 1997). It has been the belief that labels attributed to men and women and the language forms and habits adopted differentially by men and women contribute to gender inequalities in society and that linguistic intervention is possible. The chapter will attempt to review the evidence that exists to support these views and to suggest possible ways forward.

Interest in the relationship between language and gender in French has focused on three main areas. In the public sphere, job titles have had to be adjusted to reflect the growing numbers of women entering professions that were previously exclusively male. The relationship between grammatical gender and so-called 'natural' gender has been explored as a potential source of underlying social conditioning. Finally, sociolinguistic/variationist studies, generally phonological but some lexical, demonstrate the manner in which women's language differs from men's and hypothesize as to the reasons for this. We will now turn to each of these areas.

The Feminisation of Job Titles and Asymmetries in the Labelling of Men and Women

One of the most striking examples of the anomalies engendered by the retention of nouns which are masculine in gender to designate women adopting new, traditionally male, roles is cited by Yaguello (1991) in her *élargissement du capitaine Prieur* (*Captain Prieur's Widening Girth*). Captain Dominique Prieur, a secret agent involved in the Rainbow Warrior crisis in New Zealand, was habitually referred to in press reports as 'le capitaine', a noun picked up anaphorically with the anatomically correct but grammatically incongruous pronoun 'elle'(she). The incongruity is exacerbated as the captain was pregnant at the time, hence her *élargisse-ment*, and this led to statements such as: *Le* capitaine Prieur est actuelle-ment *enceinte . . . elle* pouvait être rapatriée à Paris ('Captain Prieur is currently pregnant . . . she could be repatriated to Paris').

As far back as 1984, the socialist government recognized that linguistic sexual discrimination existed and set up a terminology commission under

Yvette Roudy whose recommendations concerning the feminization of professional names are enshrined in the 1986 Circulaire. But it was not for another 11 years that the Council of Ministers decided, on 17 December 1997, that the names of administrative posts should be feminized and the recommendations could begin to be translated into real usage. Where feminine versions of male occupations existed, they often meant 'wife of', as in the pairs *ambassadeur/ambassadrice, président/présidente*. Women following professions in their own right are either referred to using the feminine article or by the addition of 'femme' (woman): *une professeur, ministre, maire; une femme-policier, une femme-chirurgien* (a teacher, minister, mayor, a woman-policeman, a woman-surgeon).

It appears that the resistance to feminization is not a linguistic problem. Masculine equivalents of traditionally female jobs such as *infirmier* (male nurse) or *assistant social* (social worker) and even *maïeuticien* for *sage-femme* (mid-wife) have been created. Feminization is well established for the so-called *petits métiers* (little jobs) such as *coiffeuse, vendeuse* and *lingère* (hair-dresser, saleswoman, washerwoman). The masculine and feminine form of the same noun used to designate professions may traditionally have very different referents. A *couturier* is a dress-**designer**, a *couturière*, a dress-**maker**. A *rédacteur* refers to a news editor whereas a *rédactrice* is the editor of a woman's magazine. Often a woman will elect to retain the masculine form because in general these indicate jobs of higher status. Consider the difference between manager and manageress in English : the term *manageress* generally refers to a small enterprise, such as a supermarket. The manager of General Motors would remain a manager, regardless of the sex of the incumbent. Similarly, *l'instituteur* (masculine) and *l'institutrice* (feminine)(primary-school teacher) exist but only *le professeur* (secondary school teacher). A doctoral supervisor is *un directeur de thèse*. To change one's title to *directrice de thèse* would involve a drop in status. There are thus reasons why even women resist the feminization of titles, as female titles are associated with lower status positions. Resistance then derives from political considerations and the connotations of low status historically attaching to women's work.

One of the recommendations of Yvette Roudy's Terminology Commission that was not adopted in the government's 1986 circular concerned words ending in 'eur', such as *professeur, ingénieur* and *auteur* (teacher, engineer and author) . Although aware that in Quebec the forms *professeure* and *auteure* have been adopted, the Commission recommended rather *professeuse* and *autrice*. The government, however, came down in favour of the use (also suggested in the report) of *un/une* with the unmarked (masculine) form of the noun. (For a list of mainly Canadian guides to non-sexist usage in French, see Fleischman, 1997: 844 and Martin and Dupuis, 1985).

In 1991, Yaguello suggested somewhat ruefully that only in the twenty-first century might we arrive at the obvious solution to the incongruity inherent in such situations as *'le' capitaine* being pregnant and referred to as 'elle', which is quite simply to move to *'la' capitaine*. In 1998, however, subsequent to the influx of women in the Jospin government put in place on 2 June 1997, Yaguello is able to report on the adoption of the title *Madame la ministre* both by the ministers concerned and (with the exception of *Le Figaro*) by the press.The new ministers immediately had plaques on their office doors, announcing 'Bureau de la Ministre'. The Académie Française was not amused: it maintains the conservative view that the masculine is the unmarked or generic form and can be used to englobe both masculine and feminine. A similar dispute continues to rage concerning the uses of 'man' in English in such expressions as fireman, chairman or indeed mankind or man-eating shark. Where alternatives are unproblematic, they are generally adopted in publishers' guidelines to authors: firefighter, chair, humanity/humankind . But what of human-eating shark? Or human overboard? Yaguello (1998: 127) argues that it is perfectly possible to retain the masculine as the generic form (*directeur de cabinet*) whilst employing the feminine (*directrice de cabinet*) for a female incumbent of the post. Several studies (Brick and Wilks, 1994; Galeazzi, 1986; Gervais-le Garff, 1998; Houdebine, 1987, 1998; Yaguello, 1998) have charted developments in the press with regard to the naming of women and the image of women which the press reflects/projects both as society's values evolve and women take what were traditionally considered to be men's positions in government and else-where. Although progress has been slow and there has been a considerable public outcry, over a ten-year period there has been a noticeable shift in the language of the press, largely reflecting the change in mores and in women's roles in society.

Female Cabinet ministers may be atypical of the population at large, the transition from the 'token' female ministers in the previous Juppé administration (dubbed *juppettes*) to those ready to name themselves, not *jospinettes* but Madame *la* Ministre is a significant move towards linguistic equality if only in the question of job titles.

The increased visibility of women in public life through the feminiza-tion of job titles has, thankfully, been matched by a reduction in the use of derogatory terms traditionally used to designate women. Denigration through the use of a range of derogatory epithets applied to women has historically played a prominent part in suggesting women's inferiority with respect to men. Yaguello (1978), in a list of synonyms for the word 'woman' notes how many are pejorative or relate to woman's function as a provider of sex for men. In the extract under 'p', we find 'pucelle, petite, poison, poufiasse, péronnelle, poule, poulette, poupée, pute, putain' ('maid, little one, misery-guts, fat bag, silly goose, bird, chick, doll, tart, whore'). Gender asymmetries also occur in the habitual collocations of lexical items. One loves *petites femmes* (little women) but admires *grands hommes* (great men). *Homme* (man) occurs in expressions indicating power and prestige *homme du monde, homme de bien, homme d'affaires* (man of the world, man of property, businessman). Women are referred to as *le beau sexe, le sexe faible* and *le deuxième sexe* (the fair sex, the weak sex, the second sex). But such linguistic categorization cuts both ways. Particularly in a world facing a 'crisis of masculinity' and in which the manufacturing industries are being run down in favour of the tertiary sector where women's jobs are more numerous, men, too, are attributed stereotypical roles (in this case, of responsibility) which are onerous to them and potentially unachievable. Both men and women are hampered by the roles allocated to them by society and enshrined in habitual lexical designations or collocations. Should he wish to, it would be difficult for a man to become a *fille de joie, fille publique, femme de ménage* or *femme de chambre* (woman of pleasure, prostitute, house-wife or chamber-maid). The Petit Robert, 1990, defines *homme* as displaying 'qualités de courage, de hardiesse, de droiture propres à son sexe' ('the qualities of bravery, daring and rectitude peculiar to their sex'). Modern man may feel that he cannot live up to this stereotypical image of what is expected of him. Happily, society has moved on and the traditionally misogynistic view encapsulated in such catch-phrases as 'sois belle et tais-toi' ('be beautiful and keep your mouth shut') or proverbs such as 'où femme il y a, silence n'y a' ('wherever women are, silence there is not') are most often regarded with wry scepticism by both sexes.

Grammatical Gender and Social Gender

Linguists generally consider that grammatical gender is arbitrary and that there is no sense in which inanimate objects such as *le mixer* or *la lampe* are linked to the biological categories of male and female. Gervais (1993: 121) notes that 90 per cent of French nouns derived from Latin have retained their Latin gender. Nearly all neuter nouns in Latin became masculine in French. There is a clear tendency for nouns ending in particular syllables to fall into one grammatical gender group or another.

This can lead to incongruities such as the German word for girl which is neuter in gender – *das Mädchen* – and a number of military words in French whose referents are without exceptions male but that are feminine in grammatical gender: *la sentinelle, la recrue, la vigie* (sentry, recruit, look-out). *Un mannequin* (model, mannequin), despite the fact that the grammatical gender of the word is masculine, is almost invariably a woman. Yaguello (1978: 91ff.), following Damourette and Pichon, and somewhat provocatively perhaps, suggests that gender allocation may provide a fundamental psychological underpinning for sexist attitudes. *L'océan* (m) is larger than *la mer* (f); *le fleuve* (m) is larger than *la rivière* (f); *le ruisseau* (m) is larger than *la source* (f); *le jour* (m) contains a 'male principle' by opposition to *la nuit* (f); likewise, *le soleil* (m) and *la lune* (f) and two of the four elements – *le feu* (m) and *l'air* (m) as opposed to *la terre* (f) and *l'eau* (f).

Whilst the argument seems to be undermined by the fact that in German, for example, sun is feminine – *die Sonne* – and moon is masculine – *der Mond* – it is certainly true that particular 'resonances' may be inherent in a language, including grammatical gender, which suggest that women are smaller, more delicate, the weaker sex and less self-sufficient and independent. This is a position that women may connive to perpetuate: abnegating responsibility can be comfortable despite the subjugation to which the dependent party is subject.

Yaguello's (1989) work, *Le Sexe des Mots* presents in dictionary form a number of intriguing examples of the tension that exists between grammatical and natural gender. In the entry under *abeille* (bee) which is grammatically feminine and where *mâle* or *femelle* must be added to specify which sex the bee is: *abeille mâle* (male bee), *abeille femelle* (female bee), Yaguello discusses the manner in which small animals (especially insects) are usually feminine in gender, whilst large are masculine and that domestic animals are usually feminine and wild animals masculine. There are innumerable exceptions to this general rule, however ; although ants and fleas are feminine – *la fourmi* and *la puce* – mosquitos and horseflies are masculine – *le moustique* and *le taon*.

Sociolinguistic Studies and the French Tradition

An area of perhaps greater concern is whether women's habitual ways of speaking doom them to a subordinate place in society, as Lakoff argued was the case for American English. Much Anglo-Saxon literature suggests that men and women 'do gender' in habitual daily acts, which include the way they use language – see, for example, Hall and Bucholtz, 1995.

Robin Lakoff's (1975) seminal work suggested that women's tendency to adopt more tentative and less forceful forms undermined their authority. Women faced a dilemma: they could become real people but renounce their femininity or be women but not real people. William Labov developed a radically different research paradigm that correlated phonological variables with such social categories as age, sex and social class. He has been concerned with the relationship between social prestige factors and linguistic change. By comparison with the Anglo-Saxon literature, the field is relatively underdeveloped for French and most authors of reviews on the subject of language and gender have, until very recently, relied heavily on data drawn from English. French writings on the subject tend to be philosophical (Luce Irigaray – see, for example, translated works published in 1985 and 1990) and/or feminist/literary (Simone de Beauvoir, Marie Cardinal, Hélène Cixous, Xavière Gauthier, Annie Leclerc). British, American and Australian (socio)linguists such as Cameron, Coates, Holmes, Labov, Lakoff and Tannen battle with concepts such as woman's adoption of more standard language than men or the relative tentativeness of women's speech and provide careful empirical and quantitative studies demonstrating such differences, but French writings have been introspective, allusive and more profound.

Amongst such French authors, the sentiment that the French language is created by men for men is frequent. Cardinal (quoted in Yaguello, 1978: 64) claims, 'Je me sens sans arrêt à l'étroit dans le vocabulaire, soit parce qu'il me manque des mots, soit parce que les mots français sont tellement investis par les hommes qu'ils me trahissent quand c'est moi, une femme, qui les emploie' (*Autrement dit*, p. 96).[1]

Simone de Beauvoir expresses a similar sentiment (in *Ophir*, 1976:13; quoted in Yaguello, 1978: 65) when she says 'Je sais que le langage courant est plein de pièges. Prétendant à l'universalité, il porte en fait la marque des mâles qui l'ont élaboré. Il reflète leurs valeurs, leurs prétentions, leurs préjugés.'[2]

There is a sense in which a value system that promotes *bon usage* (correct usage) and Cartesian rigour disappoints and frustrates the feminine urge to create rapport rather than to report facts and figures (Tannen, 1990), to 'avoid being the expert' and to 'meld' (Coates, 1997: 251) by using indirect, allusive language and hedges.[3]

Yaguello (1978: 57) summed up the stereotypical view of women's versus men's language when she said that:

Le stéréotype du langage viril implique l'usage de l'argot et de la langue verte, la pratique du jeu de mot et, singulièrement, du jeu de mot à caractère sexuel, le goût de l'injure, de l'insulte, un vocabulaire plus riche et plus étendu, la maîtrise des registres techniques, politique, intellectuel, sportif, la quasi monopole de la parole publique, le contrôle des conversations mixtes, l'exclusivité des formes de communication rituelles et codifiées, un discours autoritaire et catégorique ('tu vas voir ce que va dire ton père'), une plus grande liberté par rapport aux normes, plus de créativité que les femmes.[4]

Whilst men's language is associated with forcefulness and competence, the characteristics traditionally associated with women's language have had negative connotations:

purisme, non-créativité, goût de l'hyperbole, maîtrise de registres relevant de domaines mineurs, parole timorée, non assertive, bavardage, incapacité de manier des concepts abstraits, hypercorrection, peur des mots.[5]

Houdebine's 1979a study of the difference between men's and women's speech, presumably based on data collected for her (1979b) thesis, is one of very few early empirical investigations. It provides tentative confirmation for French of the findings of Anglo-Saxon researchers that women adopt to a much greater extent than men phonological forms which approximate to the standard or prestige form.

Aebischer and Forel (1983) collected a number of papers concerning *Parlers masculins, parlers féminins?* ('masculine ways of speaking, feminine ways of speaking') including contributions from Anglophone researchers such as Trudgill and West. Houdebine and Aebischer's papers distinguish themselves by their insight into the profounder psychological motivations behind some of the statistical evidence and the clarity and elegance of their expression. Houdebine, in particular, argues convincingly that the phonological characteristics of speakers' French shift according to the persona that they are projecting or identification they are making with a particular social group at any one time. This may vary throughout the day depending on their interlocutor and indeed throughout their lifetime as their life history evolves.

Il s'agit d'un procès d'idéalisation, d'une projection d'idéal vers quoi le sujet tend, en cherchant à s'en approprier les emblèmes, les indices, tout ce qui fait trace du groupe ou du sujet en cause: une recherche consciente et inconsciente d'identité est à l'oeuvre, un procès d'identification. (Houdebine, 1983: 130)[6]

Houdebine's (1983: 131) insistence on the tentative and non-exclusive nature of linguistic preferences, based on the shifting sands of identification, is particularly welcome:

...chaque sujet, engagé dans de tels procès d'identification, d'homogénéisation ou de singularisation linguistiques -....- privilégiant consciemment ou inconsciemment telle ou telle prononciation, la répète, la favorise, néglige l'autre et change ainsi la langue, dans la langue, intervenant du poids de sa parole dans la variation et l'évolution phonologiques et linguistiques.[7]

Houdebine also stresses that some speakers are more affected than others, more sensitive than others in the act of talking and of listening and this will depend on their own personal biography, their social position, their sex, their propensity to talk or not and the extent of their desire to integrate into a particular community by adopting their speech styles.

Houdebine's data for French concerning hypercorrection and women's supposed greater use of standard forms appear to echo the early findings of Labov and Trudgill. Her interpretation of the findings are at once more subtle, with less polarization of the sexes into separate camps, and more profound, showing deeper insight into the way that language serves as an 'emblème' or 'indice' of identification within a social group.

Aebischer's paper in the Aebischer and Forel (1983) collection is also to be welcomed for its distinction between the tendency for women to speak in a particular way and the creation of a genre dubbed 'women's language': 'le parler lié *à des* femmes devient le parler *des* femmes. Il devient une réalité présentée comme un fait accompli' (Aebischer, 1983: 178).[8]

Following the spirit of the time (with an affirmation of women's identity and a refutal of the supremacy of masculine ways of managing the world), Aebischer points up the positive side of 'bavardage' (chatter) espoused by feminists as a new mode of communication 'régi par la non-violence, l'harmonie, l'amour et par une absence de hiérarchie, de pouvoir et de leaders' (governed by non-violence, harmony, love and by an absence of hierarchy, power and leaders).

Aebischer (1985) notes that there is general agreement on women's superior verbal performance, thus seemingly contradicting the negative connotations inherent in the stereotypes presented by Yaguello (1978) and quoted above. She notes that hypercorrection is indeed a feature of French women's speech and confirms that five hypotheses first outlined by Lakoff for American English are also true for French: women employ a more subtle vocabulary particularly with reference to colour; they use euphemisms instead of swearwords or other taboo words; they use adjectives more than men (*charmant, délicieux, sidéré*) (charming, delicious, staggered/amazed); they use tags (*n'est-ce pas*) (does it not?) and they use a questioning intonation more than men.

Irigaray (1987: 122–3, quoted in Ager, 1990: 122) demonstrates in a number of contexts that women and men see the world differently and that their language use is different. When she analysed the hysterical or obsessive discourse of patients undergoing psychoanalysis, she observed that: men use *je* (I) more than women (62.5 per cent as against 42.6 per cent); women use *tu* (you) more than men (29.3 per cent as against 0 per cent). Women select 'process' verbs (*aimer, regarder, mettre)* (like, watch, put) whereas men use verbs describing utterance (*je me disais, j'ose à peine affirmer)* (I said to myself, I hardly dare to say) or verbs describing states (*je me sens libéré)* (I feel liberated*)* . Women by contrast with men use 'incomplete' rather than 'completed' tenses, preferring imperfect, present or future tenses, transitive verbs, active forms.

Women refer to concrete and inanimate objects (*robes, appartement)* (dresses, flat), whereas men refer to abstractions (*discours, difficultés, désir)* (speech, difficulties, desire). Women prefer spatial references (*dans le métro)* (in the tube) with relationship to *tu* (you), whereas men use references related to the subject *je* (I).

Women use quantitative and comparative terms (*aussi net, trop, tout)* (as clearly, too much, quite) whereas men prefer attitude descriptors (*sceptique, nerveux, à peine, encore)* (sceptical, nervous, scarcely, still).

Interesting, insightful and provocative though Irigaray's study of these patients is, it appears to beg several questions. One is whether such speech could be said to be typical – it may be that men in such conditions revert to a more egoistical and self-indulgent state than normal (as witnessed by their greater use of *je,* of statements about themselves and their state of mind) and that they hide behind generalities and abstractions more than usual. It may also be that the women's comparatively more parsimonious use of references to themselves derives from their acculturation as women, whereby it is wrong to complain or draw attention to themselves, to put the needs of others first and so on. Indeed, the speech of such patients may display in a pronounced fashion the very reasons why they became ill in the first place, relating to their sense of their own identity. These patients then through their language project a persona in keeping with an accepted stereotype. In this way they have an identity with which they can feel comfortable and maintain self-respect. Further studies will demonstrate whether such linguistic asymmetries hold true for the larger population.

Mainstream linguists in France appear dismissive both of variationist studies in general (see Gadet, 1996) and of research linking language and gender (Pillon, 1987).[9] Durand (1993: 267–70), however, usefully addresses the question of women's contribution to linguistic change and concludes, like Labov, that though in some situations women lead change in line with a statusful norm, this is not always the case. The data reported by Durand are phonological ('ne' omission, see Ashby, 1991; absence or presence of liaison, see Booij and de Jong, 1987; rolled alveolar versus uvular /R/, see Walter, 1988: 215). Durand (1993: 267) remarks that it is 'quite common in France for linguists interested in language and society to reject Labovian sociolinguistic studies on the grounds that they espouse a politically naive (consensual) view of society'. Durand provides the following corrective: 'at the very least, it must be realized that well-constructed sociolinguistic work offers a testing ground for the checking of various hypotheses concerning social stratification by opposition to speculation about language and society based on purely qualitative judgements'.

Such well-constructed sociolinguistic work is now beginning to emerge, often (though not exclusively) conducted by Anglo-Saxon researchers working in the Labovian tradition in British universities (for example, Armstrong, 1996; Coveney, 1996; Pooley, 1994; Temple, 1988). These empiricial studies paint a picture that is at once more complex and more profound than the stereotypical parody drawn by Yaguello (1978).

Early language and gender research (for example, that of Labov and Trudgill) demonstrated that women use more standard forms than men and that women's adoption of standard forms related to a lack of real status in society. It was argued that as women lacked a proper place in society because they were not part of the workforce, they invested in symbolic capital and used linguistic forms (standard or sometimes even hypercorrect forms) which gave them the status that they desired or to which they aspired. This hypothesis, however, seems unlikely, especially in view of the fact that women are now a fully participating part of working life and yet their linguistic habits appear unchanged. Indeed, Trudgill (1998) appears to have revised his initial view in favour of quite a different one, suggesting that society expects women to behave in general in ways that are more 'polite' than that which it expects from men and that this extends to the language forms which they employ. Labov's interest in gender-related language forms is motivated by an interest in the mechanisms of linguistic change. Labov (1990) attempts to explain the interrelationship between sex and social class and how this affects linguistic change. He starts from two principles, the first being that men use a higher frequency of non-standard forms than women (this seems to hold true for most societies, including French society, with some notable exceptions, for example Malagasy). The second principle states that in the majority of linguistic changes women use a higher frequency of the new forms that will subsequently spread to the rest of the community. Going back to Gauchat (1905), it is suggested that, as women are more often involved in child rearing than men, their forms are passed on to the next generation, the full implications of the term 'langue maternelle' (mother tongue) thus becoming evident.

Recent research in French seems to be leading us towards a different explanatory paradigm relating to regional (vernacular) and supra-regional (standard) forms. A significant feature of the French of the south of France and of the Languedoc in particular is the retention of schwa (the 'euh' sound) in such phrases as *la semainE prochainE* (next week). In Paris, the Es (schwas) would not be heard to anything like such an extent if at all. It would not be frivolous to suggest that the pronunciation of schwa appears to fit in with the Northerners' stereotype of the lazy south where people have time to speak slowly and pronounce more letters. It is thus associated with a relaxed but possibly non-progressive way of life. Armstrong and Unsworth (1999) not only demonstrate that women delete schwa to a much greater extent than men (thus conforming to the view that women adapt to the standard more readily) but also developed a way of measuring the degree of attachment a subject felt for their region. Women were far less committed to their region than were men. When a negative correlation between high schwa deletion rates and low regional-attachment scores was sought, it demonstrated unambiguously that the more attached a speaker is to the region, the lower their deletion rate is likely to be. This attachment of men to regional forms has been widely documented in very different societies (Cheshire 1978 and 1982 in Reading, England; Gal, 1978, in Oberwart, Austria; Labov, 1973, in Martha's Vineyard, New England, US; Milroy, Milroy, Hartley and Walshaw, 1994 in Tyneside, England). Armstrong and Unsworth (1999) suggest that females are more mobile *in principle* than males; for instance, more willing to undergo displacement for economic reasons if need be. This finding appears to be contradicted, but not vitiated, by Moreau and Bauvois' (1998) findings in Belgium. Here, the local Belgian pronunciation of words, involving a devoicing of final consonants ('mansh' instead of 'mange', 'tank' instead of 'tangue', 'fonte' instead of 'fonde', 'coute' instead of 'coude') was not dropped in formal contexts to a greater extent by the women than by the men. Despite the researchers' assertions that standard French is felt to be the 'correct' or prestige form in Belgium, it might be suggested that in these circumstances both men and women have a loyalty to their own region and continue to adopt and perpetuate its language forms.

Dewaele (1998) developed the notion of explicitness versus implicitness as a measure of formality in speech to explore gender asymmetries in learners of French. He discovered that there was a significant difference in the interlanguage of males who used similarly explicit styles to the females in formal situations but did not 'shift' to a more implicit style in an informal situation.[10] Labov (1998) invokes Chambers's (1995) review of the data which suggest that, from a biological point of view, women have better linguistic capabilities than men and for that reason are better equipped to adopt new forms and switch from one form to the other. Dewaele, too, reminds us of Kimura's (1992) findings concerning gender differences in the wiring of the brain, which might have some bearing on the subject, females putatively having greater ease in talking of emotional matters than males because the larger size of the corpus callosum in women permits greater ease of communication between the two halves of the brain.

Women's roles are changing. Historically, women had a smaller place in the economic world, fully occupied as they were with the biological processes of child rearing. Women are increasingly engaged in the public arena and job titles have had to be adjusted. Studies of the relationship between grammatical gender and social gender suggest that the feminine is smaller or daintier than the masculine and that this may lead to a form of social conditioning, but the evidence is contradictory. In some quarters women's less visible role in public life led to a downgrading of women as a sex and the adoption of misogynistic terms that seem, thankfully, to be disappearing. As far as so-called 'woman's language' is concerned, there is no evidence to suggest that women are in any way suffering from a deficit in linguistic ability. If women are subject to inequalities in society this has little or nothing to do with the language forms that they use, which, it has to be said, are different but not markedly different from those used by men. In many cases women appear, indeed, to have greater sensitivity to the social 'labels' and stigmas attached to language forms and to be better equipped to adopt different and new forms because their identifications shift more readily. If there is a difference between male and female speech patterns, it might be said to relate to woman's and man's identification with 'what is feminine' and 'what is masculine' – our projection of ourselves as men or women is fundamental and we adopt the clothing that is appropriate including appropriate language in different circumstances. It is not using women's language (if such a thing exists) but being a woman that puts woman at a disadvantage. Gradually women are entering the previously virtually exclusively male world of work – but most women want to be women, not men, and this generally involves compromising their careers to a certain degree on the altar of family and domestic duty. One of the first steps is to ensure that women are visible.

It is not so much the language women adopt as the way they are labelled that may usefully be adjusted. The so-called 'unmarked' masculine form eclipses women, renders them invisible. In Houdebine's (1998: 176) words, non-sexist people, both men and women, have been working towards 'leur non occultation linguistique' ('making women more visible linguistically').

The difference/dominance debate that has raged in Anglo-Saxon circles, whereby 'women's language' may be perceived as either an emblem of difference or as evidence of male domination over women, might thus be considered to be a fruitless dissipation of energy that could be more usefully channelled into political action. Whilst agreeing with Holmes (1995) and Preisler (1986) that the politeness and tentativeness that appear to characterize women's language are qualities, not drawbacks, we cannot deny that power and status are men's. However, the causal link appears not to be that women are not powerful because of the language they use but rather women's language is considered unpowerful because, as women, they have low status. If women had more power and status, the language forms they adopt would similarly have more status. As Holmes (1986: 18) points out 'one (female) person's feeble hedging may well be perceived as another (male) person's perspicacious qualification'. Lakoff's (1975: 83) original assertion that women's typically tentative, hesitant or polite forms are 'stifling, exclusive and oppressive' urgently needs revision. Such tentative and hedged forms are used by skilful conversationalists and indeed, academic writers, of both sexes.

Interventionist strategies are regarded by linguists with suspicion, not only because they constitute a decidedly prescriptive activity but because they are often ineffective in the face of societal pressures. The Académie Française has attempted to staunch the flow of anglicisms flooding into the French language – it has spectacularly failed. It is important to raise, however, and keep raising, the linguistic issues. Concepts enshrined in language such as the 'unmarked' masculine are difficult to dethrone. Whereas the 1986 Roudy Commission failed to shift attitudes or linguistic usage, the band of women ministers in the Jospin team appear to have gained ground and respect. They have grasped the nettle – and become madame *la* ministre.

Intervention at a lexical level is necessary but possibly ineffective and certainly insufficient to ensure equality between the sexes. As Yaguello remarked (1987: 191): 'L'action volontariste a des limites car le mal qu'elle attaque a des causes psycho-sociales qu'un bouleversement planifié ne saurait suffire à déraciner'.[11]

It appears that what is at stake is the notion put forward by Houdebine, that speakers will adopt a speech style, or approximate in speech style as closely as possible, a style projected by other individuals with whom they identify and that these speech styles may shift from addressee to addressee and throughout one's lifetime. People are not prisoners of the language they speak. Continued debate and increasing awareness of the differences between women's and men's speech may little-by-little reveal the manner in which inequalities are perpetuated. The psychosocial causes of gender inequality may thus be undermined and men and women freed to be different *and* equal.

Notes

1. 'I constantly feel hemmed in by words either because I lack the vocabulary I need or because French words have such a male bias that they betray me when it is I, a woman, who uses them.'
2. 'I know that everyday language is full of traps. Although it claims to be universal, it carries the stamp of the males who invented it. It reflects their values, their ambitions, their prejudices.'
3. Hedges are devices that are used to reduce the imposition placed on the person to whom you are speaking. They are a way of being polite, reducing the strength of an utterance. Hedging might include the use of 'Could you . . .' in front of 'put the kettle on' or the tag 'would you?' at the end of it, such as to soften the command. They also include such expressions as *sort of /kind of (thing)* and *I mean* in English. '*Hein?*','*disons*' or '*si vous voulez*' have a similar function in French when they are used to mitigate the force of what might be considered an impolitely over-emphatic utterance.
4. 'Virile language implies the use of slang and swearwords, word play and in particular sexually oriented word play; taste for insults, a richer and wider vocabulary, mastery of technical, political, intellectual and sporting registers, quasi-monopoly of public speech, control of mixed conversations, exclusive use of ritual and coded languages, authoritarian and categorial discourse ('just wait till your father gets home'), greater liberty in respect of standard usage, more creativity than women.'
5. 'Purism, non-creativity, taste for hyperbole, mastery of the registers of minor domains, timid and non-assertive speech, chit chat, incapacity

to manipulate abstract concepts, hypercorrection, fear of (non-standard uses of) words.'

6. 'What we are talking about here is an idealization process – the projection of an ideal which the speaker leans towards, attempting to take on its signs and symbols, everything which may be identified with the group or person in question: a conscious or unconscious search for identity is at work, an identification process.'

7. 'Each subject, engaged in such linguistic processes of identification, homogenization and singularization, favouring consciously or unconsciously such and such a pronunciation, repeats this form, uses it more often and the other less often and thus changes the language within the language, contributing through the weight of their own way of pronouncing a word to phonological and linguistic variation and change.'

8. 'The kind of speech which is associated with women in general becomes 'women's language'. It becomes an objective fact presented as a foregone conclusion.'

9. Variationist studies look at the social or stylistic conditions which promote the use of one linguistic term in preference to another. The latter are known as sociolinguistic variables or variants. The results of these studies give rise to variable rules which specify the social and geographical conditions which condition the use of a particular variable. The factors involved in such variation include, in addition to gender, categories such as age, social class, educational background and region.

10. The intermediate state of knowledge of a language possessed by a learner of that language. Learners go through a succession of interlanguages as they move towards greater mastery of the target language.

11. 'Interventionism has limits because the evil being attacked has psychosocial causes which cannot be uprooted and overthrown through linguistic policy alone.'

References

Aebischer, V. (1985), *Les femmes et le langage,* Paris : Presses universitaires de France.

Aebischer, V. and Forel, C. (eds) (1983), *Parlers masculins, parlers féminins?*, Paris: Delachaux & Niestlé.

Ager, D. (1990), *Sociolinguistics and Contemporary French,* Cambridge: Cambridge University Press.

Armstrong, N. (1996), 'Variable deletion of French /l/: linguistic, social and stylistic factors', *Journal of French Language Studies*, vol. 6: 1–21.

Armstrong, N. and Unsworth, S. (1999), 'Sociolinguistic variation in southern French schwa', *Linguistics* vol. 37, no. 1.

Ashby, W. (1991), 'When does variation indicate linguistic change in progress?', *Journal of French Language Studies*, vol. 1: 119–37.

Booij, G. and de Jong, D. (1987), 'The domain of liaison: theories and data', in Wenk, B, Durand, J. and Slater, C. (eds), 'French phonetics and phonology', *Linguistics*, vol. 25: 1005–25.

Brick, N. and Wilks, C. (1994), 'Et Dieu nomma la femme', *Journal of French Language Studies,* vol. 4: 235–9.

Chambers, J. K. (1995), *Sociolinguistic Theory,* Oxford: Blackwell.

Cheshire, J. (1978), 'Present tense verbs in Reading English', in Trudgill, P. (1978) *Sociolinguistic Patterns in British English.* London: Edward Arnold.

Cheshire, J. (1982), *Variation in an English Dialect: A Sociolinguistic Study,* Cambridge: Cambridge University Press.

Coates, J. (1997), 'Women's friendships, women's talk', in Wodak R. (ed.), *Gender and Discourse,* London: Thousand Oaks; New Delhi: Sage, 245–62.

Coveney, A. (1996), *Variability in Spoken French: a Sociolinguistic Study of Interrogation and Negation,* Exeter: Elm Bank Publications.

Damourette, J. and Pichon, E. (1911–1939), *Essai de grammaire de la langue française,* 7 vols, Paris: D'Artrey.

Dewaele, J. M. (1998), 'The effect of gender on the choice of speech style', *ITL Review of Applied Linguistics,* vol. 119–20: 9–25.

Durand, J. (1993), *Sociolinguistic Variation and the Linguist,* In Sanders, C. (ed.), 257–85.

Fleischman, S. (1997), 'The battle of feminism and *bon usage*: instituting non-sexist usage in French', *French Review,* 70: 834–44.

Gadet, F. (1996), 'Variabilité, variation, variété: le français d'Europe', *Journal of French Language Studies,* vol. 6: 75–98

Gal, S. (1978), 'Peasant men can't get wives : Language change and sex roles in a bilingual community', *Language in Society,* vol. 7: 1–16.

Galeazzi, C. (1986), 'Les dénominations des femmes dans deux corpus de presse féminine', *Cahiers de lexicologie,* vol. 49: 53–94.

Gauchat, L. (1905/1980), 'L'Unité phonétique dans le patois d'une commune', in *Aus Romansichen Sprachen und Literaturen. Festschrift Heinrich Morf.* Geneva: Slatkine Reprints, 175–232.

Gervais, M.-M. (1993), 'Gender and language in French', in Sanders, C. (ed.): 121–38.

Gervais-Le Garff, M.-M. (1998), 'Liberté, égalité, sororité: a new linguistic order in France?', Paper given at the annual conference of the Organization for the study of Communication, Language and Gender, Portland, University of Southern Maine, October 1998.

Hall, K. and Bucholtz, M. (eds) (1995), *Gender Articulated,* New York: Routledge.

Holmes, J. (1986), 'Functions of *you know* in women's and men's speech', *Language in Society*, 15, 1: 1–22.

Holmes, J. (1995), *Men, Women and Politeness*, London: Longman.

Houdebine, A.-M. (1979a), La différence sexuelle et la langue, *Langage et société*, vol. 7: 3–30.

Houdebine, A.-M. (1979b), *La variété et la dynamique d'un français régional. Etude phonologique à partir d'une enquête à grande échelle dans le département de la Vienne (Poitou),* Thèse de doctorat d'état, Paris: Université de Paris V – Sorbonne.

Houdebine, A.-M. (1983), 'Sur les traces de l'imaginaire linguistique', in V. Aebischer and C. Forel, (eds), 105–39.

Houdebine, A.-M. (1987), 'Le français au féminin', *La linguistique*, vol. 23(1): 13–34.

Houdebine-Gravaud, A.-M. (1998), 'Insécurité linguistique, imaginaire linguistique et féminisation des noms de métiers', in Singy, P. (ed): 155–76.

Irigaray, L. (1985), *This Sex which is Not One*, Ithaca: Cornell University Press.

Irigaray, L. (ed.) (1987), 'Le sexe linguistique', *Langages*, vol. 85.

Irigaray, L. (1990) *Je, tu, nous. Toward a Culture of Difference,* New York and London: Routledge.

Kimura, D. (1992), 'Sex differences in the brain', *Scientific American*, vol. 267(3): 80–7.

Labov, W. (1973), 'The social setting of linguistic change', in T.A. Sebeok (ed.) *Current trends in linguistics II: Diachronic, areal, and typological linguistics,* The Hague: Mouton. 195–253.

Labov, W. (1990), 'The intersection of sex and social class in the course of linguistic change', *Language variation and Change* vol. 2: 205–54.

Labov, W. (1998), 'Vers une réévaluation de l'insécurité linguistique des femmes', in Singy, P. (ed.): 25–35.

Lakoff, R. (1975), *Language and Woman's Place.* New York: Harper & Row.

Martin, A. and Dupuis, H. (1985), *La féminisation des titres et les leaders d'opinion: une étude exploratoire,* Québec: Office de la langue française.

Milroy, J., Milroy, L., Hartley, S. and Walshaw, D. (1994), 'Glottal stops and Tyneside glottalisation : competing patterns of variation and change in British English', *Language Variation and Change*, vol. 6: 327–57.

Moreau, M.-L. and Bauvois, C. (1998), 'L'accommodation comme révélateur de l'insécurité linguistique. Locuteurs et locutrices belges en interaction avec des Français et des Belges', in Singy, P. (ed.): 61–74.

Pillon, A. (1987), 'Le sexe du locuteur est-il un facteur de variation linguistique?', Revue critique. *La Linguistique*, vol. 23: 35–48.

Pooley, T. (1994), 'Word-final consonant devoicing in a variety of working-class French – a case of language contact', *Journal of French Language Studies*, vol. 4: 215–33.

Preisler, B. (1986), *Linguistic Sex-Roles in Conversation: Social Variation in the Expression of Tentativeness in English,* Berlin; New York; Amsterdam: Mouton de Gruyter.

Sanders, C. (ed.) (1993), *French Today,* Cambridge: Cambridge University Press.

Singy, P. (ed.) (1998), *Les femmes et la langue. L'insécurité linguistique en question,* Lausanne: Delachaux et Niestlé.

Tannen, D. (1990), *You Just Don't Understand: Men and Women in Conversation*, New York: Morrow.

Temple, R. (1988), 'In search of sex-specific differences in the voicing of French stop consonants', *Progress Reports from Oxford Phonetics,* vol. 3: 74–99.

Trudgill, P. (1998), 'Concept de genres, prestige latent et insécurité linguistique', in Singy, P. (ed.): 37–57.

Walter, H. (1988), *Le français dans tous les sens,* Paris: Laffont.

Yaguello, M. (1978), *Les mots et les femmes,* Paris: Payot.

Yaguello, M. (1989), *Le sexe des mots,* Paris: Belfond.

Yaguello, M. (1991), *En écoutant parler la langue,* Paris: Seuil.

Yaguello, M. (1998), *Petits faits de langue,* Paris: Seuil.

−6−

Women's Writing

Gill Rye

In common with many other countries over the last thirty years, France has seen a significant rise in the number of literary texts being published by women writers.[1] The profusion of the writing is matched by its evident richness: poetry and plays, short stories and essays, biography and autobiography, diaries, letters and novels. This chapter focuses specifically on women-authored fiction published in the 1990s; the texts considered here are posited as a site of women's personal space − not in terms of autobiography, but rather, as signalling some of the interests and concerns of contemporary women. More precisely, the chapter looks at how some of the themes raised by 1970s feminism are being developed in post-feminist women's fiction.[2]

An influential if controversial voice in 1970s French feminism, Hélène Cixous argued forcefully that women should write in order to become part of culture as (writing) subjects, inscribing their own perspectives, rather than simply being inscribed as the multifarious objects of men's desires, fears and fantasies (Cixous, 1975). Indeed, the development of feminist literary criticism has centred around concerns both to enlarge the literary canon and to study literary representations of women. Since the 1970s, the prolonged debate over whether women's writing or Cixous's formulation *écriture féminine* (Cixous, 1975) could, or even should, be considered a literary genre (Montefiore, 1987; Showalter, 1986) has given way to interest in specific authors and their oeuvres. Major critical works have focussed on a core of well-known women writers in France − Hélène Cixous, Marguerite Duras, Annie Ernaux, and Nathalie Sarraute − while others including Marie Cardinal, Chantal Chawaf, Benoîte Groult, Annie Leclerc, Marie Redonnet and Monique Wittig regularly feature on degree courses and in studies of contemporary women's writing (Fallaize, 1993; Sellers, 1991). In addition, the rise of *francophonie* as a subdiscipline of French studies has brought to the fore a diverse and diffuse group of francophone women writers from both metropolitan France and elsewhere; for example, Calixthe Beyala (Cameroon), Maryse Condé (Guadeloupe), Assia Djebar (Algeria), and *beur* writers Soraya Nini and Leila Sebbar (France).[3]

Accordingly, the chapter does not seek to identify any generic, stylistic or thematic cohesion in women's writing, but instead presents a series of snapshots of fiction by both established and new authors chosen from among the wealth of work published by women in France. The texts discussed cluster around themes of selfhood, and provide an indication of not only private and social trends but also emerging ideas. They are approached from four separate, yet interrelated, themes – mother–daughter relationships, sexuality, love, memory – and placed within the context of the debates raised by those topics.

Mother–Daughter Relationships

Modern feminism has highlighted the ambivalence of the relationship between mothers and daughters. Mothers are both idealized and denigrated; expected to be impossibly perfect, they can perhaps only fail. In both psychical and social terms, the relationship with the mother is inextricably implicated in the development of self identity. Separation from the mother is at the heart of subjectivity, but for the girl who must become a woman, the mother has a dual role to play – both as someone to identify with and as someone from whom to differentiate herself. From Mme de Lafayette's *La Princesse de Clèves* (1678) to Colette's *Sido* (1930), from Simone de Beauvoir's *Une Mort très douce* (1964) and Marie Cardinal's *Les Mots pour le dire* (1975) to Annie Ernaux's *Une femme* (1988), French women writers have always written in both idealized and painfully realistic terms about mother–daughter relationships.

Some of the most dramatic portrayals of mother–daughter relations in contemporary fiction appear in the work of 1998 Goncourt prize-winner Paule Constant.[4] This section focuses on her novel *La Fille du Gobernator* (1994), which portrays the experiences of a seven-year-old girl, Chrétienne. Set in French Guiana in the 1920s, it charts Chrétienne's 'descente aux Enfers' (descent into hell) as she goes with her parents to live in Cayenne when her father takes up a colonial appointment there as governor of the penal colony.[5] *La Fille du Gobernator* is at once comic and painful, its stylized characters and harsh poetic tone combining to evoke the child's experiences. Although both parents are implicated in their daughter's destruction, the mother–daughter relationship is revealed to be particularly painful as Chrétienne slides gradually but ineluctably towards psychological disconnection and to a loss of a sense of self. Chrétienne's mother is not the decorative colonial wife living only through her husband's position, like the character Matilde in Constant's first novel *Ouregano* (1980); rather, she has her own agenda. She is a Christian and a nurse and determined to sacrifice herself for and to the leper colonies around Cayenne. In doing so, she makes a sacrifice of her own daughter, devolving both her education and her everyday care to the band of convicts who act as the governor's domestic servants. Even the painful plaiting of her hair every morning, which Chrétienne clings to because it means physical contact with her mother, is subsequently left to whoever will do it. Her mother's ludicrous suggestion that Chrétienne get some fresh air by taking up the genteel pastime of flower-pressing only serves to highlight the gap between Chrétienne's experiences and her mother's attention to them, as Chrétienne and her convict minder hack their way through the giant tropical vegetation, squashing spiders and killing snakes before they themselves are attacked. Chrétienne's desperate trajectory takes her from aggression to pitiful attention seeking, from outspokenness to silence, from grief to psychological disconnection, and eventually, clutching a pair of her mother's shoes, she leaves Cayenne, 'plus menu, plus maigre et surtout plus petit qu'à l'arrivée' (p. 12) ('slighter, thinner, certainly smaller than when she had arrived') (pp. 1–2).

In *La Fille du Gobernator*, the narrative technique Constant employs is a crucial factor in the way Chrétienne's experience is conveyed. On the one hand, the third person narration reflects the fact that the little girl's voice is silenced and that she is denied subjectivity. On the other hand, despite this, the reader is allowed access to Chrétienne's own perspective as when the narration parallels her voice: 'il . . . prenait son zombic sur les genoux et le caressait vigoureusement. Le zombic dardait sa petite tête aveugle et l'agitait de droite à gauche avec une satisfaction qui ne faisait pas de doute' (p.102).[6] Chrétienne's idea that the convict's erect penis is some sort of strange creature called a 'zombic' is made part of the narration itself. This point is emphasized later in the novel when the narration takes slightly more distance from Chrétienne's own voice: 'Elle était ravie qu'il eût pensé à emporter son horrible zombic dont elle décrivit la tête chauve et aveugle, la dure érection contre les cuisses nues, la bave qui humectait sa bouche' (p.170).[7] Here, the use of indirect speech to convey Chrétienne's description confirms that the previous reference to 'zombic' in the narrative actually contains the little girl's own account of the convict masturbating.

The narrative voice is thus close to Chrétienne's but it is not identical; the little girl's plight is both conveyed and commented upon. To this end, two of the most painful episodes of the novel are not only juxtaposed but share the same vocabulary. Desperate for something to love, the little girl has secretly adopted a puppy but it falls ill and she is unable to care for it. As a punishment, her father forces her to shoot the half-dead, ant-eaten animal herself in order to finish it off. Chrétienne's plaintive cries for 'maman' (Mummy), just when she most needs her mother's presence, are all the more painful when it is revealed that her mother has left for good. She has achieved what she has always wanted – to become a leper – and has departed for a leper colony, never to return. According to Chrétienne's father: 'l'abandon d'un animal est un crime' (p.153) ('it is a crime to abandon an animal') (p. 123), while the narration goes on to reveal that her mother 'était partie pour toujours. Elle l'avait définitivement abandonée' (p.155) ('was gone for ever. She had abandoned her for good') (p. 125). The use of the word 'abandon' for both episodes is significant and the judgement of the reader thus elicited. If, in the view of Chrétienne's father, it is a crime to abandon an animal, it must surely be one to abandon a child. What is more, Chrétienne's father subsequently also abandons her as he goes on to abnegate responsibility for everything in order to disappear, shipwrecked, and thus fulfil his own desired destiny.

Like *Ouregano* before it, the colonial dimension of Constant's *La Fille du Gobernator* is undoubtedly relevant to the experience of the child who is its main character. In this sense, albeit to a lesser degree than Constant's first novel, it can be seen as a critique of not only the French colonial system but also those within it, but there are other valid interpretive angles. The intensity of the childhood experience is also a common theme in Constant's work, and *La Fille du Gobernator* is part of a cohesive oeuvre, in which Constant's individual novels are linked by common characters, places and themes. Chrétienne's loss of self is echoed in other novels (Constant, 1980, 1981, 1983, 1991, 1998), as is the role played by adult women in girls' psychological disconnections, whether that be in the mother–daughter relationship or the educational teacher–pupil dyad. To some extent, this feeds into the all-pervasive culture of mother blaming, but, it also accords with feminist psychological studies that point to disconnection from the self as a part of many women's psychological development (Brown and Gilligan, 1992). This is primarily to do with the importance that relationships have for women; girls lose the strong voices of their childhood as they experience the helplessness of not being listened to and compromise themselves in the relationships which are so meaningful to them. In this analysis, adult women as well as men are implicated in the process, and this is evident in Constant's *La Fille du Gobernator*. Although the very idea of a 'women's psychology' has itself been criticized by some feminist psychologists as reducing the diversity of women's experience (Burman, 1998), an interesting – and creative – outcome of the studies is that they identify a need for 'resonant relationships' between women and girls, wherein girls' voices are really listened to (Brown and Gilligan, 1992).

By dramatizing Chrétienne's psychological disconnection, by emphasizing the intense emotional investment in the person of the mother, by showing how Chrétienne is repeatedly ignored and silenced within the text itself, Constant's *La Fille du Gobernator* ultimately allows Chrétienne's voice to be heard – by the reader.[8] Thus although the problematical nature of mother–daughter relationships is still to the fore in women's fiction of the 1990s (see also Baroche, 1992; Chawaf, 1993; Darrieussecq, 1996; Detambel, 1996; Escalle, 1996; Tasma, 1997), that very fact means that the complexities and diversities of the relationship arguably most fundamental to women's identities are being communicated and explored through both writing and reading.

Sexuality

Feminist writers of the 1970s, particularly those who were concerned with sexual difference (Cixous, 1975; Leclerc 1974), called for women to express their sexual desire and sexual pleasure in writing. Within the Lacanian framework of psychoanalysis, which was then so influential on French thought, feminine sexual pleasure was deemed to be inexpressible.[9] Moreover, in cultural terms, women were historically represented as objects of (male) desire rather than as desiring subjects in their own right. The contention of feminists like Cixous and Leclerc was that women's sexuality had been repressed to the extent that women themselves did not even know anything about their own sexual desires outside the hetero-patriarchal framework within which it had been both theorized and represented. Thus the expression of eroticism is double-edged for women writers: on the one hand, the erotic transgresses the taboos that shore up social and moral orders (Bataille, 1964), whereas, on the other hand, women's expression of their own sexual experiences and fantasies also operates subversively against the phallocentrism which works both to suppress and contain it.

From Cixous's lyrical outpourings (Cixous, 1976, 1983, 1986) to Mireille Best's lesbian stories, from Annie Ernaux's account of sexual passion (1991) to Alina Reyes's erotic fiction, a growing number of contemporary women writers are publishing fictional texts that are explicitly sexual. However, feminist concerns about pornography complicate the reception of some of this work, especially where violence and degradation are an integral and sometimes sought after part of the sexual experience (Dworkin, 1981; Hughes and Ince, 1996; Russell, 1993). Despite serious attempts to differentiate between pornography and eroticism, the question of whether this type of erotic fiction simply replaces women into a victim culture or actually subverts it is continually raised. There are certainly no easy answers, and both the context of the writing and, above all, of its interpretation must be taken into account. In the two texts discussed in this section, Clotilde Escalle's *Pulsion* (1996) and Marie Darrieussecq's *Truismes* (1996), narrative style is an instrumental factor in the way we hear what women say about sex.

In Escalle's second novel *Pulsion*, Pauline, the young protagonist, is traumatized by her parents' decision that the family is to leave Morocco for France. The consequence is a catalogue of sex and violence, during which she is not only subjected to but is also complicit with sexual experiences that degrade her and cause her pain. Raped by a gang of youths, she is left battered and bleeding but the following day seeks them out again, demanding they speak in Arabic as they repeatedly use and abuse her body. Pauline's attachment to Morocco is evidently such that it is a part of her self-identity; the pain inflicted on her by the boys, 'plus forte que la douleur du départ' ('stronger than the pain of leaving') (p. 33), is undoubtedly linked to the need to feel (something) in the face of impending departure.

Subsequently, Pauline, closeted with her boyfriend François in a hotel room, becomes embroiled in a spiral of sex and violence which eventually leads to the certain death of the hotel director: Pauline both desires and submits to violent sex with him and François in turn; the hotel director is shot; and François eventually amputates the latter's gangrenous leg with his pocket knife. Notably, the narrative of *Pulsion* is simple and straightforward, recounting the events as they unfold, 'saying sex [and violence] simply with no intention other than to say' (Worton, 1998: 103). On the one hand, Pauline's passivity is emphasized: 'Elle dit qu'elle est comme cela, elle ne sait que se plier au désir des autres' (p. 82);[10] on the other hand, she is actively desiring: 'Explique-t-on ce genre de choses? Explique-t-on le désir de peaux inconnues, l'envie de les baiser là où elles approchent, cette violence, le velours qui s'écrase sous les doigts? Explique-t-on l'envie des hommes?' (p. 46).[11] Her relationship to both the sex and violence portrayed in the novel is at once passive and active. No attempt is made to reconcile her position; the contrasts simply coexist.

Such ambiguity is also at the heart of one of the most successful as well as one of the most controversial novels published in the period, Marie

Darrieussecq's first novel *Truismes*. A best-seller in France and translated into more than 30 different languages, it is the story of a woman's metamorphosis as her body alternates between the states of woman and sow, although most of the time she is a mixture of them both. *Truismes* has a recognizable but futuristic setting (millennial Europe) and uses the mode of the fantastic. Its literalization of issues surrounding women's bodies (bodily changes, self-image, sexuality, reproduction), set within the framework of a corrupt and increasingly repressive political regime, has incensed, fascinated and perplexed commentators. The *parfumerie* (perfume shop) in which the narrator is employed is more-or-less a front for prostitution. Thus power relations of all sorts have a central place in this novel but its humour is a counterweight to straightforward interpretations of these aspects. Most striking is the simple, somewhat naïve, narrative, which rather like that of *Pulsion*, albeit in the first person singular, contrasts with the sexually explicit and violent nature of the content.

> Je les trouvais charmants en général, mes clients, mignons comme tout. Ils s'intéressaient de plus en plus à mon derrière, c'était le seul problème. Je veux dire, et j'invite toutes les âmes sensibles à sauter cette page pour respect pour elles-mêmes, je veux dire que mes clients avaient de drôles d'envies, des idées tout à fait contre nature si vous voyez ce que je veux dire. Les premières fois, je m'étais dit qu'après tout, si grâce à moi la chaîne pouvait avoir de l'argent supplémentaire, je pouvais être fière et tout faire pour cela marche encore mieux. (p. 36)[12]

The exploitation of the narrator and her apparent complicity with it are both foregrounded. Thus, in *Truismes* as in *Pulsion*, the victimhood of the female protagonist is problematized. Indeed, as she becomes more sow like, the narrator becomes more sexually desiring and begins to take real pleasure in the sexual encounters with her clients to the extent that: 'je devais me souvenir de simuler comme avant avec les anciens clients' (p. 41) ('I had to remember to pretend the way I always had before with our long-time patrons') (p. 30), even though 'il est difficile de simuler quand des sensations vraies vous viennent dans le corps' (p. 42) ('it's hard to pretend when you're feeling real sensations') (p. 31). The idea of having to pretend to have an orgasm while, at the same time, having a real one is of course amusing, but this episode is also telling and worth closer scrutiny.

Women, including prostitutes, fake orgasms in sexual encounters with men for a variety of reasons. For men, the orgasm is perceived to be the ultimate and single aim of sexual intercourse. Thus a man's self-perception of himself as a good lover might well be confirmed by the idea that he is successfully giving a woman an orgasm. For women to pretend to have orgasms is, therefore, on the one hand to give men what they want and to pander to their narcissism, and on the other, to appear to comply with men's fantasies of what women's sexuality is and what women's orgasms are. In *Truismes*, it is evident that a fake orgasm is not the same as a real one, and moreover, that the narrator's real orgasm is not to be revealed. She is very conscientious and proud of giving the service her clients expect (they are used to the faked orgasms), but the double standards that render the expression of women's sexual desires unacceptable while men's are vaunted is also a factor that operates in her private life as well as in her working life, since her boyfriend rejects her increasing advances: 'Il disait que j'étais devenue, excusez-moi, une *vraie chienne*, ce sont ses propres termes' (p.41) ('He said that I'd turned into – excuse me – a *real bitch*: those were his very words') (p. 29). The narrator's real orgasm can thus be considered subversive (she enjoys what she is not supposed to enjoy; it is her secret and a space of her own, a space apart from her sexual and economic exploitation). However, her secret, subversive or transgressive orgasm can only put her in a position of power (as subject rather than object of sexual desire) if she can freely enjoy it. If she were to let her clients know she is having a real orgasm, either it would give them even greater satisfaction and thus a better service (of which she is proud), or, alternatively, it would be to admit that she had been faking it before and thus they would realize that they were not necessarily such great lovers after all. Of course, these possibilities are far from exhaustive but they suffice to show that the politics of the sexual encounter in *Truismes* are not straightforward.

Significantly, in both *Pulsion* and *Truismes*, the act of writing itself is foregrounded. In *Pulsion*, François repeatedly carves their names over the walls and ceiling of the hotel room; for her part, Pauline leaves a record of the events in a notebook, well aware of the power of writing about sex, ever since her mother had burnt her diary, horrified and frightened by what she read. The hotel staff who find Pauline's notebook are appalled by its contents but the effect of reading it forces them to face up to their own complicity in the events. Pauline's writing and *Truismes*'s narrator's account of her experiences are a mirror of Escalle's and Darrieussecq's own texts respectively. When relating the dilemma of her orgasms, the narrator of *Truismes* writes: 'Je vais essayer de m'exprimer le plus clairement possible, parce que je sais que ce n'est pas facile à comprendre, surtout pour les hommes' (p. 41), adding: 'Je conçois à quel point cela doit être choquant et désagreable de lire une jeune fille qui s'exprime de cette façon' (p. 42).[13] It is difficult for women to write about their sexuality; it is not easy for them to find the right words to describe their experiences. They have the power not only to shock and to horrify their readers, but also to lead them to interrogate their own responses. Women writing about sex are, however, also constantly at risk of being misunderstood, especially perhaps by male readers, but also by women for whom there is certainly not one common experience of sexuality. Nonetheless, among many other texts, both *Pulsion* and *Truismes* are evidence that contemporary women in France are exploring and finding different ways of writing about sex. The complex relations of power within the two accounts and the simplicity of the narratives in both instances work together to challenge common perceptions about women's sexuality. However, as the young protagonists' own writing within both *Pulsion* and *Truismes* itself implies, their readers might not always necessarily know how to read it.

Love

In both Escalle's and Darrieussecq's novels, sex is on the whole divorced from love. Love, however, is what women write about – or so the stereotypical assumption goes. Modern feminism has raised questions about the nature of romantic love, classic heterosexual coupledom and the institution of marriage, analysing the impact they have on women's identity. Nonetheless, contemporary women continue to write about love but, far from writing only romantic love stories that reproduce and reinforce the conventional heterosexual love-and-marriage recipe, love itself has become a subject of enquiry. This section focuses on a group of fiction texts by Hélène Cixous that can be read as just such an analysis of love: *Déluge* (1992), *Beethoven à jamais ou l'existence de Dieu* (1993) and *La Fiancée juive de la tentation* (1995). In contrast to the texts discussed hitherto, Cixous's body of poetical fiction is most aptly described as avant garde. It carries with it the reputation of being difficult to read, but the three texts discussed in this section, while still complex, are perhaps more accessible than the 1970s fiction by which she is often judged. Despite its non-realist style, Cixous's work is ultimately concerned with reality; each of her individual fiction texts not only self-consciously explores the process of writing itself but also examines in minute detail different elements of what could be called an internal or emotional reality. So far in this chapter, narrative style has been shown to be instrumental to the expression of women's voices as writing subjects. This point is also applicable to Cixous's fiction, although her narratives are of a very different style, but in the three texts discussed here it also has a somewhat different outcome. In contrast to Cixous's resolutely women-centred earlier work, all three of these texts focus on a heterosexual couple. However, by means of multi-layered narratives, slippery textual figures, poetical writing and even the books' titles with their various biblical connotations, the particular couple is allowed to become conceptualized, and thus Cixous's discussion of love oscillates between the individual, the general and the universal.

Déluge is primarily a meditation on loving and hurting through the account of a specific loss – a broken relationship. Images and vocabulary of death convey the intense pain of loss: 'la maladie mortelle' (p. 183) ('mortal illness'), 'un assassinat' (p. 32) ('an assassination'), 'le désert' (p. 74) ('desert'), 'un trou noir' ('a black hole') and 'un gouffre' (p. 168) ('an abyss'). The process of grieving is explored in minute detail, as 'amputation de voix' (p. 50) ('amputated voice') and 'cette plaie sans bords' (p. 55) ('this endless wound'). Although recounting the end of a specific relationship, on many occasions the narrative slides from *je* to *nous* (from 'I' to 'we'), and thus *Déluge* also becomes a reflection on loving and hurting more generally. By means of a consideration of a wealth of different perspectives – chapters entitled 'Points de vue 1–4' ('Points of view 1–4') as well as extended speculation on the topic – it becomes clear that the potential to hurt forms part of any loving relationship. In *Déluge*, the person we love most, simply by being the person we love most, is the person who can hurt us most. Similarly, we can all hurt those who love us and we may do so without even realizing it.

For Cixous, fear of being hurt is part of every loving relationship but the next text, *Beethoven à jamais ou l'existence de Dieu*, focuses specifically on the problems and negotiations involved in becoming a couple. The diaries, notebooks, letters, songs and narrative that together make up the account reveal the full extent of the emotional experiences of a relationship: the intensity of love, fear of loss, joy, hurt, togetherness and separation. In a similar way to *Déluge*, *Beethoven à jamais ou l'existence de Dieu* is centred on an individual couple but in this text the plethora of slippages between narrative levels, between textual figures (and couples), between historical periods and between love stories of fact and fiction means that the individual relationship portrayed also figures in a more conceptual manner. Here, promises play an important and particularly creative role in the way the relationship is both lived and developed. The man's 'je te serai toujours infidèle, comme à moi-même' (pp. 71–2) ('I will always be unfaithful to you as I am to myself') and 'je ne t'épouserai jamais' (p. 82) ('I will never marry you') are of course hardly the classic pledges of a conventional heterosexual love affair. Nonetheless, they are shown to have real meaning. Marriage is deemed to be undesirable, appropriative and sterile, but rejection of it does not preclude commitment. Ultimately, the couple succeed in saying 'jetaime' (pp. 234–5) ('Iloveyou'). This phrase, run together in the text, is thus emphasized as a cliché, loaded as it is with culturally determined emotional investment. However, this particular couple is able to use it creatively, because they have negotiated its meaningfulness within the context of their own individual relationship.[14]

Promises are also what count most in *La Fiancée juive de la tentation*, a text that uses mythical references to universalize its analysis of passion and commitment. As in *Beethoven à jamais ou l'existence de Dieu*, marriage is not a desirable outcome, but in both texts the pledge or promise between lovers is what is considered to be most valuable and creative. Like *Beethoven à jamais ou l'existence de Dieu*, *La Fiancée juive de la tentation* deals with the fundamental pledges on which a relationship is constructed, but it also explores the problematics of seemingly simple everyday commitments like promising to phone:

> Quand je te dis 'je t'appellerai' ne comprends pas 'ne m'appelle pas' ne comprends pas quand je te dis je t'appellerai ne m'appelle pas je ne te comprends pas tu as l'air de penser que je ne souhaite pas que tu m'appelles, tu me troubles, j'ai oublié de te dire, tu peux m'appeler, j'ai oublié de te dire que ça allait de soi quand tu veux tu peux m'appeler quand tu veux.
>
> Mais comment mon amour appelerai-je 'quand-je-veux' alors que je ne peux vouloir appeler que quand tu veux et que dans l'obscurité de l'éloignement il m'est difficile de juger à ton visage quand c'est le quand. (p. 88)[15]

The discussion continues over three pages of the book, Cixous's lyrical language teasing out the complex network of emotions, needs, desires and fears which create misunderstandings in loving relationships. The first voice (the first paragraph) of the above extract is that of a man and the second a woman, and thus the scenario notionally re-places the male/female couple into conventional gender hierarchies. On one level, here just as in old-fashioned boy-meets-girl love stories, the woman seems to take the passive role and waits for the man to phone. However, there is certainly more to *La Fiancée juive de la tentation* than this, and indeed, in a similar way to *Déluge*'s multiple perspectives and *Beethoven à jamais ou l'existence de Dieu*'s creative promises, this re-placement calls into question that very placing.

Taken together, these three fiction texts by Cixous explore and analyse the finer points of the everyday experiences of loving relations. They foreground the difficulties of being a loving subject, which, despite the best of intentions, is not as simple as it might seem. Although dealing with relationships based on mutual respect, they show the problems of negotiating loving relations with others in practice. The specific couples around whom the texts are centred are all heterosexual couples and on the surface they might seem to play into conventional gender stereotypes that make masculinity equivalent with activity and femininity with passivity (whether this is theorized as natural or socially constructed). Nonetheless, the narrative slippages which are a feature of Cixous's writing de-particularize the analysis of these individual relationships. Indeed, the focus on love rather than sex in these texts extends the questions they raise about how we love one another beyond the limitations of one particular (heterosexual) sexual orientation. In this way, apparently conventional gender hierarchies are nuanced, love is in the process of being re-theorized, and Cixous's texts, *Déluge, Beethoven à jamais ou l'existence de Dieu* and *La Fiancée juive de la tentation* become a creative space for thinking differently about loving relationships.

Memory

Memory is emphatically about the past, but it is also an intrinsic part of the present. In many different ways, memory makes a significant contribution to identity formation – to what we are and to what we are perceived to be. Both cultural and personal memory are implicated in individual selfhood as well as impacting on a variety of notions of community and collective identities. On the one hand, as feminist theory has shown, cultural production (including literature) contributes to the way women's identities are constituted – as a group, as diverse groups, and as individuals. On the other hand, personal memories are an important part of the way we constitute ourselves. Life stories, not only in the form of biography and autobiography but also as letters, diaries and memoirs have long been part of women's writing, and they are certainly privileged literary productions of memory. Fiction, however, is able to throw light on the interaction between memory and selfhood in a rather more self-conscious way and, to this end, this section focuses on prize-winning short-story writer Christiane Baroche's third full-length novel, *La Rage au bois dormant* (1995).

La Rage au bois dormant is the story of the lives of two friends, Adèle Dausse and Judith Fautrelot, both now in old age. Their life stories are built up during the course of the novel. The narration consists of the two women, separately and together, talking about themselves and each other, going back over the past and recounting their memories. Their contributions are supplemented by those of their lawyer and friend, Georges Falloires, who fills in some of the gaps in their stories and provides a different, although equally subjective, perspective. This structure reveals the differences between the two women's relationship to past memories. Adèle, motivated by the desire to keep hold of the past in order to counter the effects of ageing – the loss of youth, beauty, loved ones and even memories – tends to romanticize it: 'A cinq ans, Judith, j'avais des cheveux si blonds, bouclés si court qu'on m'habillait d'une peau de mouton, la nuit de Noël, et qu'on me couchait dans la paille de la crèche. Qui peut se vanter comme moi d'avoir remplacé l'enfant Jésus? Tu vois bien, tu vois bien' (p. 19).[16] Adèle's description of her part in the Christmas crèche evokes children's picture book portrayals of the nativity. For Judith, on the other hand, remembering means reliving bitter realities: suffering with childhood eczema, finding her father in bed with another man, losing first her lover and then her son in two different wars. However, Judith is a strong, active character whose exploits enliven the humdrum of everyday life: speculating on Judith's frequent absences, Adèle imagines her friend as 'un robot dangereux' (p. 279) ('a dangerous robot'), seducing men but indifferent to them, using her sexuality to get the better of them; to the local townspeople, Judith is larger-than-life and said to have a sort of mythical affinity to animals. Judith herself veers from amusement to anger at Adèle's story-making, ultimately refusing to be enclosed in the 'belles images' (p. 318) ('pretty pictures') or 'roman rose' (p. 292) ('erotic novel') that her friend is weaving around their lives. Far from being a mythical siren, tempting men to their ruin, Judith makes it clear that she was simply – banally – away working; her own account of her life reveals the extent to which Adèle's perceptions of her are fed by imagination and fantasy.

In this way, Baroche's novel shows time and time again how our identities are made up not only of how we perceive ourselves but also of the ways in which others perceive us. It also demonstrates the extent to which we implicate other people in our own identities. Adèle is pretty, coquettish, gossipy, a prostitute, then a wife and mother; in contrast, Judith is active, educated, a leader, a mother, a wife *and* a businesswoman who enjoys power. In these respects, Adèle fits the stereotypes of traditional femininity while Judith is the epitome of a liberated woman; the friends are like two sides of the same coin – of women's identity. Moreover, Judith is such a constant source of fascination to Adèle that she forms part of Adèle's own perception of herself: 'je n'ai pas eu d'histoire sans tes histoires, c'est simple' (p. 279) ('without all the things you get up to, I don't have a story, it's quite simple'). In one sense, therefore, Adèle lives passively and vicariously through Judith, but in another sense, the Judith Adèle fantasizes (about) is the woman that she herself would like to be. Judith is thus Adèle's 'other' – someone from whom she differentiates herself and at the same time with whom she identifies.

In *La Rage au bois dormant*, multiple layers of fiction affirm the importance of narrative itself: the title evokes the classic fairy tale 'La Belle au bois dormant' (Sleeping Beauty), the form of the novel is theatricalesque (complete with monologues, dialogues, cast list and scene setting), and multiple references are made to the women's lives as a *roman* (romance, saga – or novel). The last chapter is also entitled 'La Rage au bois dormant', and is the only chapter narrated by an unknown narrator. The ending to Baroche's novel, it is also a fictional ending to a fictional novel (the *roman* Judith and Adèle create out of their lives and memories). This last chapter thus creates a circular open-ended structure to the novel, which ultimately leaves Adèle still imagining, still speculating, and still fantasizing. In this way, the narrative, the form and the structure of *La Rage au bois dormant* combine to testify to the extent to which fiction, in the form of creative interpretation, is implicated in the process of remembering, but the effect of these factors also goes further. Baroche's novel demonstrates not only that the memories, imagination, speculation, fantasy and the narratives (stories, fiction) we forge are part of our life but also the extent to which they are actually constitutive of both our own and others' identities.

The last section on the roles of narrative and fiction brings this chapter full circle, since it underlines the connections between writing and women's identities with which it started. The fiction discussed here represents only a small number of examples of the diverse experiences that make up women's lives. Nonetheless, these texts provide ample evidence that the perspectives of women as (writing) subjects are now included in contemporary French cultural production to a greater degree than ever before. Accordingly, this fiction shows how 1990s post-feminist writing builds on and develops some of the issues and themes surrounding women's identities that were raised by feminist thinkers of the 1970s. Identity and selfhood are foregrounded – in mother-daughter relations, in sexuality, in love and in the stories we tell about ourselves. Individual identities are closely intertwined with others and, to a large extent, constituted through relationships with them. Most of the texts discussed deal in some way or another with loss – of the mother, of the self, of love, of youth. In the 1970s, loss was theorized as being at the heart of women's identity in both psychoanalytical and sociocultural terms, but here, in women's writing of the 1990s, loss within the texts is treated as part of life itself. Indeed, this body of fiction testifies to women's survival – and creativity – in the face of loss of all kinds.

The variety of different forms and genres that make up this fiction is evidence of the aesthetic richness of the writing. Narrative styles and structures contribute to its originality and the settings and references to different time periods and cultures enable fictional spaces to be established that are different from the actual context of writing. Thus this fiction not only portrays the experiences and memories of contemporary women but also explores new and innovative ways of thinking and being, offering its readers plenty of food for thought.

Above all, the self-conscious nature of the writing discussed in this chapter itself proclaims the importance of contemporary women's fiction – for understanding, for exploring and for speculating on women's identities. It affirms the value of telling new stories as well as confirming the worth of retelling the old ones, although in a different way. In doing so, it signals that not only the writing but also, crucially, the reading of new fiction forms part of the complex, tortuous processes of both renewal and change.

Notes

1. There are no readily available statistics of publishing by gender, but the effects of modern feminism on women's writing are evident by the number of studies devoted to it. Athlone's 'Women in Context' series provides a country-by-country survey of women's literature (see especially, Holmes, 1996); for general introductions to contemporary French women's writing, see Fallaize, 1993; Sellers, 1991; Sorrell, 1995; *Into the Mainstream* (Gerrard, 1989) is one of the few studies to focus on changes in publishing trends, albeit in a predominantly anglophone context. As far as French reading and publishing practices are concerned, it is significant that several of the authors whose work is discussed in this chapter have written either best sellers or prize-winning fiction.

2. Here, 'post-feminist fiction' means fiction that is not necessarily explicitly feminist but is both written and read at a cultural moment which implicitly includes feminist thinking.

3. *Beur* means someone of North African descent who is born in France.

4. The *Prix Goncourt* is the most prestigious French literary prize awarded for fiction writing.
5. *La Fille du Gobernator*, back cover; all other translations are from *The Governor's Daughter* (1998).
6. 'He ... took his zombic on his lap, and petted it vigorously. The zombic lifted its little blind head and waved it from right to left with a satisfaction that left no room for doubt' (pp. 79–80).
7. 'She was delighted that he had thought to take with him his zombic, and pictured its blind, bald head, and its hard erection against naked thighs, and the drool wetting its mouth' (p. 137).
8. For a fuller discussion of this point (Rye, 2000a).
9. The work of Jacques Lacan, a French psychoanalyst and interpreter of Freud's theories, emphasizes the connections between language and subjectivity. According to Lacan, when a child enters into language, s/he also enters the social order with its (patriarchal) laws and rituals. For Freud and Lacan, female sexuality is a 'dark continent', unknown and unsymbolized. It cannot, therefore, be expressed within the terms of the symbolic (the all-determining social order theorized by Lacan). For lucid and accessible accounts, see Mitchell and Rose, 1982 (editors' introductions); Sellers, 1991; Wright, 1992 ('sexuality' entry).
10. 'She says that is how she is, that she has to give in to the desires of others.' (My translation.)
11. 'Can you explain that sort of thing? Can you explain the desire for unknown bodies, the desire to fuck them wherever they approach you, that violence, the velvet that gets crushed by touch? Can you explain the desire for men?' (My translation.)
12. Translations are from *Pig Tales* (1997). 'In general, I found my clients charming, cute as could be. They were growing increasingly interested in my derrière, that was the only problem. What I mean is – and I urge all sensitive souls not to read this page, for their own self-respect – that my customers had some peculiar predilections, some completely unnatural ideas, if you follow me. The first times, I told myself that after all, if the chain could earn some extra money thanks to me, I should be eager to do anything to help things go even better' (pp. 25–6).
13. 'I'll try to express myself as clearly as possible, because I know it's not easy to understand, especially for men' (p. 30); 'I can imagine how shocking and disagreeable it must be to read this sort of thing from a young girl' (p. 31).
14. For a fuller discussion of these points (Rye, 2000b).

15. 'When I say 'I'll call you' don't take it as meaning 'don't call me' don't think I mean don't call me when I say I'll call you I don't understand you, you seem to think that I hope you won't call me, you are confusing me, I forgot to say, you can call me, I forgot to say that it goes without saying that when you want you can call me when you want. But how my love will I call 'when-I-want' when I only want to call when you want and when we are far apart it is difficult for me to judge from your face when is the when.' (My translation.)

16. 'When I was five, Judith, I had such short blond, curly hair that on Christmas Eve I was wrapped in a sheepskin and put to bed in the straw of the crèche. Who else could boast they'd taken the place of the baby Jesus? You see, you see . . .' (My translation.)

References

Baroche, C. (1992), *Les Ports du silence*, Paris: Grasset.

—— (1995), *La Rage au bois dormant*, Paris: Grasset.

Bataille, G. (1964), *L'Erotisme*, Paris: UGE.

Beauvoir, S. de. (1964), *Une Mort très douce*, Paris: Gallimard.

Brown, L.M. and Gilligan, C. (1992), *Meeting at the Crossroads: Women's Psychology and Girls' Development*, London: Harvard University Press.

Burman, E. (ed.) (1998), *Deconstructing Feminist Psychology*, London: Sage.

Cardinal, M. (1975), *Les Mots pour le dire*, Paris: Grasset.

Chawaf, C. (1993), *Vers la lumière*, Paris: Des femmes.

Cixous, H. (1976), *La*, Paris: Gallimard.

—— (1983), *Le Livre de Promethea*, Paris: Gallimard.

—— (1986), *La Bataille d'Arcachon*, Laval: Editions Trois.

—— (1992), *Déluge*, Paris: Des femmes.

—— (1993), *Beethoven à jamais ou l'existence de Dieu*, Paris: Des femmes.

—— (1995), *La Fiancée juive de la tentation*, Paris: Des femmes.

—— and Clément, C. (1975), *La Jeune Née*, Paris: U.G.E.; (1986), *The Newly Born*.

Woman, translated by Betsy Wing, Manchester: Manchester University Press.

Colette, (1930; 1961), *Sido, suivi de Les Vrilles de la vigne*, Paris: Hachette.

Constant, P. (1980), *Ouregano*, Paris: Gallimard.

—— (1981), *Propriété privée*, Paris: Gallimard.

—— (1983), *Balta*, Paris: Gallimard.

—— (1991), *Le Grand Ghâpal*, Paris: Gallimard.

—— (1994), *La Fille du Gobernator*, Paris: Gallimard; (1998) *The Governor's Daughter*, translated by Betsy Wing, Lincoln: University of Nebraska Press.

—— (1998), *Confidence pour confidence*, Paris: Gallimard.

Darrieussecq, M. (1996), *Truismes*, Paris: P.O.L.; (1997), *Pig Tales*, translated by Linda Coverdale, London: Faber.

Detambel, R. (1996), *La Verrière*, Paris: Gallimard.

Dworkin, A. (1981), *Pornography: Men Possessing Women*, London: The Women's Press.

Ernaux, A. (1988), *Une femme*, Paris: Gallimard.

—— (1991), *Passion simple*, Paris: Gallimard.

Escalle, C. (1996), *Pulsion*, Paris: Zulma.

Fallaize, E. (1993), *French Women's Writing: Recent Fiction*, New York: St. Martin's Press.

Gerrard, N. (1989), *Into the Mainstream*, London: Pandora.

Holmes, D. (1996), *French Women's Writing 1848–1994*, London: Athlone.

Hughes, A. and Ince, K. (eds) (1996), *French Erotic Fiction: Women's Desiring Writing 1880–1990*, Oxford: Berg.

La Fayette, Mme. de. (1678; 1958), *La Princesse de Clèves*, Paris: LGF.

Leclerc, A. (1974), *Parole de femme*, Paris: Grasset & Fasquelle.

Mitchell, J. and Rose, J. (eds) (1982), *Feminine Sexuality, Jacques Lacan and the Ecole Freudienne*, London: Macmillan.

Montefiore, J. (1987), *Feminism and Poetry: Language, Experience, Identity in Women's Writing,* London: Pandora.

Russell, D.E.H. (ed.) (1993), *Making Violence Sexy: Feminist Views on Pornography*, Buckingham: Open University Press.

Rye, G. (2000a), 'Re(dis)covering One/self: Julia Kristeva's *expérience littéraire* and Paule Constant's Little Girls', *Journal of the Institute of Romance Studies* vol. 7, forthcoming.

Rye, G. (2000b), 'Agony or Ecstasy? Reading Cixous's Recent Fiction', *Paragraph*, vol. 23, forthcoming.

Sellers, S. (1991), *Language and Sexual Difference: Feminist Writing in France,* Basingstoke: Macmillan.

Showalter, E. (ed.) (1991), *The New Feminist Criticism: Essays on Women, Literature and Theory*, London: Virago.

Sorrell, M. (ed.) (1995), *Elles: A Bilingual Anthology of Modern French Poetry by Women*, Exeter: University of Exeter Press.

Tasma, S. (1997), *Désolation et destruction*, Paris: Editions de l'Olivier/ Le Seuil.

Worton, M. (1998), 'Looking for Kicks: Promiscuity and Violence in Contemporary French Fiction', *Nottingham French Studies*, vol. 37: 89–105.

Wright, E. (ed.) (1992), *Feminism and Psychoanalysis: A Critical Dictionary*, Oxford: Blackwell.

—7—

Immigrant and Ethnic Minority Women
Jane Freedman

The experiences and problems of immigrant and ethnic minority women in France are often specific ones that cannot be generalized either in relation to other French women or to men of immigrant and ethnic minority origin. The multiple nature of immigrant women's identities and experiences has therefore sometimes been overlooked both by feminists seeking to generalize women's experience based on that of white French women, and by analysts of immigration who have failed to take proper account of the gendered processes involved in the immigrant experience, rendering women 'invisible' or considering them only in their position as wives and mothers (Barison and Catarino, 1997; Golub, Morokvasic and Quiminal, 1997; Bentichou, 1997). This chapter will attempt to provide some account of the particular experiences of these immigrant and ethnic minority women and to point out how these experiences differ both from those of white French women and from men of immigrant and ethnic minority origin.

A first point that must be underlined in talking about the experiences of immigrant and ethnic minority women in France is that we are not dealing with a homogeneous category. Immigrant women in France come from many different countries of origin in Europe, Asia and Africa, and there are obviously various different ethnic minority communities within French society. Clearly one should not assume that the mere process of immigration overrides these differences of origin and ethnic identity. Similarly, within different ethnic communities there are differences of class, age, ability and so forth. As Yuval-Davis points out: 'Gender, class, political, religious and other differences play central roles in the constructions of specific ethnic politics, and different ethnic projects of the same collectivity can be engaged in intense competitive struggles for hegemonic positions.'(Yuval-Davis, 1997: 44). It would thus be foolish to try to construct a generalized model for immigrant women without taking account of these cross-cutting divisions. Having said this, however, it will be impossible in a chapter of this length to provide a detailed account of the experiences of all immigrant and ethnic minority women and this task is made harder by the relative lack of information available concerning women from some ethnic minority communities – for example, Vietnamese women in France. We will thus aim to try to point out some of the possible common factors in these women's position, without assuming that such common factors signify a totally shared experience. The first section of this chapter will thus examine the general experiences of immigrant and ethnic minority women in France, highlighting some of the difficulties that they face in French society and also some of the strategies they have developed to ease their integration into this society. We will also highlight two high-profile issues in French politics and society that have posed particular problems for immigrant women. The middle section of the chapter will thus examine the question of the *sans-papiers* and the final section will take a look at the *Affaire des foulards* (Islamic headscarf affair), both of which have had a particular significance for immigrant women and for gender relations within ethnic minority communities in France. Before beginnning this exposé we will briefly outline the context in which the immigration of ethnic minority women into France began.

The question of immigrants and ethnic minority communities is a highly sensitive one in contemporary France.[1] There is not space here to explore the history of immigration into France or the complexities of the political situation that has resulted.[2] Suffice it to say that France has a long history of immigration, with various waves of migrants arriving first in the nineteenth and early twentieth centuries, mainly from within Europe and then, after World War Two with the process of decolonization, from France's ex-colonies in Asia and Africa. Although immigration was originally tolerated, if not welcomed, as an answer to labour shortages in French industry, in 1974 the French government officially suspended immigration in response to the economic crisis. This 'suspension' has not meant the end of immigration, however, despite efforts by successive governments to stop the influx. As a member of the European Union, France cannot stop immigration from other EU countries, but what French politicians, and public opinion, have been more worried about is immigration from Africa and Asia. Attempts to halt this immigration have not been successful for several reasons, not least of which is that France has not been able to prevent immigration for family reunification which is protected under international law (although a very rigid interpretation of conditions necessary for immigration for family reunification has been applied (Prencipe, 1994)). This immigration for family reunification has accelerated the process of sedenterization of immigrant communities from Africa and Asia, which began principally in the 1960s, and has changed the nature of debates over immigration. As Nicollet points out with regard to African women, the sedenterization of the immigrant community and the greater presence of women and children amongst the immigrant population has given gender relations a particular importance, and to the previous debates over immigrants and the labour force have been added questions over families, marriage, polygamy, excision and so forth. (Nicollet, 1993). This is true not only for African immigrants but for all other immigrant communities. The immigration of women rather than men poses different questions for French society, and the experience of immigration is clearly a gendered one, lived differently by men and women.

The Experience of Ethnic and Immigrant Women in France

In the case of immigration into France women and men have immigrated at different times and for different reasons. For a long time the immigrant population in France numbered many more men than women, as men came to France to find work, or were recruited by French industry, but since the 1960s the number of women immigrants has grown so that today there are almost as many women as men amongst most ethnic minority communities. In 1990 figures show that amongst European immigrant communities there was an almost equal gender balance, whilst around 41 per cent of the Maghrebi and Sub-Saharan African and 45 per cent of the Asian populations were women.[3] Whilst the general assumption is that men immigrated to work and women then followed to rejoin their husbands, or to find a husband in France, and whilst this may be true in many cases, it can be seen as an over-simplification of the situation. Contrary to received opinion, women immigrants are not only women who have 'followed their husbands', women do migrate alone and for their own particular reasons. Similarly it is not true that marriage is the only reason and means of entry for immigrant women in France, many women immigrate alone and find a partner afterwards, others leave their husbands behind in their country of origin (Golub et al., 1997; Silberman, 1991). So the choice to emigrate from their country of origin and come to France is not merely a passive one for women, and indeed research has shown that for many women immigration is a positive life choice as they hope to find a freer society or a more urban lifestyle than that which they experienced in their country of origin. For example, a survey carried out amongst Algerian women in France has shown that these women have specific ideas behind their migratory projects, hoping to find a better life in French society, and that, in contrast to Algerian men immigrants, they have little desire to return to their country of origin:

> Cette émigration féminine traduit pour beaucoup d'entre elles un véritable choix de société: une idée de liberté, le choix de l'urbain, la consommation ... Dans les enquêtes que nous avons effectuées, les femmes n'ont pas beaucoup de projet de retour au pays. Ainsi, l'une d'entre elles nous dira: 'mon pays c'est là où il y a mes enfants et ma famille.' Chez les hommes, par contre, l'idée du retour existe. Dans cette idée, il y a l'appartenance à la communauté d'origine, à la terre, aux racines. Les femmes, elles, ont une idée beaucoup plus individualisée, avec des projets, des rêves, comme si tout était Avenir.[4] (Boulahbel-Villac, 1992: 107)

But whilst women's migratory projects are varied and cannot be attributed merely to a desire to follow their husbands, this variety is often overlooked and within dominant French culture, immigrant women either remain 'invisible' (which seems particularly to be the case for immigrant women of Asian origin), or if they are not 'invisible' these women are principally represented as wives and mothers and as such are seen as the key to the integration of immigrants in France. Represented in their role as 'mothers' of families, it is seen to be their duty to ensure the stability of the ethnic minority population and to see to it that their children integrate or assimilate and become 'French'. So we can argue that these women face a particular weight of expectation and are under specific pressure from French society. At the same time there are powerful forces acting to exclude these women from this same society, depending on their particular situation. For many first-generation immigrant women in particular, adaptation to French society may be difficult. They have broken with systems of solidarity and affiliation in their countries of origin and have to reconstruct their social position in a foreign society. They may find themselves isolated, especially if they have a limited command of the French language. Housing for immigrants is often poor, and one can argue that this has a particular effect on women, who, in many immigrant and ethnic minority communities are almost entirely responsible for the management of the domestic space. Moreover, for women of immigrant origin, access to salaried work has been limited both because of domestic and social pressure from within their communities – women of Maghrebi and Turkish origin have the lowest rates of formal employment due in part to the norms in their countries of origin (Hargreaves, 1995) – and because of reluctance by French employers to hire immigrant women, especially those from the ex-colonies (there is a general differentiation in French opinion between immigrants of European origin and those from Africa and Asia who are more readily referred to as '*immigrés*' and can be seen to suffer greater discrimination from employers and others). Thus in contrast with many immigrant men who arrived in France to fulfil demands for manual labour, immigrant women have not been able to count on integration through waged employment, particularly in a time of economic recession. Those who do find waged employment are often employed in low-paid service sector jobs, many in temporary and part-time positions with no security. As Quiminal explains, immigrant women may be less prone to overt racist attacks than men, but at the same time, they are expected to occupy a particular place and there is no room in the French imagination for these women to expand their role, take advantage of education and job training opportunities and enter the labour force. French attitudes to immigrant women, particularly from the ex-colonies can be resumed thus:

> On les tolère comme femmes au foyer, s'occupant des tâches domestiques, de l'éducation des enfants, responsables de l'intégration de leur famille. Les femmes immigrées sont véritablement assignées à une place, et en période de crise, de chômage, elles ne doivent absolument pas 'déborder'cette place, et lorsqu'elles demandent des formations, par exemple, elles ne sont absolument pas entendues.[5] (Golub et al., 1997: 25)

Even when immigrant women are offered help with training programmes, for example, these programmes often underestimate their knowledge and experience as this is not considered valid in terms of dominant French culture (Beski, 1997). It might therefore be argued that women face an almost impossible task: they are expected to ease the process of integration of immigrants into French society but at the same time they face many barriers to integration, and these barriers may not be taken into account by administrative structures and social institutions in the host society. Immigrant women in France are not alone in facing these types of difficulties, it is a problem that may be seen to apply to immigrant women of different origins throughout Europe as a survey for the European Community demonstrates. Summarizing the findings of this survey, Costa-Lascoux argues:

> Women immigrants are in a paradoxical situation: they are those from whom one expects the most, particularly in maintaining family stability, bringing up the children of the 'second generation' and transmitting values and, at the same time, hardly any attention has been given to their own education and socio-economic integration. This failure to consider their socio-cultural and

political role goes hand in hand with ignorance of their status and their projects. (Costa-Lascoux, 1995: 18)

It might be expected that this lack of attention by official institutions to the problems of immigrant women and the barriers to their integration would be in part remedied by the efforts of feminist and anti-racist movements to struggle against sexist and racist dominations and oppressions. In France, however, one can point to a *rendez-vous manqué* between feminisms and anti-racisms (Lloyd, 1998), with both sides tending to prioritize one axis of domination (either sexist or racist) and failing to take full account of the multiple nature of immigrant women's identities, experiences and situations.[6] As Barison and Catarino argue:

> Ignorant ou voulant ignorer que les femmes immigrées se situent dans une position stratégique, car à l'intersection des rapports sociaux de domination qui se jouent entre les sexes, les classes et les groupes ethniques, le corpus de recherche sur la migration et les recherches féministes qui ont porté sur des thèmes généraux (travail, famille . . .) ont respectivement, pendant des années, négligé les femmes et les immigrés.[7] (Barison and Catarino, 1997: 17)

As well as a lack of research on immigrant women, one can point to a general lack of co-ordination between feminist and anti-racist movements in France, as Lloyd argues: 'Despite the key themes of equality and difference, there has been until recently little contact between the organised women's movement and the anti-racist movement in France' (Lloyd, 1998: 71). This lack of contact between feminists and anti-racists has meant that the specific experiences and problems of immigrant women have often been ignored in their campaigns.

Having said this, however, immigrant and ethnic minority women should not be seen as helpless victims with no resources of their own. Despite the lack of support from feminist and anti-racist movements, and the barriers they face in their encounters with French institutions, they have certainly developed their own particular strategies to deal with the problems posed by life in French society. One important manifestation of this is the formation of women's associations to provide solidarity and self-help for immigrant women. A well-known example of a women's association is that of the Nanas Beurs (now known as the Meufs Rebeus or Voix d'Elles Rebelles) an association for young Maghrebi women. One of the founding members describes how she and other young women from the North African immigrant community set up this association to defend their interests as:

Women's concerns were often overlooked in the ideological battle for equal opportunities for immigrants. None of the slogans or campaigns showed how young women of North African origin were the victims of discrimination or oppression. (Benani, 1995a: 79)

Their association provides help for women having trouble with their residence or nationality papers, refugees, unmarried mothers and battered wives amongst others. They also stage debates and public meetings on topics of concern to immigrant women and act as a point of liaison between immigrant women and the French authorities in the forms of social and welfare workers, courts and police. And the Nanas Beurs are not the only such organization of immigrant women; there are numerous other associations of immigrant women of different origins, providing self-help in negotiating a path towards an easier life in France. As Quiminal comments with regard to African women's associations:

These assocations can be considered as creating innovatory social networks. As intermediary groups, in the Durkheimian sense, they are means of integration in today's world, spaces where women can meet one another and redefine one another, their identities and their relation to others. (Quiminal, 1997: 7)

This redefinition of identities and relations to others is clearly important for immigrant women as they make the transition from their society of origin to French society, often negotiating a path between tradition and modernity. The formation of new social relations and identities is visible in the transformation of family norms, particularly those concerning marriage, with a growth in the number of 'mixed' marriages – marriages between a partner of immigrant origin and a French partner. Statistics also show that women of immigrant origin are marrying at an older age than their mothers did largely as a result of increased scolarization of young immigrant women (Bentaieb, 1991). These changes reflect an evolution in the family structures within immigrant and ethnic minority communities as immigrant women mediate a path between the traditions of their community and the norms of French society. This is not always easy and there are sometimes clashes as immigrant women, particularly of the 'second generation' attempt to assert their own identities (Lacoste-Dujardin, 1992). What is clear, however, is that immigrant women should not be regarded merely as 'tools' of integration of immigrant and ethnic minority communities into French society. Even as these women adapt to life in France they retain a sense of their origins, a sense of belonging to their community (Geesey, 1995). This need to retain their particular heritage and identities whilst adapting to life in France is demonstrated in the increasingly popular and successful cultural productions of women of immigrant origin in France – cultural productions that draw from and reflect on their specific experiences and identities. More and more young women of immigrant origin are emerging as novelists and film makers, for example. Amongst others it is interesting to note the commercial success of a recent documentary *Mémoires d'Immigrés*, a film in which Yamina Benguigui, the daughter of Algerian immigrants to France, explores the history of Algerian immigration in order to explore her own personal history. Thus although intergenerational tensions do certainly exist amongst women of immigrant origin in France, young women of the 'second' and 'third' generations find the experiences and identities of their mothers valuable markers in the quest for their own identities (Lacoste-Dujardin, 1992). And as Geesey comments (perhaps somewhat optimistically in her view of the image French society has of women immigrants) with regard to children of North African women immigrants:

> As the children of Maghrebian women immigrants in France grow into adulthood, they will not only look to their mothers for a sense of identity as French citizens who are a bit 'different', but they will rehabilitate the equivocal image French society has of North African women immigrants. Members of the Beur generation increasingly acknowledge the Arab heritage transmitted by their mothers, as they recognize the courage displayed by women *primo-arrivantes* in France. Without sophisticated tools of cultural and sociological analysis, their mothers undertook to live in a society of 'radical alterity', to negotiate the expectations of change and adaptation, and yet they were able to conciously maintain a sense of *enracinement* in the culture of their ancestors. (Geesey, 1995: 149)

Having briefly examined some of the issues surrounding women and immigration in France, we will now go on to examine some more specific cases, namely that of the women *sans-papières* and the so-called *Affaire des foulards*.

Immigrant Women, Nationality and Citizenship: Les sans-papières

One of the key problems facing immigrant and ethnic minority women in France today is that of citizenship and nationality. The issue of nationality has been a particularly sensitive and difficult one in France since the mid-1980s when the Right-wing government, under pressure from the Front National, started a campaign to change the nationality code and restrict French nationality. Reforms in the nationality code since 1993 (with the *lois Pasquas* and other subsequent laws)[8] have made it harder for immigrants to obtain French nationality. Again there is not space here to describe in detail the debates over nationality law or the changes that have been made to laws on immigration and nationality. We will, however, attempt to look at ways in which these changes have affected women in particular. One of the major outcomes of the changes in nationality and immigration law has been the rapid development of the *sans-papiers* movement. In March 1996, 300 Africans occupied the church of Saint-Ambroise in Paris to demand the regularization of their residence papers. Facing forced explusion from France, these so-called illegal immigrants or *clandestins*, started hunger strikes to try to force the government to review these cases. After expulsion from the church the *sans-papiers* moved to different locations, and despite attempts by the government to end the protest (using CRS to evict *sans-papiers* from the church of Saint-Bernard in Paris) the movement has spread throughout France. The election of a Left-wing government in 1997 brought hopes of a resolution to the *sans-papiers'* problem with new legislation on nationality and immigration (see note 8), but there are still thousands living in France with no formal papers and threatened with expulsion.

Women have been active in the *sans-papiers* movement since the beginning, taking part in the occupation of churches and in hunger strikes alongside the men and claiming leading roles in the movement. As Madjiguène Cissé, who emerged as a spokesperson for the *sans-papiers* explains, women had to fight against traditional masculine domination in order to gain their role as leaders of the movement: 'Car au début il semblait acquis que les femmes ne participeraient pas à l'assemblée générale: ce n'était pas nécessaire, puisque les maris étaient là!'[9] (Cissé, 1996: 11). Once they had managed to assert their presence in the General Assembly, however, women were soon at the forefront of the movement, and were particularly able to gain public attention through actions like a women's march in May 1996. Cissé explains this high profile of women *sans-papières* with reference to a long tradition of women's combativity and self-organisation in Senegal and other African countries. (Cissé, 1996). The women *sans-papières* have thus shown themselves not to be passive victims but capable of strong and organized action, overcoming dominations from within and without their community. Despite their struggle, however, there still remain many immigrant women in difficult situations with regard to French nationality and citizenship, and as 'non-citizens' they are denied basic rights with regard to welfare, health, education and work. As women from a collective of *sans-papiers* in Lille argue, the situation of all *sans-papiers* is difficult but it is even more so for women because of their position in the family: 'Cette situation est encore aggravée pour les femmes sans-papiers. En effet, sur elles reposent le plus souvent la charge de l'éducation des enfants et de la tenue du ménage.'[10] Without wishing to essentialize women's role in the family or as mothers of children, it is true in practice that the responsibility for bringing up children and looking after the household does usually fall to them which makes their situation as *sans-papières* even more difficult.

In addition, an issue that has particularly affected women *sans-papières* and other women of immigrant origin is that surrounding the nationality of children born to immigrant parents resident in France. Again it would be wrong to essentialize women's role as mothers, but it is perhaps fair to say that the question of children's nationality has affected them more than it has men of immigrant origin. In the past children born to immigrant parents resident in France would naturally receive French nationality, but under new laws (see note 8) this is no longer the case and children of immigrants who are born and grow up in France can no longer automatically become French citizens. This affects women particularly in that their children no longer have the same legal status as French citizens which puts them in an ambiguous position with regard to welfare rights. For example, women whose children do not have French nationality cannot claim the same family allowances as French women. A woman *sans-papières* in Toulouse recounts her experience:

> Ça fait six ans qui je vis en France. Je suis venue pour rejoindre mon mari, qui était artisan. J'ai quatre enfants: quinze ans, douze ans, huit ans, cinq ans. Le dernier est né ici. Mon mari est parti, je vis seule avec les quatre enfants. Je faisais partie du Collectif des sans-papiers de Toulouse et j'ai été une des premières à être régularisées, avec la circulaire Chevènement. Mais ça n'a pratiquement rien changé, parce que mes enfants, eux ne sont toujours pas régularisés. C'est comme s'ils n'existaient pas. Ça fait que je n'ai pas droit aux allocations familiales, je n'ai droit à rien. Avec quoi je vis?[11]

This problem of their children's nationality is not unique to those women who form part of the *sans-papiers* movement. Benani points to the example of Maghrebi single mothers who, because of their status as women and immigrants, have children with no nationality:

> Les femmes sont plus fragilisées par leur statut de femmes et d'immigrées ou de filles d'immigrées. Le phénomène des mères célibataires maghrébines est à cet égard significatif: Celles qui n'ont pas acquis la citoyenneté française et

sont mères d'enfants nés sur le territoire français élèvent des enfants qui ne sont reconnus par aucun pays. Ils ne sont pas français (et ne le seront pas avant l'âge de seize ou de dix-huit ans), en vertu des lois Pasqua, et pas davantage marocains, algériens ou tunisiens, les codes de la famille, au Maghreb, ne reconnaissent pas le statut des mères célibataires, et pas davantage un statut juridique de l'enfant naturel ... Ces enfants, dès leur naissance, vont vivre sous le statut de l'exclusion.[12] (Benani, 1995b: 217)

Thus women are in some ways doubly excluded by their status as women and immigrants. Even those women who are not officially classified as *sans-papières* may have specific problems related to nationality and citizenship, stemming from their lack of autonomous legal status. Because of this problem a campaigning network[13] has been set up to argue for the introduction of an autonomous legal status for immigrant women. Campaigners argue that without such a status, immigrant women are prevented from accessing the rights they should have as individuals. It seems that until the problems of immigrant women in regard to nationality and citizenship are considered specifically and apart from general issues relating to these subjects, women will continue to be the victims of particular exclusions. Despite the efforts of the women *sans-papières* to organize and struggle against these exclusions, there is still a long way to go before immigrant women achieve equal citizenship status.

The *Affaire des Foulards*

Another issue which has brought one group of ethnic minority women into the spotlight of the media and French public opinion is the so-called *Affaire des foulards*. The question of the Islamic headscarf (*le voile* or *le foulard*) first hit the headlines in October 1989 when a headmaster in Creil, near Paris, refused to allow three Maghrebi girls to come to school wearing headscarves on the grounds that this would contravene the republican principle of *laïcité* (secularism). This incident provoked a national debate involving media, politicians and intellectuals, and despite a ruling by the then Minister of Education in the Socialist government, Lionel Jospin, supported by the Conseil d'Etat, that girls should not be excluded from school for wearing a headscarf, the issue has not died away, and was indeed, relaunched by a circular published by François Bayrou, Minister of Education in a Right-wing government in 1994, affirming that 'ostentatious' religious symbols – the Islamic headscarf – should not be allowed in schools. The issue of the *foulard* was one which was picked up by the extreme-Right and those who were anti-immigration and used to stigmatize Islam, branding all Muslims as *intégristes* (funda-mentalists), and criticizing immigrants and populations of immigrant origin as a whole. For the Left, the issue was more complex, pitting their tolerance of ethnic minority communities against their defence of the secularism of the republican school system. But what has often seemingly been forgotten (or ignored) in the debate over headscarves is the gendered nature of the issue, and whilst many men spoke out and gave their opinion on the affair, the voices of women, and particularly Maghrebi women were more rarely heard. As Bloul comments:

> These debates were also monopolized by men, notwithstanding their apparent concern with the question of women's rights in Islam. French men, Muslim men, male intellectuals and politicians, male personalities gave their opinion ad nauseam over the wearing of the scarves and its sociopolitical and cultural consequences. Women, on the other hand, whether Muslim, Maghrebi or French, were hardly heard. (Bloul, 1996: 259)

The young women who chose to wear headscarves to school were represented by many media reports as mere passive agents: either victims of dominating fathers who insisted on them wearing headscarves, or unwitting tools of Islamic organizations who manipulated them for their own purposes. Those who opposed the wearing of headscarves argued that they were protecting Muslim girls from a patriarchal order that restricted their freedom. Even those who supported these girls' right to attend school wearing headscarves argued that the French school system would help integrate them into French society and 'liberate' them from Islamic pressure within their families and communities, implying a superiority of French society over patriarchal Islamic society whilst ignoring the presence of male domination within their own French society. These reports denied Muslim women the capacity to make their own choices, to decide to wear headscarves as expressions of their own particular identity, and not as a result of pressure from a patriarchal social order. In fact, in a study of the meaning of the headscarf for women of immigrant origin in France, Gaspard and Khosrokhavar found that for many young women, often those most 'integrated' into French society, the choice to wear a headscarf was an autonomous one taken not for militant religious or political reasons, but as an affirmation of identity, an attempt to open up a new space where French and Islamic identity could be combined without conflict:

Il ne s'agit pas de conquérir la société (ni même la communauté islamique en France), mais d'aménager un espace pour soi. Dans la très grande majorité des case, il n'existe pas de 'militantisme voilé', mais une tendance à concilier les multiples exigences d'une identité qui ressent le besoin de se différencier par rapport à l'extérieur.[14] (Gaspard and Khosrokhavar, 1995: 115)

But whilst for some women the choice of wearing a *foulard* can be seen as an expression of their identity as French and Islamic women, others oppose the wearing of the headscarf on the grounds that it is an expression of patriarchal power, legitimating the control of fathers and husbands over women. Whilst opposing the exclusion of girls from school, Maghrebi women from organizations like Expressions Maghrébiennes au Féminin (EMAF) and women from SOS-Racisme and France Plus argued that the headscarf symbolized the oppression of Muslim women and the limitation of their freedom (Lloyd 1998). Benani argues that: 'Légitimer le port du voile, c'est mettre sous pression toutes celles qui se battent pour leur émancipation et leur liberté'[15] (Benani 1995b: 216).

There are, therefore, differences of opinion amongst Muslim women over the significance of the headscarf, some choosing to wear it as a symbol of identity, others condemning it as a symbol of oppression. But what seems most significant about this *affaire des foulards* is the way in which it demonstrates the stereotyping of immigrant women and the failure of both the French and of immigrant men to listen to their points of view. The debate over the *foulard* can be seen as a reflection of a previously noted tendency in dominant French culture to represent women as the key to the integration of immigrant populations: persuading or forcing women to remove their headscarves is seen as releasing them from the domination of Islamic culture, and an important step to their 'integration' into French society. What seems important is that the choice to wear or to remove their *foulard* should be that of the women alone. As with other issues it is important that immigrant women should be able to forge their own identities and assert their autonomy as French women of immigrant origin.

As the examples of the women *sans-papières* and the *affaire des foulards* have shown, immigrant women in contemporary France face a constant struggle against exclusions and a struggle to assert their own identity and become 'visible' within dominant French culture and representations. Clearly not all immigrant women are *sans-papières*, and the debate over the *foulard* has not affected all immigrant women directly, but the issues raised by these experiences are valid examples of the types of problems immigrant women face. Faced with a sometimes hostile, often ignorant French society, and with forms of domination from within their own communities they must renegotiate a position for themselves, making a path between tradition and modernity. Despite the problems they face, however, the picture is not all bleak. Immigrant women have shown themselves capable of adaptation and self-organization, using tools such as associations to carve out a place for themselves in French society and to assert their own particular identities. This process seems certain to continue with the new generations of women of immigrant origin.

Notes

1. The debate over 'immigration' in France refers not only to the process of migration itself but to the settlement of post-migratory or 'foreign' communities within France. Those belonging to ethnic minority communities are often referred to as 'immigrants' even though they may have been born in France and have French nationality. There is not space in this chapter to explore the complexities of this question, but when we refer to 'immigrants' this term may be taken to include people of ethnic minorities resident in France.
2. For a general account of immigrantion and ethnic minorities in France see (amongst others) P. Weil (1991) *La France et ses étrangers,* Paris: Calmann-Lévy, or A. Hargreaves (1995) *Immigration, 'Race' and Ethnicity in Contemporary France,* London: Routledge.
3. Source: Institut National de la Statistique et des Etudes Economiques (1992) *Recensement de la population de 1990: nationalités, résultats du sondage au quart,* Table 10.
4. 'For many of the women, emigration signals a positive social choice: an idea of liberty, the choice of the urban, consumption . . . In the interviews we carried out, women did not express plans to return to their country of origin. Thus one of them said to us: 'my country is where my children and family are.' Amongst men, by contrast, there is a strong idea of return to the homeland. This idea contains feelings of belonging to one's community of origin, to the land, to one's roots. Women on the other hand have a much more individualistic idea with their own projects and dreams, as if everything was in the future.'
5. 'They are tolerated as housewives, taking care of domestic tasks, bringing up children, responsible for the integration of their family.

Women immigrants are assigned a place, and in times of economic crisis, of unemployment, they must absolutely not 'spill out' of that place, so when they ask for vocational training, for example, they are completely ignored.'

6. Notable exceptions to this trend are Colette Guillaumin and, more recently, Françoise Gaspard (see for example Guillaumin, C. (1992), *Sexe, race et pratique du pouvoir,* Paris: Côté-femmes, or Gaspard, F. and Khosrokhavar, F. (1994), 'Sur la problématique de l'exclusion: de la relation des garçons et des filles de culture musulmance dans les quartiers défavorisés', *Revue française des affaires sociales,* vol. 2: 4–15.)

7. 'Not realizing, or not wishing to realize that women immigrants are situated in a strategic position at the intersection of the social relations of domination that exist between sexes, classes and ethnic groups, the corpus of research on migration and feminist research which have focused on general themes such as work and family, have respectively, over the years, neglected women and immigrants.'

8. The *loi Pasqua* of 1993 made it more difficult for foreigners living in France to obtain residency papers and made the conditions for family regroupment more strict. It was also made easier for the French authorities to expel foreigners from French territory. At the same time, under the *loi Méhaignerie* (often subsumed under the general term of the *lois Pasquas*), conditions for obtaining French nationality were changed for children of foreign parents resident in France who could previously obtain French nationality automatically but now had to wait until the age of sixteen to twenty and then make a declaration announcing their wish to obtain French nationality. These laws were made even more rigorous by the *loi Debré* of 1997. The Socialist government currently in power had promised to reform the Pasqua and Debré laws, but the *loi Chevènement* did not return the situation to the pre-1993 state. Conditions for gaining entry to France and residency papers are still difficult, and there are still many who remain without papers and whose situation has not been regularized. Similarly, under the *loi Guigou*, the right to automatic nationality for children born to foreign parents resident in France has not been re-established. These children still have to wait until eighteen to obtain French nationality although they no longer have to make a declaration of intention. For a full account of the way in which these laws have affected immigrant families see, for example, Rude-Antoine, E. (1997), *Des vies et des familles: Les immigrés, la loi et la coutume,* Paris: Odile Jacob.

9. 'Because at the beginning it was taken for granted that women would not take part in the General Assembly: it was not necessary as their husbands were there!'
10. Appel des femmes du comité des sans-papiers de Lille, January 1997: 'This situation is made even worse for women *sans-papiers* because, in effect, they are most often responsible for bringing up the children and looking after the household.'
11. 'I've lived in France for six years. I came to join my husband who was an artisan. I have four children aged fifteen, twelve, eight and ten. The youngest was born here. My husband left and I live alone with the four children. I became part of the Collective of *sans-papiers* in Toulouse and I was one of the first to be regularized under the Chèvenement directive. But that hardly changed anything because my children have still not been regularized. It's as if they didn't exist. Which means that I have no right to family allowances. I have not right to anything. What can I live off?'
12. 'Women are made more fragile by their status as women and immigrants or daughters of immigrants. The phenomenon of Maghrebi single mothers is significant in this respect: Those who have not acquired French citizenship and are mothers of children born in French territory, are bringing up children who are not recognized by any country. They are not French (and will not be before the age of sixteen or eighteen), by virtue of the Pasqua laws, and neither are they Moroccan, Algerian or Tunisian, as family law in the Maghreb does not recognize the status of single mothers, nor is there a legal status for natural children . . . These children are living in a condition of exclusion from birth.'
13. The 'Réseau pour l'autonomie juridique des femmes immigrées et réfugiées'.
14. 'It is not a question of conquering society (or even the Islamic community in France), but of creating a space for oneself. In the great majority of cases, there is no 'veiled militantism' but instead an attempt to reconcile the multiple demands of an identity which feels the need to differentiate itself from the outside.'
15. 'To legitimize the wearing of the headscarf is to put under pressure all those who are fighting for their emancipation and their liberty.'

References

Barison, N. and Catarino, C. (1997), 'Les femmes immigrées en France et en Europe', *Migrations Société*, vol. 9, 52: 17–19.

Benani, S. (1995a), 'Les Nanas Beurs', in *Immigrant Women and Integration*, Strasbourg: Council of Europe Publications.

Benani, S. (1995b), 'Le voile et la citoyenneté', in M. Riot-Sarcey (ed), *Démocratie et représentation*, Paris: Kimé.

Benguigui, Y. (1997), *Mémoires d'Immigrés*, Paris: Albin Michel.

Bentaieb, M. (1991), 'Les femmes étrangères en France', *Hommes et migrations*, vol. 1141: 4–12.

Bentichou, N. (ed.) (1997), *Les femmes de l'immigration au quotidien*, Paris: L'Harmattan.

Beski, C. (1997), 'Les difficultés spécifiques aux jeunes filles issues de l'immigration Maghrébine', in N. Bentichou (ed.), *Les femmes de l'immigration au quotidien*, Paris: L'Harmattan.

Bloul, R. (1996), 'Victims or Offenders? 'Other Women in French Sexual Politics', *European Journal of Women's Studies*, vol. 3(3): 251–68.

Boulahbel-Villac, Y. (1992), 'Les femmes algériennes en France', *Revue française des affaires sociales*, vol. 46(2): 105–23.

Cissé, M. (1996), 'Sans-papiers: les premiers enseignements', *Politique la revue*, vol. 2: 9–14.

Costa-Lascoux, J. (1995), 'Immigrant women: out of the shadows and on to the stage', in *Immigrant Women and Integration*, Strasbourg: Council of Europe Publications.

Gaspard, F. and Khosrokhavar, F. (1995), *Le foulard et la République*, Paris: La Découverte.

Geesey, P. (1995), 'North African Women Immigrants in France: Integration and Change', *SubStance*, vol. 24(1): 137–53.

Golub, A; Morokvasic, M. and Quiminal, C. (1997), 'Evolution de la production des connaissances sur les femmes immigrées en France et en Europe', *Migrations Société*, vol. 9(52): 17–36.

Hargreaves, A. (1995), *Immigration, 'Race' and Ethnicity in Contemporary France*, London: Routledge.

Lacoste-Dujardin, C. (1992), *Yasmina et les autres de Nanterre et d'ailleurs: Filles de parents maghrébins en France*, Paris: La Découverte.

Lloyd, C. (1998), 'Rendez-vous manqués: feminism and anti-racisms in France', *Modern and Contemporary France*, vol. 6(1): 61–73.

Nicollet, A. (1993), *Femmes d'Afrique noire en France*, Paris: L'Harmattan.

Prencipe, L. (1994), 'Famille-Migrations-Europe: Quelles relations possibles?', *Migrations Société*, vol. 6(35): 27–42.

Quiminal, C. (1997), 'The associative movement of African women and new forms of citizenship', paper presented at the Centre for Cross-Cultural Research on Women, Oxford, November 1997.

Silberman, R, (1991), 'Regroupement familial: ce que disent les statistiques', *Hommes et Migrations,* vol. 114: 13–17.

Zehraoui, A. (1996), 'Processus différentiels d'intégration au sein des familles algériennes en France', *Revue française de sociologie*, vol. 37(2): 237–61.

—8—

Visible Subjects: Lesbians in Contemporary France

Ursula Tidd

In 1997, Marie-Jo Bonnet argued that lesbians are subject to three forms of discrimination (Bonnet 1997b: 9). Firstly, lesbians experience the traditional discrimination against women by patriarchy; secondly, they experience discrimination as lesbians within the gay movement which has traditionally assumed male homosexuality as the key referent and site of struggle; and finally, she argues that there is discrimination against lesbians within feminism, which has not been able to legitimize primary, sexual relationships between women as an emancipatory strategy within patriarchal society. One might add that lesbians also experience discrimination as lesbians living in hetero-normative society. Indeed, the situation of lesbians in France, as a traditionally Catholic, patriarchal and heterosexual-centred society that privileges the extended family, continues to be precarious in the apparently 'liberated' late 1990s, as this chapter will outline.

Before exploring these issues further, some methodological caveats are necessary. In a brief discussion of this type, an initial question arises concerning the identity of the subject group in question: who are lesbians in France? Defining the subject group is problematic, for one runs the risk of exploring only the issues of a visible minority of 'out' lesbians who are politically active within struggles concerning identity politics within the French lesbian and gay movement. This may disregard the role played by politically active lesbians who have always campaigned within the French women's movement (MLF) for issues which affect all women.[1] Further, focusing on 'visible' lesbians engaged in a variety of political activity disregards women who do not explicitly identify themselves as lesbians yet live or wish to live in a primary erotic relationship with another woman and experience some or all of the oppression shared by other groups of lesbians. Recognizing, then, the impossibility of exploring all the issues faced by the variety of lesbians living in metropolitan France in the late 1990s, this discussion will seek to highlight some of the key issues for (some) French lesbians in recent years. It does not seek – *pace* Foucault – to reduce lesbians uniquely to their erotic choice or position them passively as an object of academic study, but rather seeks to conceptualize lesbian activity in the sociopolitical field as a dynamic affirmation of subjectivity for certain women living in a patriarchal society (Foucault, 1976: 55–9). As such, then, the ensuing discussion seeks to be pluralist in its attempt to represent a range of lesbian activity in recent years in France, while acknowledging that for lesbians to be visible at all with the prevailing hetero-normative society is nevertheless politically subversive.

The context for the discussion will initially be Simone de Beauvoir's groundbreaking chapter on 'La Lesbienne' in *Le Deuxième Sexe* back in 1949, which constituted one of the earliest theoretical discussions of the situation of lesbians in France. Then, the particular role of lesbians in the origins of the modern French gay liberation struggle will be sketched. Over the last thirty years, some lesbians have been active within feminist groups, whereas others have preferred to work within explicitly lesbian and/or gay groups which seek to promote lesbian and gay visibility as a statement of political identity and to contest the workings of hetero-sexuality as a political regime. The chapter will explore the role of lesbians in various groups such as Arcadie, the MLF, FHAR (Front homosexuel d'action révolutionnaire) and the Gouines rouges to analyse some key moments of struggle for French lesbians since 1970. The chapter will then briefly explore the impact of the PaCS partnership agreement for lesbians, and raise issues concerning the many tensions that exist between affirming lesbian identity as a site of resistance and autonomy, which challenges the patriarchal category of 'woman', and affirming lesbianism as a minority lifestyle that seeks to be inscribed within current forms of social and political organization. For, as will be suggested, lesbianism continues to pose far-reaching questions for feminism and its relationship to heterosexuality as a political regime that prefers to problematize lesbianism rather than problematize its own political constructions of sexuality, as Monique Wittig has argued (Wittig, 1992). Before reaching its conclusions, the chapter will then briefly survey some of the lesbian activity in France in the late 1990s.

Beauvoir and *Le Deuxième Sexe*

Back in 1949, Simone de Beauvoir provided one of the earliest discussions of the situation of lesbians in France in *Le Deuxième Sexe*. Arguing against the pathologization of lesbians by psychoanalysis and patriarchal society more generally, Beauvoir's account of lesbianism is surprisingly radical for its time. In the aftermath of World War Two, the substance of homophobic Vichy legislation proscribing homosexuality was preserved by the provisional government. Homosexuality was illegal under the age of twenty-one and there was a range of legislation passed between 1946–9 aiming to preserve 'good morals' in society that, in practice, was used to discriminate against gays (Robinson, 1995: 3–4).

In Beauvoir's portrayal of sexual relationships in *Le Deuxième Sexe*, she offers a more positive account of lesbian sexuality than heterosexuality, although viewed together, the inconsistencies between the two accounts suggest that Beauvoir had not developed a coherent theory of female sexuality in her account of gendered subjectivity. The chapter on 'La Lesbienne' is positioned between 'L'Initiation sexuelle' and 'La Femme mariée', and interestingly, closes the 'Formation' section, which suggests that Beauvoir did not envisage lesbianism as a lifelong choice for women. She argues that within a patriarchal society, a lesbian relationship is at least as valid as any heterosexual relationship, and that 'l'homosexualité peut être pour la femme une manière de fuir sa condition ou une manière de l'assumer' (Beauvoir, 1949: 172) ('homosexuality can be for woman a mode of flight from her situation or a way of accepting it'). Characteristically, Beauvoir argues here that one is neither irrevocably heterosexual nor homosexual, one chooses one's sexuality perpetually and what is more pertinent is the authenticity of the choice (Beauvoir, 1949:173). She challenges here the notion of 'the lesbian' as a discrete identity and argues that all women are predisposed – in a rather 'adolescent' way – to have a physical affinity with women, thereby lapsing into a certain essentialism herself (Beauvoir, 1949: 173):

> Et si l'on invoque la nature, on peut dire que naturellement toute femme est homosexuelle. La lesbienne se caractérise en effet par son refus du mâle et son goût pour la chair féminine; mais toute adolescente redoute la pénétration, la domination masculine, elle éprouve à l'égard du corps de l'homme une certaine répulsion; en revanche le corps féminin est pour elle comme pour l'homme un objet de désir.[2]

Beauvoir also dismisses certain heterosexist received ideas about lesbian identity – for example that it can be modelled on gender-differentiated roles within the traditional heterosexual couple and neatly categorized as 'butch' or 'femme': 'A y regarder de plus près on s'aperçoit que - sauf dans des cas limites – leur sexualité est ambiguë'. (Beauvoir,

1949: 186) ('On closer observation it is to be seen that, except in a few cases, their sexuality is ambiguous'.) Such gender roles need rather to be interpreted in the context of a lesbian's choice not to depend financially or affectively on a man:

> Ce qui donne aux femmes enfermées dans l'homosexualité un caractère viril, ce n'est pas leur vie érotique qui, au contraire, les confine dans un univers féminin: c'est l'ensemble des responsabilités qu'elles sont obligées d'assumer du fait qu'elles se passent des hommes. (Beauvoir, 1949:189) [3]

Although Beauvoir's account of lesbianism was groundbreaking, there is no sustained attempt to address the issue of heterosexuality as a political institution in *Le Deuxième Sexe* – Beauvoir appears to assume that most women are irrevocably heterosexual. Furthermore, as Toril Moi has noted, Beauvoir oscillates between arguing, on the one hand, for the authenticity of lesbianism and on the other, describing its narcissistic character (Moi, 1994: 199–203). Moi says:

> True reciprocity, Beauvoir implies, presupposes difference: too much similarity reduces sexual interaction to a narcissistic mirroring of the Other: it is not a coincidence that she speaks of the 'miracle of the mirror' precisely in the context of lesbian sexuality. (Moi, 1994: 203)

In *Le Deuxième Sexe,* as Ann Ferguson has noted, Beauvoir does not consider the social, historical and political significance of assuming a lesbian identity and instead conceptualizes lesbianism narrowly as an effect of choice (in al-Hibri and Simons, 1990: 285). This is surprising because the majority of Beauvoir's text is devoted to the social, historical and political implications of living as a (heterosexual) woman. Following her analysis, one might logically conclude therefore that lesbians do not exist in a social, political or historical framework. Yet despite its flaws, Beauvoir's chapter on lesbianism in *Le Deuxième Sexe* constituted a key moment in advancing debates concerning women's sexuality in France, although many of her arguments were not addressed until the 1970s.

Lesbians and the Gay Movement in France

Prior to May 1968, lesbian and gay politics were discreet and reformist rather than militant (Robinson, 1995: 25–7). In addition to existing legislation which discriminated against gays, in July 1960, homosexuality was declared a 'social plague' as were alcoholism, tuberculosis, heart disease and prostitution (Robinson, 1995: 4). In this climate, Beauvoir's chapter on lesbianism, published in 1949, was ground breaking. The only major gay organization, Arcadie, began as a Catholic-oriented, 'homophile' literary review founded by André Baudry in 1954. By 1957, Arcadie was organizing its own cultural events and evenings and functioned essentially as a non-political, male-dominated association, acting as a forum for gay men and some lesbians to meet. Yet, amid the upheaval of 1968, Arcadie's masculinism and political conservatism seemed increasingly out of touch with current political concerns, and a group of lesbians, among them Françoise d'Eaubonne and Anne-Marie Fauré, formed a splinter group which began to meet to promote a radical political agenda.

Women played a key role in the incipient stages of the modern gay liberation movement in France, which emerged in the wake of May 1968. Various groups of women – some from the MLF's female sexuality group meeting at Antoinette Fouque's appartment, others who were involved in the 'Petites Marguerites' group which met at Monique Wittig's as well as those from Arcadie – met at Arcadie to work out a new political agenda for lesbian rights. Since the beginnings of the MLF, there were lesbians who were involved in fighting for key campaign issues such as abortion and contraception although such issues did not affect them personally. Women, such as Cathy Bernheim, were happy to subordinate the issue of lesbian rights to wider issues which concerned the female population at large:

> Au départ, on ne considérait pas que c'était important. L'important, c'était les femmes, toutes les femmes, homos ou hétéros. Même aux Gouines rouges, qui s'est constitué plus tard, on se considérait plus comme des lesbiennes féministes que comme des lesbiennes radicales. (Bernheim, 1998:13) [4]

Yet she says that heterosexual women did not reciprocate and support lesbian issues:

> Je me rends compte que j'ai signé par exemple 'le Manifeste des 343' . . . Alors que les féministes ne collaient pas les affiches des lesbiennes. Même au sein du mouvement des femmes, on était considérées comme anormales. [5]

Within the MLF in the early 1970s, it seems that although the practical boundaries between lesbians and heterosexual women were quite fluid as heterosexual women experimented with lesbian eroticism, the sites for political struggle were nevertheless largely regulated as heterosexual. Marie-Jo Bonnet has noted that although women were campaigning for the emancipation of their bodies, this did not extend to campaigning for the free expression of women's desire and sexuality when it included lesbianism (Bonnet, 1998: 97–8). Yet Christine Delphy has argued that this was a strategic decision on the part of the MLF. As patriarchy attempts to order everything towards its own self-perpetuation, the MLF realized that any feminist struggle which also campaigned vociferously for lesbian rights would be dismissed as a lesbian struggle and perceived as unrepresentative. In order to campaign effectively, it was important that the movement was perceived as representing women more generally and not just lesbians.[6] Indeed, today it remains inconceivable that lesbian oppression will disappear as long as women are oppressed within the prevailing patriarchal organization of French society, and the political consequences of lesbian desire continue to prove a thorny issue for society to address.

Three actions took place in early 1971 that were to be important for the subsequent lesbian struggle in France: firstly, the MLF spectacularly disrupted two pro-life rallies on 10 February and 5 March by the 'Laissez-les vivre' association over which Jérôme Lejeune presided. These actions were organized by a coalition from the MLF, the newly-formed FHAR, and left-wing sympathizers, and formed part of a much wider campaign to legalise abortion in France. Secondly, the first lesbian group from the MLF led an action on 10 March to disrupt a live radio talk show on 'l'homosexualité, ce douloureux problème' hosted by Ménie Grégoire, which was being recorded at the Salle Pleyel for RTL (Radio-Télé Luxembourg). It had assembled André Baudry from Arcadie – the conservative face of homosexuality in France – and a number of churchmen, doctors and legal specialists to address the 'problem' of homosexuality. The programme was interrupted by lesbians shouting 'On ne souffre pas!' ('we're not suffering!') and 'A bas les hétéro-flics!' ('down with the straight-police!'). Following this action, the women present decide to meet on a regular basis and the FHAR was born. It would become a key early group in revolutionary lesbian and gay politics in France and refused restrictive gay identity politics, proclaiming 'la polysexualité pour tous!' Yet, if women played a leading role in the early days of the FHAR, which readily adopted some of the key themes of the MLF's struggle, it also became increasingly male dominated and inattentive to the politics of sexual equality within its own ranks. Initially, the FHAR had been anti-hierarchical, eschewing spokespeople and leaders, seeking to function as a 'mixed' group for gays, lesbians, drag queens and kings, transsexuals, bisexuals and every 'queer' permutation. Soon, distinct lesbian and gay sites of political struggle would emerge.

Yet one of the significant joint lesbian and gay initiatives by the FHAR was the April 1971 special issue of *Tout*, devoted to gay politics and co-ordinated by Guy Hocquenghem, who would subsequently become a key figure in the FHAR and in French gay politics. *Tout* was a radical left-wing review, published by a libertarian Maoist group, Vive la Révolution, whose editor-in-chief was Jean-Paul Sartre and was the first review to run this special issue on homosexuality.

By April 1971, political differences between lesbians and gay men in the FHAR began to be articulated as the men proclaimed their active/passive sexual roles and male groups such as 'Les Gazolines' paraded in drag. For some women in FHAR, such behaviour reinforced sexism for it replicated the traditional patriarchal gender roles and power structure from which, as women, they were trying to escape. Marie-Jo Bonnet, a one-time member of the FHAR, has noted the misogyny of certain men within the group who saw the FHAR as a forum for the free expression of male gay desire (Bonnet, 1998b: 94). This encouraged lesbians to break away and meet separately, feeling neither at home in the FHAR, as an increasingly masculine sexualized space, or in the heterosexual-dominated MLF groupings.

Subsequently, women from the lesbian-consciousness group in the MLF met together informally to form Les Gouines rouges. One of their actions was to promote lesbian visibility within the MLF at the 'Journées de dénonciation des crimes commis contre les femmes' (Days of Denunciation of Crimes against Women), which took place at the Mutualité from 13–14 May 1972. Although Les Gouines rouges group was short-lived, like many sub-groups of the MLF at the time, it nevertheless served to highlight the presence of lesbians within the movement. Indeed, despite the relative lack of lesbian visibility within the MLF, lesbians tended to gravitate there rather than to 'Psychanalyse et politique', whose focus on sexual difference, conceptualized through the rose-coloured, obscurantist glasses of Lacanian psychoanalysis, offered little to empower lesbian subjecthood. In 1973, in *Le Nouvel Observateur*, 'Psych et po' proclaimed: 'l'homosexualité primaire des femmes devrait n'être qu'un passage vers une hétérosexualité retrouvée et vraiment libre' ('reactionary lesbianism should only be a transition to the rediscovery of a genuinely free heterosexuality') (*NO*, 27 August 1973).

Within the MLF, lesbians worked on key campaign issues such as abortion, contraception, rape and pornography. In 1974, a lesbian couple who were raped in the Marseille region while on holiday agreed to press charges against the perpetrators. Gisèle Halimi, the lawyer who had worked with Simone de Beauvoir on the Djamila Boupacha case in 1960, later took up their case.[7] These women were obliged to assume their lesbian sexuality publicly during the trial proceedings and for this reason the case is significant in the recent history of French lesbians. The perpetrators were finally jailed in 1978, after the Court of Appeal acknowledged that the case merited criminal proceedings.

Divergent views on rape and pornography proved to be two key issues that divided lesbians from sectors of the gay male community in the late 1970s. Writing in *Libération* in March 1977, Guy Hocquenghem dismissed the specificity of rape as a crime against women and condemned feminists for supporting bourgeois justice in pressing for criminal convictions for rape (Martel 1996: 115–16). Outside the gay community, lesbian and gay issues were gaining greater visibility and political momentum, for example the first French Gay Pride march – another initiative by women – took place on 25 June 1977. This was mooted by women from the MLF, particularly Christine Delphy, a key figure in post-1968 French materialist feminism and former 'Gouine rouge'. Delphy had worked closely with Simone de Beauvoir on issues such as abortion in the MLF and secured Beauvoir and Sartre's support to launch a petition for gay rights. Moreover, in Lyon – already by this time a key site for radical lesbian and gay politics – the first lesbian magazine, *Quand les Femmes s'aiment*, was launched and was published from 1978–80.

Questions Féministes, a theoretical radical feminist journal, was launched in 1977 by women who had been active in or sympathised politically with the 'Féministes révolutionnaires'. Its original collective included Christine Delphy, Emmanuèle de Lesseps, Nicole-Claude Mathieu, Colette Capitan and Monique Plaza. Within the MLF and specifically among women involved in *Questions Féministes*, theoretical debates continued concerning the role of lesbians within patriarchal society and within the women's movement itself. Simone de Beauvoir acted as the journal's titular editor-in-chief. Although she was not closely involved with the journal at a day-to-day level, her support was entirely logical because *Questions Féministes* (*QF*) approached women's oppression from a materialist perspective and was 'dedicated to the analysis of patriarchy as a social system in which women and men constitute different classes with opposing interests' (Jackson, 1996: 22).

In 1978, a year after the founding of *QF*, Christine Delphy invited Monique Wittig to join the collective. Like Delphy, Wittig had been active in feminist politics from the beginning of the MLF, in groups such as Les Petites Marguerites, which later became known as Féministes Révolutionnaires although major political differences were to emerge between the two women. In February 1980, Wittig published an important article, 'la pensée Straight' in which she argued that heterosexuality operates as a universalizing political discourse that orders everything towards its own self-perpetuation. The category 'woman', according to

Wittig, has no meaning outside the political institution of heterosexuality for women are only 'women' in relation to men – thus, lesbians are not women because they live outside the heterosexual political economy. In a further article published in the next issue, 'On ne naît pas femme', Wittig elaborated further that 'women' and 'men' were political and economic categories that should be abolished. Further, she argued that lesbians were fugitive slaves from the class of women because they were not women in economic, political or ideological terms. In response to Wittig, Emmanuèle de Lesseps published an article in *Questions Féministes* exploring whether it was possible to be both heterosexual and a feminist.

Questions Féministes existed for approximately three years before it was dissolved in the context of a major political rift within the MLF more generally concerning the relationship between lesbianism and feminism (Duchen, 1986: 22–25). The rift between lesbians and straight feminists within the MLF came from outside the *QF* group, as certain 'lesbiennes radicales' adopted exclusionary policies towards heterosexual feminists. As Stevi Jackson has noted, the terms of this debate within *QF* and the MLF more generally were not specific to France, for the issue of how to pursue a radical feminist agenda and maintain personal and economic relationships with men divided radical feminists in Britain and elsewhere (Jackson, 1996: 23). In France, however, the debate had flared up somewhat later because radical feminists sought to retain a united front in public against the Psych et po' 'sexual difference' tendency, who were actively 'opposed' to the materialist feminist groups within the MLF. Psych et po' advocated the existence of a repressed 'natural' female difference which would only emerge – in their view – if 'phallocratic' societal structures were completely dismantled. As discourses of 'sexual difference' have been traditionally been exploited by patriarchy to oppress women, materialist feminists rejected any recourse to notions of repressed female difference as a means to combat women's oppression.

Amid these debates, Delphy and others argued that lesbians and heterosexual women should work together in the MLF each taking account of their respective demands. *Nouvelles Questions Féministes* was launched by Delphy and again supported by Beauvoir as titular editor, who condemned the radical lesbian position of Wittig and her supporters, accusing them of excluding straight women from the class of women.[8]

The questions of the relationship of lesbianism to feminism and of sexual differentialist versus materialist analyses of women's oppression in patriarchal society had been present since the beginnings of the second-wave feminist movement in France. A decade later, these issues proved intractable and the women's movement – which was composed of diverse, anti-hierarchical, ephemeral groupings – fragmented further. Moreover, following the political victories of abortion and contraception, there was a loss of political impetus and energy within the movement.

Following the election of the socialists in 1981, who were widely supported by women voters, there was optimism in the lesbian and gay community. This optimism was particularly focused on the campaign to lower the age of consent for gay men, and proved well-founded in that respect for the necessary legislation was passed in 1982 following a high profile campaign led by Gisèle Halimi (now a socialist Deputy) and Robert Badinter, the Garde des Sceaux (Minister for Justice). As far as lesbians were concerned, some continued to devote their energies to working within the MLF. Within the mixed federation of groups known as the CUARH (Comité d'Urgence Anti-Répression Homosexuelle), the MIEL (Mouvement d'Informations et d'Expressions Lesbiennes) was formed in 1982. It was based at the Paris Maison des femmes, which had been recently set up with government funding from the Ministère des Droits de la Femme, headed by Yvette Roudy. MIEL thereby maintained links with the MLF and the *Nouvelles Questions Féministes* group. Another group, emanating from the Front des lesbiennes radicales, a splinter group formed at the time of the dissolution of the *Questions Féministes* collective, centred around the lesbian archive centre, known as ARCL, set up in 1984 by Claudie Lesselier. Thus, throughout the 1980s, despite a certain loss of political momentum, there was a range of lesbian groupings in Paris and the provinces.

Other initiatives, such as the launch of *Lesbia* magazine are also important during this period. *Lesbia* was founded in 1982 by Christiane Jouve and Catherine Marjollet and, unlike *QF* or *NQF*, did not aspire to be a serious theoretical journal but rather a monthly magazine that covered areas of general, largely cultural, interest to lesbians. Relying heavily on volunteers, *Lesbia* lacked the commercial format of gay men's magazines and initially, at least, could not rely on a broad, affluent readership (unlike publications aimed at a gay, male readership). *Lesbia* continues to be published and also organizes social events in Paris and is affiliated to ILGA (International Lesbian and Gay Association) and the Coordination Lesbienne Nationale. It continues to play a significant role in linking its readership to the wide network of lesbian groups which now exist throughout France. Although some may dismiss it as lightweight and non-aligned in its political stance, *Lesbia* continues to be important for reducing the isolation of some gay women in France.

In the early 1980s, lesbian and gay lifestyles had less and less in common, according to a 1984 study (Martel, 1996: 200). While certain gay men often preferred to 'cruise' and spend their 'pink' francs on the increasingly commercialized male gay 'scene', lesbians, benefiting usually from less disposable income and fewer women-only bars and clubs, socialized more outside the commercial gay scene, meeting in small friendship or political groups or in couples. Yet these behaviour patterns among lesbians are not specific to France and seem increasingly to be less prevalent in the 1990s. Younger lesbians now benefit from a greater range of social opportunities and venues, aimed at a lesbian 'market'. Moreover, with an increased confidence in the expression of their sexuality, young lesbians in the 1990s have less difficulty 'cruising' the lesbian 'scene' – even if this means that feminism no longer holds the political urgency or even relevance it did for earlier generations of gay women.

For those women who continued to be politically active in the 1980s, some became involved in the fight against AIDS, working in Aides and Act Up. In 1993, 43 per cent of volunteers at Aides were women, of which 12 per cent were lesbians (Martel, 1996: 376). Although lesbians are usually considered a low-risk group for contracting HIV, unless they are haeomophiliacs, take drugs, are raped or engage in bisexual practices, they nevertheless do contract HIV and develop full-blown AIDS, although at the time of writing there have not been any studies in France devoted uniquely to lesbians and AIDS. Women became involved in the fight against AIDS in France also through solidarity with gay male friends in the face of blatant homophobia that was prevalent in the early years of the AIDS epidemic. Lesbian groups were created within both Aides and Act Up and these women constituted a new generation of lesbians for whom feminism was no longer necessarily their political springboard. In late 1994, the 'Lesbiennes se déchaînent' group was formed along the same militant lines as Act Up, distancing itself from feminism and working with gay men's groups.

Into the 1990s

The strand of specifically lesbian radicalism that had taken off in the mid-1980s continues to the present day both in Paris and in the provinces. Over the last decade, lesbians have remained politically active in specific arenas, such as the campaigns for political parity and equal pay or for solidarity with women in the former Yugoslavia. According to Thérèse Clerc of the 'Réseau femmes pour la parité', the majority of women involved in the campaign for political parity are lesbians (Martel, 1996: 378). Lesbians are also involved in the CADAC (Coordination des associations de défense de l'avortement et de la contraception), a federation of groups that was formed in the early 1990s to fight against the anti-abortion lobby. At a more general level, *Nouvelles Questions Féministes* (*NQF*) continues to publish theoretical articles on lesbianism and the *NQF* board is composed of a majority of lesbians. In 1998, the Collectif national des droits des femmes, regrouping representatives from over 140 organizations, has included the defence of lesbian rights in its platform. This is a significant step for it is the first time that lesbian rights have specifically been endorsed by the French feminist movement.

An increasingly well-organized lesbian movement is slowly emerging through the 1990s in France. A major evolution has been the nationwide development of a network of lesbian groups. Between 1985–97, more than twenty lesbian organizations were formed throughout France – in Rennes, Nantes, Toulouse, Marseille, Grenoble, Lyon, Bordeaux, Lille and elsewhere. These are orchestrated by the Coordination Nationale Lesbienne, created in 1997, which also lobbies on behalf of lesbian rights, advises groups on campaign tactics and organises lesbian participation in the annual Lesbian and Gay Pride march as well as events throughout the year. Advances in telecommunications and information technology such as Minitel and the Internet have faciliated the development of virtual lesbian networks and communities, for there is an increasing number of Francophone lesbian-authored sites on the Internet offering discussion groups, small ads services, and articles of interest to lesbians.

From the late 1970s, women's film events were organized which attracted a great number of lesbians. In 1978, the Festival international de films de femmes de Sceaux took place and thanks to its success, led to the Créteil women's film festivals as well as offshoots such as the 'Quand les lesbiennes se font du cinéma' festival.

A key debate within the lesbian and gay community generally since the early 1990s has concerned the partnership agreement, known variously as the CUS/CUCS (Contrat d'union sociale and Contrat d'union civile et sociale), the PIC (Pacte d'intérêt commun) and most recently, the PaCS (Pacte Civil de solidarité). The background – in brief – to this complex debate was an increasing recognition that state legislature was out of step with the the existence of co-habiting lesbian, gay and heterosexual couples. Since the AIDS epidemic gained ground in the early 1980s, it became increasingly apparent that during the illness and eventual death of gay men and lesbians from AIDS, the rights of their partners were often ignored by the AIDS sufferer's family. The wider lack of social, political and legal recognition of gay and lesbian couples and its attendant homophobia, reinforced by the Catholic Church and many on the political

Right and Left, meant that lesbians and gay men were completely isolated and with few enforceable rights at a time of personal trauma. Moreover, the lack of enforceable rights for lesbian and gay partnerships left a significant sector of the population vulnerable to exploitation.

The first civil partnership Bill was introduced in the French Senate in May 1990 by Jean-Luc Mélanchon, but it was not debated. Then, in late 1991, the issue finally began to be seriously discussed as the 'Contrat d'union civile' (CUC), with Elisabeth Badinter as one of its main supporters. Some of the key benefits of the CUC – which was open to gay and lesbian couples, heterosexual couples and siblings – were common taxation, reductions in inheritance tax and that the relationship could be taken into account for immigration purposes. By May 1992, 72 per cent of the French population supported the broad principle of the CUC (Martel, 1996: 388). A second Bill was introduced in November 1992 by a socialist Deputy, Jean-Pierre Michel, but again, the text was not debated in the French National Assembly. However, once the RPR was re-elected in 1993, they made it clear that they intended to drop the CUC from their political agenda. This stance was out-of-step with developments at European level. Following the 1994 Roth report detailing the extent of discrimination against lesbians and gays throughout the EU, the European Parliament issued a resolution recommending to all EU member states that they should work to abolish any legal, administrative and social discrimination towards homosexuals and give legal status to gay and lesbian couples (OJ 1994 C 61/40). In France by late 1995, the CUS (contrat d'union sociale) as it was now termed, was still being derailed. Although in early 1997 both the Parti Socialiste and the Parti Communiste introduced new Bills concerning the partnership agreement – effectively signalling their support for the lesbian and gay community – the dissolution of the French Assembly in April 1997 again delayed any discussion of the partnership question. A version of the Bill was adopted at its first reading in the National Assembly on 9 December 1998 with 316 to 249 votes. But on March 18, the Senate rejected it and formulated an alternative proposal which rejected a Left-wing amendment that the two people wishing to take out a PaCS together could be of the same sex. The text then went back and forth between the National Assembly and the Senate, which rejected it a second and third time, before it was adopted on its fourth and final reading by the National Assembly on 13 October 1999. The PaCS finally became law in France on 16 November 1999.

Unlike the CUCS, the PaCS only applies to individuals who are in an intimate relationship, and applies to co-habiting lesbian and gay couples who cannot marry, as well as co-habiting heterosexual couples who can marry. The agreement has to be taken out for a minimum of three months and cannot apply to anyone who already has a PaCS or is currently married. Benefits of the PaCS include common taxation (after three years), a greater reduction in inheritance tax than the previous CUS or CUCS, social security benefits as a couple and the right to take over the lease of a partner who leaves the common home or who has died. But the PaCS does not accord gay couples the same rights as a married couple. For example, it does not allow a gay couple to adopt children jointly and it does not allow automatic immigration rights to partners who are not French nationals (although French nationality is not required to sign a PaCS).

The various proposals for a partnership agreement have been subjected to rigorous debate and severe criticism in France from all sides of the political spectrum, as well as by the Catholic Church. Some of the arguments against the PaCS have been, firstly, that the state should not recognize a minority lifestyle, considered by some as a 'sterile' relationship. Secondly, the PaCS has been criticized as an ineffective means of regulating the issues of property and inheritance relating to co-habiting couples of whatever sexual orientation. Thirdly, some believed that the state should not legislate on the basis of affective links between individuals but rather – as in the case of marriage – on the basis of the social role of the relationship and its perceived wider social benefit. Lastly, some feminists and lesbian feminists are opposed to the PaCS on the grounds that it is rooted in the institution of patriarchal bourgeois marriage, which has traditionally kept women in a state of oppression. Moreover, they view the PaCS as an assimilationist and conservative political strategy, which annihilates the politically subversive potential of lesbian and gay relationships in a patriarchal, hetero-normative society. For example, Christine Delphy, who opposes marriage for homosexuals and heterosexuals, has argued that the PaCS is also divisive within the lesbian and gay community because it creates a potential hierarchy between married and unmarried partnerships.[9]

The PaCS fails to tackle the question of lesbian and gay couples' parenting rights. This affects primarily two groups of lesbians: those who have a child from a previous heterosexual relationship and those who wish to have and raise a child within a lesbian relationship or as a single parent. Currently, artificial insemination and adoption are not available to lesbian couples in France; moreover, custody of a child from a previous heterosexual relationship is often denied to lesbian mothers as are parenting rights to lesbian partners on the grounds of their sexual orientation. Since 1986, the Association des parents et futurs parents gays et lesbiens (APGL) has existed to campaign on these issues and to provide a meeting ground and telephone support line for lesbian and gay parents. It currently has over 900 members and between 1995–8, saw its membership increase tenfold, resulting in the creation of regional APGL groups. The APGL is a self-financing, mixed group, with (to date) equal numbers of lesbians and gay men amongst its members. The rapid increase of its membership and activity suggests that the issue of lesbian and gay parenting rights has acquired political momentum in the 1990s in France. Yet there remains a vociferous and violent lobby that seeks to protect the 'traditional' family – as was evident on 31 January 1999 when an estimated 100,000 people, including right-wing Deputies and National Front supporters, demonstrated against the PaCS on the streets of Paris, expressing extreme homophobia, such as calls for 'les pédés au bûcher!' ('burn the queers!')

If the many opinion polls which are regularly conducted in France hold any credence, lesbian and gay parenting remains a controversial issue: in a poll conducted in September 1998 by BVA for *Valeurs*, 68 per cent of French people were against any legislation which might permit lesbian and gays to adopt children. In a June 1998 survey conducted by the Institut de sondage CSA for *L'Evénement du jeudi*, 67 per cent of French respondents opposed artificial insemination for lesbians and 54 per cent opposed their right to marry.

Yet if issues concerning lesbian citizenship rights have been slow to gain ground in France, well-established, nationwide groups are tackling the diversity of questions affecting lesbians. Moreover, lesbians are beginning slowly to have an autonomous cultural presence in France, evident in film, contemporary writing and song, which does not seek to gratify and reassure the heterosexual male gaze.

A prime example of the increasing importance of autonomous lesbian cultural production is the annual Paris-based festival 'Quand les lesbiennes se font du cinéma', noted earlier, which has taken place since 1989. This self-financing, highly successful lesbian film festival, which happens annually in October, is organized by Cinéffable as a forum for debate amongst women as well as a means to promote women's political control over the image-making process.

Within mainstream cinema, a recent example of an attempt to represent lesbianism – albeit made by a heterosexual film director – is Josiane Balasko's *Gazon maudit* (1995) (*French Twist*), a comedy which exploits the farcical situation of the ménage-à-trois to explore the impact of a lesbian relationship upon a stale marriage.[10] Although the film uses a stereotypical representation of lesbianism in the butch Marijo, with whom Loli falls in love as a vast improvement on her philandering, inattentive husband, Laurent, the film nevertheless attempts to provide a critique of gay and straight relationship possibilities in the 1990s. It does not represent lesbianism simplistically as an object of gratification for the heterosexual male voyeur and raises a set of questions about relationships – gay or straight – including the issue of gay/straight parenting. Although it can be argued that Marijo's role as a gender outlaw is 'redeemed' by her pregnancy and, thereafter, her sexuality is a less subversive, managed element in the film. Surprisingly, *Gazon maudit* was seen by four million filmgoers when it was released in France.

Lesbian visibility in the cultural sphere is politically significant. One of the persistent questions affecting lesbians and gays is that of negotiating the double-edged sword of visibility. If films, book and television debates promote more positive images of lesbianism then it may help to render lesbian existence and experience more commonplace. But as recent debates concerning the PaCS have indicated, the notion of homosexuality becoming a 'commonplace' alarms the politically conservative and traditionalist sectors of society who experience any banalization of homosexuality as a threat to the political institution of the hetero-patriarchy. Among the right-wing in France, lesbian and gay rights lobbies are seen as evidence of American-inspired 'communitarianism' and consequently as a threat to the universalist, republican tradition. Negotiating lesbian visibility remains problematic as long as lesbians do not exist in the legislative and political sphere as full citizens, for homophobia remains a feature of contemporary French society.

The 1998 annual report of SOS Homophobie, an organization that monitors homophobia in France and runs a telephone helpline, indicates that approximately 70 per cent of calls received from lesbian and gay men are concerning physical and verbal attacks or problems relating to their workplace, neighbours or family. Although only 17 per cent of the callers were lesbians who apparently tend less to report incidents of verbal or physical aggression, Christine Le Doaré, President of SOS Homophobie, has argued that this is not because lesbians are less likely to experience homophobic harassment but rather because lesbians are generally much less visible in society (Le Doaré, 1999: 38). Le Doaré also notes that homophobia is expressed for different reasons towards lesbians and gay men: homophobic men physically or verbally assault lesbians because – according to Le Doaré – lesbians threaten their ability to dominate and seduce women, whereas gay men threaten heterosexual men's sense of masculinity and are subject to homophobic abuse for that reason.

In conclusion, at the beginning of the third millenium, many French lesbians can live more openly than their predecessors and lesbian couples who take out a PaCS now have some legally enforceable rights. Yet, much still needs to change in French society for lesbians to be able to assume their roles as full citizens and for lesbian 'equality in difference' to be respected. The profound social and political transformations that have taken place in the post-1968 era have not led to the inscription of lesbian citizenship in all areas of society for it poses perhaps an impossible challenge to French patriarchy.[11]

Notes

1. The abbreviation 'MLF' is used in this chapter to refer to the French Women's Movement in general rather than to the group known as 'Psychanalyse et politique', who registered the logo 'MLF' as their own trademark and the 'Mouvement de libération des femmes' as their property in 1979.
2. 'And if nature is to be invoked, one can say that all women are naturally homosexual. The lesbian, in fact, is distinguished by her refusal of the male and her liking for feminine flesh; but every adolescent female fears penetration and masculine domination, and she feels a certain repulsion for the male body; on the other hand, the female body is for her, as for the male, an object of desire.'
3. 'What gives homosexual women a masculine cast is not their erotic life, which, on the contrary, confines them to a feminine universe; it is rather the whole group of responsibilities they are forced to assume because they dispense with men.'
4. 'At the beginning we didn't think it was important. What was important was women, gay or straight. Even in the Gouines rouges, which was formed later on, we thought of ourselves more as lesbian feminists than radical lesbians.'
5. 'I realise that I signed the 'Manifesto of the 343' [campaigning for the right to abortion]. Even though heterosexual feminists didn't put up lesbian posters. Even within the women's movement, lesbians were seen as abnormal.'
6. Christine Delphy, in correspondence with author.

7. Djamila Boupacha was an Algerian Muslim and member of the FLN, who was accused of planting a bomb in Algiers in 1959 during the Algerian War. The bomb was defused; however, Boupacha was arrested, tortured and raped by French soldiers. Beauvoir was invited by Gisèle Halimi, Boupacha's lawyer, to help her publicize the case so that an official enquiry would be held and the perpetrators brought to justice. For a full account of the case, see Simone de Beauvoir and Gisèle Halimi (1962) *Djamila Boupacha*, Paris: Gallimard.
8. The notion that women and men constitute distinct classes is fundamental to French radical feminism and to Christine Delphy, in particular, see Delphy 1977 and 1984. For a general analysis of this position, see Jackson 1996: 92–114.
9. Christine Delphy, in correspondence with author.
10. For an interesting reading of *Gazon maudit*, see Hayward 1998.
11. I would like to thank Christine Delphy, Avril Horner and Harriet Lukens for their comments on earlier drafts of this chapter; I would also like to thank Christine Delphy, Catherine Gonnard and Marie-Jo Bonnet for providing me with information on specific aspects of the situation of French lesbians.

References

Association des parents et futurs parents gays et lesbiens, http://www.France.qrd.org/assocs/apgl.
Beauvoir, Simone de (1949). *Le Deuxième Sexe*, Paris: Gallimard.
—— (1972). *The Second Sex*, Harmondsworth: Penguin Books.
Bernheim, C. (1998) 'Plutôt lesbienne féministe que radicale', *3 Keller, le mensuel du Centre gai et lesbien*, no. 38: 12–13.
Bonnet, M.-J. (1995). *Les Relations amoureuses entre les femmes*, Paris: Odile Jacob.
—— (1997a) 'Le Lesbianisme est toujours tabou', *Ex Aequo*, no. 6: 30.
—— (1997b) 'Retour sur la lesbian and gay pride (suite)', *Alternative Libertaire*, no. 58: 9–10.
—— (1998a) 'CUS: la norme et ses impasses', *Ex Aequo*, no. 16: 34.
—— (1998b). 'De l'émancipation amoureuse des femmes dans la cité', *Les Temps modernes*, no. 598: 85–112.
Delphy, C. (1977) *The Main Enemy*, London: Women's Research and Resources Centre.

—— (1984). *Close to Home: A Materialist Analysis of Women's Oppression*, trans. and ed. D. Leonard. London: Hutchinson.

Duchen, C. (1986) *Feminism in France, From May '68 to Mitterand*, London: Routledge.

—— (1987) *French Connections, Voices from the Women's Movement in France*, London: Hutchinson.

D'Eaubonne, F. (1998) 'Mai 68: le Pink Bang', *3 Keller, le mensuel du Centre gai et lesbien*, no. 38: 8–10.

Ferguson, A. (1990) 'Lesbian Identity, Beauvoir and History' in *Hypatia Reborn*, ed. A. Y. al-Hibri and M.A. Simons, Bloomington and Indianapolis: Indiana University Press, 280–9.

Foucault, M. (1976) *Histoire de la sexualité I, La Volonté de savoir*, Paris: Gallimard.

French Queer Resources Directory, http://www.casti.com/FQRD/texts/index-articles.html.

Hayward, S. (1998) '"Hardly Grazing", Josiane Balasko's *Gazon Maudit* (1995): The *mise-en-textes* and *mise-en-scène* of Sexuality/ies' in Heathcote, O., Hughes, A. and Williams, J., *Gay Signatures, Gay and Lesbian Theory, Fiction and Film in France, 1945–1995*, Oxford: Berg.

Jackson, S. (1996) *Christine Delphy*, London: Sage Publications.

Journées nationales d'étude contre les discriminations liées à l'homosexualité, 26–27 April 1998 (conference proceedings), edited by the Comité National du Parti Communiste Français, Paris.

Le Doaré, C. (1999), 'La Lutte contre l'homophobie ne peut se passer des lesbiennes!', *Lesbia Magazine*, no. 178: 38.

Marks, E. (1979) ' Lesbian Intertextuality' in Stambolian, G. and Marks, E. (eds) *Homosexualities and French Literature*, Ithaca and London: Cornell University Press.

Martel, F. (1996). *Le Rose et le noir, les homosexuels en France depuis 1968*, Paris: Editions du Seuil.

Mécary C. and Pradelle, G.de La (1997) *Les Droits des homosexuel/les*, Paris: PUF.

Moi, T. (1994) *Simone de Beauvoir, The Making of an Intellectual Woman*, Oxford-UK and Cambridge-USA: Blackwell.

Picq, Françoise (1993) *Libération des femmes. Les années mouvement*, Paris: Seuil.

'Les revendications du Centre Gai et Lesbien', http://www.cglparis.org/revendications.html

Robinson, C. (1995) *Scandal in the Ink, Male and Female Homosexuality in Twentieth- Century French Literature*, London: Cassell.

Roussel, Y. (1995) 'Le mouvement homosexuel français face aux stratégies identitaires', *Les Temps modernes*, no. 582.

Schulz, M. (1998) 'Les silences du droit', *Les Temps modernes*, no. 598: 113–55.

SOS Homophobie (1998), *Rapport 1998 sur l'homophobie*, Paris, 62 pp.

Wittig, M. (1980) 'On ne naît pas femme', *Questions Féministes*, no. 8: 75–84.

—— (1992) *The Straight Mind and Other Essays*, Hemel Hempstead: Harvester Wheatsheaf.

–9–

Women in Rural France
Marion Demossier

In France, serious study of rural women began with the emergence of ethnology as an academic discipline in the 1930s. These early works dealt with most aspects of rural life, but from a rather descriptive and dogmatic perspective. When scholars considered the position of women they did so in an unsystematic fashion, commenting mainly on female labour and the effects of technical change upon it (Lagrave, 1983). Before 1950, France was still a predominantly agricultural society, and the place of women was well defined within it. Their lives were structured around the family farm and the village, and their economic, social and political activities rarely went beyond those boundaries. Agricultural production and the family were, therefore, fundamental to their identity.

In the decade after 1968, this traditional, rather one-dimensional, view of rural women was challenged. In their remarkable studies of Minot (Jolas, Pingaud, Verdier and Zonabend, 1990), a Burgundian village, Tina Jolas, Marie-Claude Pingaud (1978), Yvonne Verdier (1979) and Fran-çoise Zonabend (1980), 'our four Parisian ladies' as the locals described them, transformed the traditional interpretation of women's role in rural France. Their works, and a series of ethnological monographs of rural cultures that they inspired, revealed a more sophisticated picture of feminine social space, the rites of passage of women and their vital place in rural society. Yet this research, conducted in the 1970s, coincided with the modernization of the rural economy, which saw an exodus from the countryside headed mainly by young women. The village communities and their culture were thus disappearing before the eyes of the researchers, taking with them the world described by 'the four ladies'.

Amongst more recent studies, those by Martine Segalen (1980) and Susan Carol Rogers (1975 and 1980) are particularly noteworthy, not least because they highlight two distinct academic traditions, that of a French ethnologist on the one hand and that of an American feminist anthropologist on the other. Through their respective studies of Brittany and of Lorraine, they have explored the role of gender relative to the division of labour, the transmission of property and feminine space and power within rural France. Both scholars have challenged the myth of male dominance in rural societies by looking at the female forms of power in a very detailed fashion. Since the publication of the works of Rogers and Segalen, the rapid pace of change in agricultural life has continued. The 1980s saw large-scale restructuring, not least because of the effects of reforms within the Common Agricultural Policy. In twenty years, the agriculturally active population has decreased from four million to one million in France. Now only five per cent of the active population is employed in agriculture. Women's participation in French agriculture is also declining and has been estimated at only 34.4 per cent of total employment in the sector (Braithwaite, 1994) as is demonstrated by Table 9.1 below.

Table 9.1 Percentage of Female Employment in Agriculture, European Community, 1990

Belgium	26
Denmark	23.1
Germany	43.9
Greece	44.5
Spain	27.1
France	34.4
Ireland	10.4
Luxembourg	33.3
Netherlands	27.3
Portugal	49.7
Italy	35.4

Source: Braithwaite, M. (1994). *Le rôle économique et la situation de la femme dans les sociétés rurales,* L'Europe verte, n⁰1, Luxembourg: Office des publications officielles des communautés européennes: 59.

Paradoxically, it was at a time when the employment of women within the rural sector was declining (except in the Low-Countries), and when women were increasingly working outside of the family farm, that they became a distinct subject of sociological enquiry (Braithwaite, 1994). When we examine the research published since 1980,[1] it is clear that the vast majority of authors have in common the aim of defining the role of gender in rural studies.[2] As Whatmore (1994: 1) has argued, this work.

represents important departures in the development of feminist research perspectives in the arena; extending the analysis of gender construction of rurality beyond the family farm; highlighting the contested and heterogeneous nature of 'rural women's' experience; and exploring a greater diversity of threads in feminist theories of gender as an axis of social power and identity.

This chapter will examine the role of contemporary women in rural France in light of recent changes in both the agricultural economy and society. The first section will look at their new roles in relation to the family and the community before moving onto the persistence of traditional gender roles in rural France achieved by assessing women's position relative to the division of labour and to kinship networks.

Section I: New Roles for Women in Rural France

New Professional Roles

On account of its history and culture, France is one of the few European countries to have clearly defined the concept of the rural zone.[3] Any community of less than 2,000 inhabitants is classed by the INSEE as rural. These rural zones represent approximately 85 per cent of French territory, but include only 27 per cent of its inhabitants with an average population density of 15 per square kilometre. In these rural areas, farming families, although declining in number, still dominate the life of the community. Today, one Frenchwoman in four lives in a rural community and, of these, 2.6 million are considered to be economically active. According to Braithwaite (1994), there are proportionally more young women living in rural communities than urban ones, but when they are old enough to work they leave the countryside for the towns. The result is an overrepresentation of elderly women and an underrepresentation of those between the ages of twenty and thirty-nine years.

Overall, despite the decline in agricultural employment, farmwomen still occupy a key position in this society. But what do we mean by farmwomen? For the purpose of this chapter, we intend to define farmwomen as those who are declared as economically active in agriculture, or who are married, or live, in households where one or more members is involved in agriculture.[4] This conceptual definition embraces a wide range of positions including women who own farms in their own right, those who work full time or part time on a farm and even professional women employed in a non-agricultural sector.

In 1970, 84 per cent of women living on a farm worked in some capacity as part of the enterprise, but by 1988 this percentage had fallen to 64 per cent (INSEE, 1993). In 1997 there were an estimated 216,000 *actives agricoles* (women economically active in agriculture) whose principal or secondary activity was centred on the farm. They represented 37 per cent of farmers according to the census of 1990 (and 35 per cent in 1997 according to the *Enquête Emploi*). Among farmwomen over fifteen years of age living in farming families, the proportion working on the farm is falling rapidly: whereas 67 per cent were active in 1970, and 58 per cent in 1979, only 54 per cent were thus classified in 1988 (Barthez, 1993). We should, however, note that more women are now described as full-time employees in agriculture, with official statistics showing a rise from ten to nineteen per cent between 1979 and 1988 (INSEE, 1993). This reflects a longer term trend towards salarization in agriculture (Bouillaguet-Bernard, Gauvin-Ayel, and Outin, 1981).

Rural women increasingly work outside the farm and it is especially true for farmers' wives under 35 years of age (40 per cent of wives in this age group). Indeed, according to the INSEE (1993), among farmers' wives under 40 years of age, only 34 per cent are classed as farmers by profession as opposed to 58 per cent of those over 40. The effect of this trend has been to reduce the proportion of family revenue derived directly from the farm from 72 per cent in 1970 to 58 per cent in 1988 (INSEE, 1993). By 1993, a quarter of all farmers' wives exercised a main profession unconnected with agriculture, which was twice the number recorded in 1979. Indeed, the level of economic activity of rural women is identical to that of their urban counterparts. In rural zones, the most recent statistics for the period 1990–7 revealed that for those women aged between 25 and 39 there has been an increase from 72 per cent to 78 per cent of women classed as active, while the national figure for the same age group has risen from 75 to 78 per cent (Toutain, 1998).

Since the 1970s, the nature of women's employment has changed significantly, and the farmer's wife who a generation ago was involved in *petit commerce* (small trade) is now working as an employee outside of the farm: 50.3 per cent of the total in 1988 (see Table 9.2). These women have been able to claim a professional and personal identity independent of the farm and the values it represents. One of the most important consequences of their action is the breakdown of the frontiers separating rural France from its urban counterpart, leading to the gradual homogenization of values and lifestyles.

The growth in the number of women who are the head of the family farm contrasts with the general pattern of decline. Between 1979 and

Table 9.2 Main Occupations of Farmers' Wives (in percentages)

Main Occupations*	1970	1988
Artisans, commerçants, petits		
commerçants dont directeurs industriels (1)	39.2	10.6
	36.9	–
Cadres supérieurs (2)	1.7	2.9
Cadres moyens (3)	14.0	19.9
Employés dont femmes de ménages et		
techniciens de surface	26.0	50.3
	12.3	12.9
Ouvriers (5)	17.4	13.9
Autres (6)	1.7	2.4
Total des femmes dans profession non agricole (7)	100	100

* *Note:*

(1) Artisans, shopkeepers, small traders including directors of industrial concerns

(2) Senior executives

(3) Middle managers

(4) Employee including domestic and commercial cleaners

(5) Factory workers

(6) Others

Source: INSEE (1993) SCEES, agricultural census of 1970 and 1988, Table 2, p.27.

1988, they have increased from 116,000 to 150,000, a 29 per cent rise, whereas the percentage of male heads of family farms has fallen by 24 per cent (Barthez, 1993). The number of women in this position is increasing (INSEE, 1993) but we should remember that for many it is a responsibility assumed by chance rather than by design and it is often held on a temporary basis. Many women have been obliged to take over the farm because of the ill health or advanced age of their husbands. In such a situation, they are acting as *co-exploitante* (partner) with the married couple defining the farm and not the individual. For agricultural spokesmen, trade unions and politicians, farming is frequently represented as a profession for a married couple and as a social ideal that should be protected. The law of 1980, referred to below, which defined the status of *agricultrice* (farmwoman), provides the most telling example of this desire for association and fusion of men and women in the same profession (Barthez, 1993).

Legislation and Social Status: Facilitating Change

In France, the civil law code names the head of the family as the head of the farm. Furthermore when it comes to the inheritance of property and land preference is given to the male line. As a result of the strong influence of the Jeunesse agricole catholique (JAC)(Young Catholic Farmers) during the 1960s, government legislation frequently reflected this male *techniciste* (technologically progressive) view inspired by earlier agricultural laws. Yet the idea of women as *mère de famille, travailleuse et militantiste* (mothers, workers and union activist) (Lagrave, 1983: 22) has gradually developed with women divided between the family farm and their own search for a professional identity.

It was not until 1965 that farmers' wives obtained the status of farmers in their own right and they were obliged to wait for the orientation laws of 4 July 1980 before being recognized as co-owner or manager of the farm. With the development of new forms of economic organization such as the *societé civile d'exploitation* (SCE)(operating company), women are increasingly acquiring the status of shareholder providing them with a status of legal equality with their husbands. But despite this improvement in their position, their rights are still restricted by the ban on wives participating in the *Groupement agricole d'exploitation en commun* (GAEC) (Farmers' economic interest group). Moreover it was not until 1988, with the creation of the *Etablissement agricole à responsabilités limitées* (EARL)(limited liability agricultural holding) that it was finally permitted for women to benefit from state grants and economic assistance on the same terms as men. Thus farmwomen have only partially won the battle for legal equality and the control of their social and professional lives.

Although the number of independent farmwomen has increased, it remains true that their farms are smaller both physically and economically than those controlled by men. In 1994, 46.8 per cent were working in what the INSEE classified as a 'small farm' and only 33.3 per cent in a 'large farm' as indicated in Table 9.3 overleaf.

Women as Mediators between Tradition and Modernity

The opening of rural France towards the rest of society is not the only result of the increasing education and professional independence of women. Another consequence is the convergence of agricultural and urban lifestyles. As a link between a profession that is still extremely insular and the outside world, rural women travel between two distinct cultures. In addition to their professional contacts, they visit the towns both to buy domestic goods and to attend to the educational and cultural needs of their children. It is women who mediate and broaden the contacts between their husband and non-agricultural society, offering the possibility for social and cultural exchange.

Table 9.3 Women Farmers by Size of Farm

Socio- professional category	Number of women		Percentage of working women		Percentage of women working in the category	
	1982	1994	1982	1994	1982	1994
Farmers	592,027	315,941	6.8	3.3	38.3	36.9
Farmers on small farms	289,594	89,248	3.4	0.9	41.1	46.8
Farmers on medium sized farms	186,975	89,181	2.1	0.9	37.2	35.3
Farmers on large farms	115,458	137,512	1.3	1.4	34.1	33.3

Source: INSEE (1995) *Les Femmes: contours et caractères*, Paris: La Documentation Française: 121.

Recent studies of rural women have emphasized the vital role they play as mediators, linking tradition and modernity (GREP, 1998). Generally closer to their children and more conscious of the problems they are liable to confront, women have understood the demands of a modern world and its influence over the economic and social life of the village. Women have thus adapted their traditional role of instructing and 'socializing' their children. In the past, they transmitted, amongst others things, religious practice and belief and general moral codes and rules of behaviour. Today, their vision and experience has expanded to encompass the functioning of wider French society and its economy, allowing them to prepare their children, irrespective of whether their future lies on the farm. These mothers are responsible for encouraging their children, both male and female, to continue their education to a higher level. They also have great influence over the career choices of their children, even to the extent of encouraging them to follow a profession other than farming.

Although there is a shortage of detailed studies of the influence of women on the socialization of their children, the evidence available suggests that mothers are the mediators between generations and especially between the father and the son who is to succeed him (Jacques-Jouvenot, 1997). Harmony and the smooth transition of the patrimony are only possible if the son does not challenge the authority of the father openly. The social destiny of mothers and sons are therefore tightly connected. It appears that the professional emancipation of one and the other is linked. Women's search for professional recognition beyond the farm has been accompanied by a refusal to be treated as unpaid labour, and it has been mirrored by the demands of their sons to be made head of the farm, or at least full partners, sooner rather than later. The authority of the father is thus challenged, and in such circumstances families are not harmonious associates but social actors in a conflicting relationship. As Michèle Salmona (1980) has shown, it is women who are decisive in ensuring that the conflict is kept to a minimum and who act to maintain or restore harmony within the family. Generally speaking, it is clear that the wives of farmers have a positive attitude and discourse relative to their husbands' profession, even if, unlike their husbands, they are more willing to express their unhappiness with the idea of their sons following the same career.

Clearly individual circumstances affect the attitude of women towards the question of inheritance but, in the majority of cases, they distinguish in their discourse between two generations, those of the grandfather forced to take over a family farm and those fathers who had the choice to do so. The right to choose is considered to be the fundamental reason why employment as a farmer can be treated on equal terms with other professions. The desire to have a choice of profession explains, in part, why the educational qualifications of young farmers are so superior to those of previous generations. Here is a classic example of the alliance between mothers and sons with the women determined that their boys should have a choice. Farm women are now consistently educated to a higher level than were their own mothers, or mothers-in-law, or their husbands (SEGESA, 1995). Mothers and sons thus form an alliance in which the claim to a professional and educational status is a defining feature of their identities (Jacques-Jouvenot, 1997).

Beyond the Community

The gender division of social space and of labour is now more clearly defined in terms of public/private or feminine/masculine than was previously the case. The idea of a couple scarcely existed in traditional agricultural society and ties of family or generational solidarity were given priority (Barthez, 1982). This social pattern has been transformed as a consequence of the movement of women into the labour market, and their acquisition of an independent professional status. These changes have undoubtedly affected the relationship between farming families and the rest of society, but it is still important to recognize that they have maintained distinctive features that are not found in other social groups.

The convergence of agricultural and urban lifestyles can be demonstrated by the new willingness to 'go out' whether to restaurants, cinema or theatre as well as by the decline in male time spent in cafés as opposed to watching television. Today farmers spend as much time at home in front of the television as other Frenchman. They have also embraced the once taboo concept of the vacation. In 1994, official figures revealed that the number of holidays taken by families living in rural zones had tripled compared to the situation in 1982 (Braithwaite, 1994). One of the reasons for this is the development of different forms of business organization that enable the family to go away. Another feature of the trend towards greater contact with the outside world is a development of activities alongside the farm that encourage links with townspeople. The sale to the public of farm products and the growth of rural tourism are particularly pertinent examples of this trend. In the majority of cases, women have been responsible for the development of these sectors and they exercise direct control over the organization involved (GREP, 1998).

Nevertheless, social relationships amongst farmers provide an example of their relative isolation compared to other professional groups (SEGESA, 1995 and Braithwaite, 1994). Table 9.4 overleaf gives us some indication on the nature of their network of relationships.

The three categories of interlocutors that together form 70 per cent of the whole for both men and women are the relationships of work, friendship and family. It is, however, the case that farmwomen have generally richer networks founded upon strong ties of extended kinship, and frequent contacts with shopkeepers and services providers. Rogers (Lamarche, Rogers, and Karnoouh, 1980) has already underlined the importance of these networks in her study of village life in Lorraine. In rural communities, which are frequently sparsely inhabited, access to crèches, nurseries and leisure or sporting activities for children is more restricted, making life more difficult for women and obliging them to take the initiative themselves in order to fill the gap. This encourages them to join or form associations that are separate from the life of the farm (Braithwaite, 1994). But whether they belong to local associations or in the case of older women to a *club du troisième âge* (club for retired people), their participation is nearly always connected to social matters. Thus despite farmwomen having a rate of membership of associations that matches that of the men, the nature of the associations they join is different and it is only when they are retired that couples are likely to belong to the same social organization. Women are almost completely absent from the trades unions (Mouchtouris, 1994), as they have traditionally been at a national level, and from other professional bodies of

Table 9.4 The Composition of Network of Interlocutors (Outside Work)

Gender and profession (1)	Average number of interlocutors in a week						
	Friendship	Work colleagues	Diverse (2)	Shopkeepers and service providers	Neighbours	Family	Total
Men: Total of economically active	4.7	5.1	2.3	1.5	1.6	3.9	19.1
Farmers	4.7	1.6	2.1	1.9	2.8	5.2	18.3
Artisans, Shopkeepers, Managers	5.8	3.8	2.3	1.4	1.6	3.0	17.8
Women: Total of economically active	4.5	4.5	2.3	2.2	1.5	4.4	19.4
Farmers							
Artisans,	4.3	0.6	2.2	2.9	2.8	6.3	19.1
Shopkeepers, Managers	3.5	4.1	2.4	2.3	1.4	4.3	17.8

(1) Most recent profession (2) Acquaintance, door-to-door salesperson, member of an association
Source: INSEE (1993) *Les Agriculteurs: contours et caractères*, Paris: INSEE:101, Table 1.

farmers. However, the most recent president of the *Centre National des Jeunes Agriculteurs* (CNJA) (National Centre of Young farmers) was a woman farmer from Brittany, and more women are now playing a major role in rural development (GREP, 1998). Overall some six per cent of French women are active members of an association of any sort but only 3.6 per cent of *agricultrices* belong to such an organization, primarily because of the limits on their time. Once again, rural women display a different pattern of behaviour from the norm, even if they are gradually converging with the lifestyles of French women as whole. As in the rest of France, most rural women stay outside formal political and institutional life (GREP, 1998). There are many reasons for this situation: family and public services do not mix well together and women are still affected by the perception that it is above all *une affaire d'hommes* (men's business). The lack of technical knowledge reduces their scope for participation in agricultural organizations (GREP, 1998).

There are, however, some signs of change, when we examine women's participation in the public life of villages as councillors or mayors. In 1994, some 17 per cent of councillors elected to municipal councils in *communes* with fewer than 3,500 inhabitants were women, but the corresponding figure in 1996 had risen to 22 per cent. As for the number of women elected as mayor, the figures for the same period were 5.4 per cent and 7.7 per cent respectively which again suggests a growing representation. This increase is, however, slower when we examine the *conseils régionaux* (regional councils) and especially the *conseils généraux* (departmental councils) (Toutain, 1998). Recent debates about the need to choose women representatives for agricultural trade unions and national professional bodies such as the CNJA attest to the fracturing of traditional patterns of thought and behaviour. It could be argued that the changes taking place are piecemeal rather than obeying any particular dynamic, but they are nevertheless leading rural women to redefine their own identities and to balance tradition and modernity within a more fragmented French society.

Section II: The Persistence of Traditional Gender Roles in Rural France

Women's Traditional Roles

If the position of women in rural France has been transformed by economic and social change, it is still necessary to recognize the persistence of more traditional forms of social behaviour. Alice Barthez (1982) has demonstrated that the issue of professional recognition for women remains problematic because they are still wives, mothers and partners in the family enterprise.[5]

However, we should note that the degree of women's emancipation depends to some extent on the agricultural sector concerned. When we look at the presence of women in terms of regions and particular agricultural sectors (INSEE, 1989; 1991), it is clear that women are especially well-represented in dairy farming and in the breeding of small livestock. There are clearly strong regional variations with sharp contrasts between the west and the east of France. In the west, women are most active in livestock and dairy farming, whereas in the south-east, and in particular in the Languedoc and Corsica, where viticulture or sheep farming predominate, female participation has traditionally been very limited. In the north and north-east of France, on the other hand, agriculture is not a major employer of either men or women.

If we take the example of two generations of women in Burgundian viticulture it is possible to see the ongoing weight of tradition on women in rural France as well as the impact of change since the 1970s as women engage in the search for professional and personal autonomy (Demossier, 1999). The Chardin family, winegrowers for several generations, is today composed of Alex and his wife Sandra and their three children, plus

Sandra's mother, who inherited the estates on the death of her husband. Sandra's mother today claims to have suffered from the lack of recognized social status within the estate, despite having brought her own vineyards into the family when she married. Her daughter, although joint owner and manager of the domain with her husband, is not recognized professionally and socially as the head of the vineyard. On the other hand, in addition to overseeing the business accounts and finances and participating in the process of wine making, Sandra teaches several hours per week in the local school of viticulture. Whereas her mother identifies herself above all in relation to her late husband and the family domain, Sandra has established an independent professional identity.

There are two opposing views that can be applied to women's role in French rural society. Firstly, there is that of Susan Carol Rogers (Lamarche et al., 1980). In her study of power and authority in Lorraine she challenged several assumptions about women in rural society, notably the notions of overwhelming masculine dominance and the relatively inferior status of women's domestic labour. According to Rogers (Lamarche et al., 1980), the process of socialization of children, the networks of gossip and a complex system of rewards define the traditional role of women in the village; through their control of social activity, women are central to the exercise of informal authority. So, although both men and women behave as if the men are dominant, the actual situation is very different: 'male peasants seem to be characterised by a felt lack of power' (Rogers, 1975: 752). Another view is the one expressed by Christine Delphy (1984) according to her, if women are outside formal, recognized power networks, the 'informal' power which they may like to believe they hold is worth very little and easily withdrawn. I would, however, argue that while most women in rural France are not consciously aware of the power they hold, their role within the community is nevertheless essential in the production of social norms. Women exercise a decisive role in the financial management of the farm, and through their strengthened legal position can determine the economic future of the family business. As we have seen, women play a crucial part in the education and socialization of their children even to the extent of directing their sons towards non-agricultural employment.

However, if the profession of farmer is acceptable for men, that of *paysanne* (peasant) is often rejected by women. It is one of the reasons why young women are more likely to pursue their studies for longer and to a higher level than young men as official statistics regularly confirm. Recent figures (INSEE, 1993) have demonstrated that amongst the economically active population under thirty-five, the proportion of farmwomen with educational qualifications of secondary school or university level is nearly twice that of men (see also Barthez, 1980) – despite the fact that they do not usually receive much in the way of professional training. When women do pursue agricultural studies they concentrate upon a narrow range of technical skills that reflect the sexual division of young students in agriculture. One of four pathways is followed by the majority of women: basket weaving, laboratory technician, distribution and commercialization of agricultural products and agricultural economy (INSEE, 1995). The result of this is that women are still restricted to what are essentially traditional activities.

The Traditional Division of Labour

From the few studies that have attempted an in-depth analysis of daily life and the division of labour a certain number of themes emerge that would appear to be unique to rural women. As we have seen, the sexual division of labour is a defining feature of traditional peasant society. Questions such as who is responsible for milking the cows, or whether or not women work in the fields, provide clues as to the organization of the farm and to the spheres of influence of the sexes. In those regions where women assist the men in nearly all of their labours, without having any specific tasks assigned to themselves other than the *basse-cour* (looking after the poultry), they are in effect both domestic and agricultural workers and any control they exert over the management of the farm is derived from their personal influence over their husband. However, in the majority of cases, the activities of men and women are clearly segregated, although the trend is for women to assume ever more responsibility for the essential instruments of farm management.

For economically active rural women, it is more difficult than for urban women to reconcile their professional and domestic occupations. For farmwomen, the amount of time that needs to be devoted to household and other domestic tasks is greater because of their connection to the work of the farm. Of all the women in rural France, it is the farmwomen who have the least amount of free time in the day (Braithwaite, 1994). Although the number of farming households with at least one car has increased (INSEE, 1993), women have less ready access to a car than the men which adds an additional complication to life, especially for those women with children, that is to say the majority. For women with outside professions their work is differentiated from the potential confusion with domestic activities. It is thus defined as labour in its own right, providing the women with an independent professional and social identity. In addition, their absence from the home and the farm creates a clear distinction between 'paid work' and 'domestic work', inviting them to negotiate a fairer division of unpaid work. However, in common with many non-rural French women (see Chapter 2), such women find themselves facing the problem of the 'double day': domestic tasks are still divided on gender lines and their husbands rarely participate.

Marriage and Inheritance

The participation of women in the two essential moments in the patrimonial cycle – marriage and inheritance – is vital. Both are central to rural and agricultural society and on them depends the successful transmission of land and property within the family group. In rural France, marriage has always been viewed as an economic and social wager, a gamble that requires the birth of an heir and the stability of the couple to succeed. Marriage is a serious matter involving the future of the patrimony, and not just the happiness of the couple concerned. Amongst farming families, where rates of endogamy are extremely high, two distinct strategies coexist. Amongst the poorest farmers, there are remarkably high rates of bachelorhood and at the same time a growing number of farmers who are marrying women employed in non-agricultural occupations, especially *cadres moyens* (middle management). According to R.-M. Lagrave (1987), these apparently conflicting strategies are a response to the need of farming families to protect themselves economically and to acquire educational and cultural capital. Marrying a farmer no longer means automatically becoming an *agricultrice*, and this is further evidence that the term *agricultrice* is more complex than was previously the case. However marriage remains the fundamental means to ensure the continuity of the farm. All the evidence indicates that unmarried couples are only a tiny fraction of the farming population and divorce is extremely rare.

There were 1,700,000 unmarried couples in 1990 in France, that is to say 12.4 per cent of the overall total number of households (see Table 9.5). This was a huge increase on the total of 800,000 recorded in 1982. Amongst farming families, however, only 4.4 per cent were unmarried in 1990, although this was an increase compared to 1982. We should, however, note that for agricultural labourers the number of unmarried couples is much higher.

In the agricultural milieu there remains a stark contradiction between the legal principle of equality for all children and the principle of not subdividing the estate. Attempts to reconcile these conflicting aspirations

Table 9.5 Proportion of Unmarried Couples in 1990, according to the husband's age (for 100 couples)

	Under 35	Between 35 and 59	Over 60	Total
Farms	15.6	3.9	5.8	4.4
all farms	19.8	6.3	8.7	7.4
– Medium-sized farm	15.7	3.2	5.6	4.2
– Large farm	11.7	2.4	3.8	2.6
Workers	33.0	8.9	7.4	17.8
of which agricultural workers	35.4	9.1	6.0	19.0
Total of households	31.9	8.1	4.5	12.4

Source: INSEE (1993) *Les Agriculteurs: contours et caractères*, Paris: INSEE: 49, Table 1.

vary from region to region and are determined by law, local custom and practices of inheritance where we distinguish *dévolution préciputaire*[6] and *dévolution égalitaire.*[7] Ethnological studies have revealed the existence of cultural areas where women can become the heir, as, for example in the Basque country, or in Brittany where girls and boys are treated equally in matters of inheritance. In Béarn, on the other hand, if the eldest child is a girl, it is possible to *faire l'aîné*, that is to say overlook her inheritance rights to the advantage of a younger brother. Where the only possible heirs are women, other strategies can be employed. In the Burgundian vineyards, for example, we have observed cases where the inheritance has been turned to the advantage of the second daughter because she married a winemaker. The crucial matter is to transmit the farm or vineyard to the most competent and stable couple (Demossier, 1999).

However, as a general rule, inheritance favours the eldest male. Given the inherent inequality of the inheritance system, there is a need for heirs to be socialized into acceptance (Bertaux, 1977). The choice of a successor in agricultural communities is associated with a system of joint management, for example the transfer of a farm from father to son is usually marked by a period when they work together as partners on the farm. The patrimony thus creates the link between different generations and, it has to be said, women are frequently excluded from this process. Even if the number of women controlling farms is growing, they are still rarely heirs to the patrimony. Rather than inherit directly themselves or being able to claim the right to family estates, they acquire their farms after the death of a brother or husband. They can, however, inherit from their father in families that either lack male heirs or men willing to take on the farm. This conscious strategy to disadvantage women relative to the family succession is apparent at various points in the lives of farmwomen. In effect, they and their daughters are used by their families as a means of bonding the family unit.

Women as the Hub of Kinship Relationship

Despite the pressures of change, life on the farm has retained its uniqueness. The sense of isolation – or independence – traditionally affected lifestyles with farmwomen spending time perfecting the domestic arts. As Verdier (1979) and Zonabend (1980) demonstrated in their study of Minot, the garden, like the kitchen, was a feminine sphere and young girls learned from their grandmothers the secrets of the tasks that formed the daily routine of women: to wash, cook, garden and sew. This domestic sphere had its own 'techniques, traditions, language, its scale of competence and proficiency, its topography and its rhythms' (Verdier, 1979: 80) but it is now in crisis. This feminine culture has been eroded by social change and by the breakdown of rural societies. It is perhaps in reaction to this decline that there has recently been something of a revival of interest in these 'feminine arts', for example, through the rediscovery of traditional products and cuisine.

Traditionally several generations lived under the same roof and this provided the *agricultrice* with increased flexibility in managing her time. Although this was one of the chief characteristics of rural families, it is now being replaced by the tendency of young couples to establish their own independent households. A recent survey concluded that only 14 per cent of farming households are now composed of a family plus a grandparent or a grandchild (INSEE, 1993). Yet family values are essential to the continuity of the group. Despite the apparent disintegration of the peasant family, rural households continue to maintain extremely tight relations amongst themselves. Everyone will share the same allotment, and when a pig or other livestock is killed there will be something for everybody's freezer. With mothers increasingly away from the farm, it is grandmothers who assume much of the responsibility for the care and education of the children. This is a change from the traditional pattern when the three generations lived and worked under the same roof, but it is an example of the persistence of strong bonds of kinship amongst rural families. Similarly, the kinship network has been recreated with a more informal and flexible structure with what Mendras (1984: 280) calls the *parentèle localisée* (local relations) linking different households groups. Women are fundamental in holding together the kinship network.

There remains enormous scope for further study into the role of women in both agriculture and rural society more generally. This chapter has attempted to sketch out the effects of social and economic change on women, their family relationships and their interaction with French society as a whole. Since the mid-1970s, a silent revolution has been taking place with many women not only breaking free from the farm and redefining their own identity, but also coming to act as the key mediators between the farm and the society beyond it. It is clear that women have often acted as innovators especially if their economic situation enabled them to do so, and their emancipation, through their quest for a professional identity, has contributed to the transformation of both agriculture and rural society. Through their contribution to strategies of social reproduction, they complement the role of their husbands. They now prefer to call themselves *agricultrices* instead of *paysannes*. This is partly due to the more assertive attitude of the women themselves, but it also reflects a more general movement that, since the 1980s, has redefined the profession of farmer in French society in a more positive light (Bourdieu, 1977). It is likely in the future that women will play a major role in the restructuration of the social fabric of contemporary France. Their contribution will be based upon their uniqueness as mediators and agents of change. However, given the tendency to talk about this society as entering a post-industrial, even post-modern phase, it is also important to reflect here upon the remarkable capacity for resistance and redefinition that is to be found in a rural France that continues to plough its own furrow and maintain its distinctiveness at the beginning of the twenty-first century.

Notes

I would like to thank Anne Thierry, ethnologist, and the Cpéderf for their help in preparing the different materials for this article.

1. For a European perspective on this topic, see the special issues of the *Rural Sociologist* in 1981, *Sociologia Ruralis* in 1988 and *Journal of Rural Studies* in 1991. For a survey of French publications on women in rural France, see Lagrave (1983).
2. For a discussion of methodological issues, see GREP (1998), Whatmore (1988) and Barthez (1982).
3. A detailed discussion of the concept of the rural zone has been provided by Toutain in GREP (1998).

4. The statistics compiled by the INSEE and by the SCESS (Service central d'études et enquêtes statistiques) of the French Ministry of Agriculture reflect the fluid nature of this social group. Only those women working on a farm can be classed as *agricultrices* (farmwomen), but this definition excludes groups that are not always reflected in the official statistics because the women involved fail to recognize themselves in the official categories, or underestimate their own contribution to the family enterprise. For statisticians, farmwomen form part of what we might describe as the unclassified, identified sometimes as family help and labour or even as economically inactive, depending on their matrimonial status or their own self-perception.

5. Women working in agriculture provide an excellent example of how important it is to study the family and the farm as a single unit of observation, and it is misleading to study the role of women and their work without reference to the prevailing social structure. For the INSEE, an agricultural family is defined as a group of people who are not necessarily related by ties of kinship or living in the same household, who work together on the same farm or estate. Such an artificial distinction, although comforting for bureaucrats, is misleading. To place work and the family into separate spheres makes the concept of work completely incomprehensible for farmwomen. Moreover the growing significance of women's involvement in the labour market beyond the farm raises serious doubts about this artificial division requiring us to reconsider the theoretical field and provide a definition that will take into account the informal economy of household tasks, subsidiary activities, and seasonal employment as different forms of work (Braithwaite, 1994).

6. Portion of an estate or inheritance that devolves upon one of the coheirs over and above his equal share with the others.

7. Equal share of the inheritance.

References

Association des Ruralistes français. (1984). *La pluriactivité dans les familles agricoles*. Paris: ARF.

Augustins, G. (1990), 'Les transmissions entre générations dans les sociétés paysannes contemporaines', in *Patrimoines en Folies*, Paris:

Ministère de la Culture et de la Communication, Editions de la maison des sciences de l'homme.

Barthez, A.(1982), *Famille, Travail et Agriculture*, Paris: Economica.

Barthez, A. (1984), 'Femmes dans l'agriculture et travail familial', *Sociologie du Travail*, no. 3–84, July–September: 255–67.

Barthez, A. (1993), 'Une agriculture en mutation', in *Données sociales*, Paris: INSEE.

Bertaux, D. (1977), *Destins personnels et structures de classes*, Paris: PUF, coll Politiques.

Bonnet, J. (1988), *La terre des femmes et ses magies*, Paris: Editions Robert Laffont.

Bouillaguet-Bernard, P., Gauvin-Ayel, A. and Outin, J-L. (1981) *Femmes au travail. Prosperité et crise*, Paris: Economica.

Bourdieu, P. (1977), 'La paysannerie, une classe objet', *Actes de la recherche en sciences sociales*, 17–18.

Bourdieu, P. (1980), *Le sens pratique*, Paris: Editions de Minuit.

Braithwaite, M. (1994*), Le rôle économique et la situation de la femme dans les sociétés rurales*. L'Europe verte, nº1, Luxembourg: Office des Publications Officielles des Communautés Européennes: 59–65 and 75–8.

Caisse Nationale des Allocations Familiales (1990) *Familles en milieu rural*, Paris: Caisse Nationale des Allocations Familiales.

Delphy, C. (1984). *Close to Home : a Materialist Analysis of Women's Oppression*, London : Hutchinson.

Demossier, M. (1999). *Hommes et Vins, une anthropologie du vignoble bourguignon*, Dijon: Presses Universitaires de Dijon.

De Singly, F. (1993), *Sociologie de la famille contemporaine*, Paris: Nathan.

Duby, G.(ed) (1976), *Histoire de la France rurale*, Paris: Seuil, vol. 4.

GREP (Groupe de Recherches pour l'Education et la Prospective). (1998) *Actes du séminaire Femmes en milieu rural: nouvelles activités, nouvelles qualifications 1995–7 et 1998–2000, bilan et perspective*, Paris: Europea.

Grignon, C. (1975), 'Le paysan inclassable', *Actes de la recherche en sciences sociales*, vol. 4, July: 82–7.

Heritska, HH. (1995). *La participation des femmes dans les processus décisionnels du monde agricole et rural*, Bruxelles: CEPFAR.

INSEE (1989), 'L'activité féminine dans les régions', *Emploi-Revenus*, vol. 10(1): 46.

INSEE (1991), 'L'activité féminine', *Démographie-Société*, vol. 10, January.

INSEE (1993), *Les Agriculteurs: contours et caractères*, Paris: INSEE.

INSEE (1995), *Les Femmes: contours et caractères*, Paris: INSEE.

INSEE (1998), *Tableaux de l'économie française 1998–1999*, Paris: INSEE.

Jacques-Jouvenot, D. (1997), *Choix du successeur et transmission patrimoniale*, Paris: L'Harmattan.

Jolas, T., Pingaud, M-C., Verdier, Y. and Zonabend, F. (1990), *Une campagne voisine*, Paris: Editions MSH.

Kayser, B. (1990). *La renaissance rurale. Sociologie des campagnes du monde occidental*,Paris : Colin, Collection U.

Lagrave, R-M. (1983), 'Bilan critique des recherches sur les agricultrices en France', *Etudes Rurales*, October–December, 1983, vol. 92: 9–40.

Lagrave, R-M. (1987), *Celles de la Terre; Agricultrice, invention politique d'un métier*, Paris: EHESS.

Lamarche, H., Rogers S-C. and Karnoouh, C. (1980), *Paysans, femmes et citoyens*, Le Paradou: Actes Sud.

Lantz, P. (1980), *Le travail des femmes*, Besançon: Actes du colloque.

Mannheim, K. (1990), *Le problème des générations*, Paris: Nathan.

Maresca, S. (1983), *Les dirigeants paysans*, Paris: Minuit.

Maresca, S. (1991), *L'autoportrait. Six agricultrices en quête d'image*, Toulouse: Presses Universitaires du Mirail, INRA.

Maresca, S. (1995), 'Traquez le naturel, il revient mis en scène; des agricultrices en quête d'image', *L'ethnographie*, 91(2): 131–45.

Mendras, H. (1984), *La fin des paysans*, Arles: Actes Sud, Collection Babel.

Mouchtouris, A. (1994). *Le féminin rural. Aspirations sociales et culturelles*, Paris: L'Harmattan.

Moscovici, M. (1960), 'Le changement social en milieu rural et le rôle des femmes', *Revue française de sociologie*, vol. I: 314–22.

Pingaud, M-C. (1978), *Paysans en Bourgogne, les Gens de Minot*, Paris: Flammarion.

Pour (1998), *Femmes en milieu rural. Nouvelles activités, nouvelles compétences*, no. 158, June.

Rogers, S.C. (1975), 'Female forms of power and the myth of male dominance: a model of female: male interaction in peasant society', *American Ethnologist*, vol. 2(4): 727–56.

Rogers, S.C. (1979), 'Espace masculin, espace féminin. Essai sur la différence', *Etudes Rurales*, April–June, vol. 74: 87–110.

Rogers, S.C. (1991), *Shaping Modern Times in Rural France. The Transformation and Reproduction of an Aveyronnais community*, Princeton: Princeton University Press.

Salmona, M. (1980), *Travail dans la cellule de production familiale, fatigue et imaginaire*, Paris: CAE.SAR.

Salmona, M. (1994), *Les paysans français*, Paris: L'Harmattan, Collection Alternatives rurales.

Service des droits de femmes/SEGESA (1995) *Femmes en milieu rural: des initiatives pour l'animation, le développement des services de l'emploi*, Paris: Service des droits des femmes/Societé d'Etudes Géographiques Economiques et Sociologiques (SEGESA).

Segalen, M. (1980), *Mari et femme dans la société paysanne*, Paris: Flammarion.

Segalen, M. (1991), *Jeux des familles*, Paris: Presses de CNRS.

Terrail, J.-P. (1995), *La dynamique des générations*, Paris: Editions l'Harmattan.

Toutain, X., Velard, L. and Mathieu, N. (1992). *Les femmes en milieu rural. Pour une meilleure connaissance de leur situation*, Collection: Droits des femmes (Secrétariat d'Etat), Paris: SEGESA.

Toutain, X. and Velard, L. (1993). *La situation des femmes et le rôle des agricultrices en milieu rural*, Paris: SEGESA.

Toutain, X. (1998), 'La situation socio-économique des femmes en milieu rural', *Pour*, no. 158, June.

Verdier, Y. (1979), *Façons de dire, façons de faire : la laveuse, la cuisinière, la couturière*, Paris: Gallimard.

Whatmore, S., Marsden, T. and Lowe, P. (1994), *Gender and Rurality*, London: David Fulton Publishers.

Whatmore, S. (1988), 'From Women's roles to gender relations, developing perspectives in the analysis of farmwomen', *Sociologia Ruralis*, vol. XXVIII-4: 239–47.

Zarca, B. (1990). *Situation professionnelle, statuts, rôles et individualisation des droits des femmes d'indépendants non agricoles*, Paris: Centre de Recherche pour l'Etude et l'Observation des Conditions de Vie (CREDOC), June.

Zonabend, F. (1980), *La Mémoire Longue. Temps et histoire au village*, Paris: PUF.

Conclusion

In this book we have sought to analyse aspects of the situation of women in contemporary France. Was Bourdieu correct in his view that persistent, relative inequalities between women and men remain, despite the increased range in opportunities for women in French society (Bourdieu, 1998: 97)? Are there grounds for optimism in the new millennium?

Throughout the postwar period, the situation of Frenchwomen has evolved rapidly and a diverse range of laws has been passed by successive governments to attempt to improve women's rights, status and opportunities. Moreover, such evolution in the status of Frenchwomen has challenged the universalist republican tradition. Despite the declarations of its founding text, adopted by the Assemblée nationale in 1789, which accorded the civil rights of freedom, property, security and resistance to oppression to 'l'homme et le citoyen', French Republican universalism has largely failed to recognize the diverse specificity of its citizens and collapsed differences of gender, ethnic group and sexual orientation into white, male heterosexual self sameness. In the postwar period of twentieth century France, it is by invoking the rights guaranteed by the falsely universalist republican tradition that women, Algerians and lesbians and gay men have fought for their freedom to be recognized and respected. In the case of women, as Mona Ozouf has argued, it is the principle of universalism that has paradoxically kept them out of political power (Ozouf 1995).

However, the evidence assembled in this book would tend to support Bourdieu's contention. For example, we have seen in Abigail Gregory's chapter that women have made significant inroads in the field of paid work in France (with increasing activity levels and continuity in employment, reduced occupational segregation and pay inequality compared with men). Maggie Allison points notably to French women's increased presence in journalism and the media, and Marion Demossier has shown that even in agriculture, a sector in the French economy that has been relatively resistant to change, women have been able to increasingly assert their identity over recent years and, in doing so, have contributed to the transformation of both agriculture and rural society. These developments are being matched by other positive changes regarding women as our contributors have shown. These include a greater awareness of the need to make women linguistically visible and the feminization of formerly male titles given to women (Kate Beeching), a growing desire by the French public to see women in positions of greater responsibility in politics (Máire Cross) and evidence that new and established women writers are tackling a greater diversity of thematical concerns (Gill Rye).

Yet our contributors also provide abundant evidence that persistent and fundamental inequalities remain between women and men and that certain groups of women face specific difficulties. For example, in the realm of paid work Abigail Gregory shows that women remain concentrated in the less well-paid jobs and find it hard to reach the most senior posts. They are also, particularly when young, increasingly suffering from new 'flexible' forms of employment as well as unemployment. Simultaneously, as Jan Windebank shows, French women continue to assume responsibility for the vast majority of unpaid work and as a result benefit from significantly less 'leisure' time than French men. Marion Demossier demonstrates that this situation is particularly acute for women in rural France, and that such women also tend to be disadvantaged in other ways – for example, they remain discriminated against in property succession, and the types of activities they carry out remain strongly sex-typed. In the case of other minority groups of women in French society, such as immigrant and ethnic minority women and lesbians, as respectively Jane Freedman and Ursula Tidd show, they have to fight to assert their own autonomous identity to become visible within dominant French and hetero-normative culture and representations and, indeed, to confront sexism from within their own communities.

In view of this situation, are there grounds for optimism at the start of the new millennium? While some positive trends can be highlighted in French women's situation in recent years, we are forced to conclude this book on a more pessimistic note. In the context of recent challenges to French republican universalism constituted for example by the recent campaign for political parity that has ignited a sense of fair play in the public consciousness as regards gender equality, there has also been a vociferous backlash over the last decade to circumscribe and diminish any improvement in women's status (Frischer, 1997). For example, the Front national has campaigned for maternal salaries in a bid to get women back into the home and to rescind the 1979 Veil abortion law. From 1990–2, pro-life activists and members of the far Right participated in commando-style raids on hospital and abortion clinics in a violent bid to curtail women's freedom (Cesbron, 1997: 14; Mossuz-Lavau, 1999: 85).

Moreover, women's access to non-surgical abortion continues to be threatened by the militant pro-life lobby who have instigated boycotts against the pharmaceutical companies who manufacture and distribute the RU 486 (morning-after pill) in France (Aulagnon, 1999). Despite legislation passed in 1993 to protect women's right to abortion, such signs of backlash demonstrate that women still need to fight to protect basic rights – such as the right to control their own fertility – which many now regard as being fundamental to women's autonomy in everyday life.

In sum, although it has been consistently argued in the preceding chapters of this book that women are contributing more than ever before to public life, there is substantial evidence that patriarchal values which permeate public institutions, organizations and structures continue to facilitate and promote traditionally masculine lifestyles and working practices. For example, the fact of increasing numbers of women 'on the ground' in diverse employment sectors does not necessarily correlate with the media representation of those professions, with an increased symbolic power enjoyed by those women, or with material change in the division of labour between men and women. Indeed, crucially, ideological appropriation of women's diverse contribution to society may be widespread. As Ramonet has noted, although 60 per cent of paediatricians in France are women, twenty out of twenty-one children's books surveyed that featured doctors represented them as male figures. Similarly in these same books, only in 5 per cent of cases was there any reference to working mothers even though 75 per cent of mothers work outside the home (Ramonet, 1999: 7). If, despite legislative gains and amendments to the French constitution designed to improve women's status, women are sidelined in this way as 'only' wives and mothers or represented by the media as little more than sexual objects who are readily available for male consumption, this militates against a public perception of women as autonomous citizens. Such representations of women in a society whose institutions and organizational cultures remain largely patriarchal tend only to incite and perpetuate misogynistic practices.

Tackling the sexism inherent in the ideological apparatus which is operant in French society is a complex issue for it is perpetuated by both men and women who derive comfort and convenience from accepting the status quo of oppressive gender relations, however personally and professionally disabling. As the new millennium dawns, many of the key laws to enshrine women's equal status in society have been passed in France, the next challenge will be to preserve those gains and to dismantle the patriarchal ideological apparatus that perpetuates gender discrimination and oppression in favour of positive, enabling representations of gender roles in society and policies which respect equality in difference and favour the aspirations of all. As Gisèle Halimi has argued:[1]

> L'égalité consiste à avoir la même voix, la même importance, à peser de la même manière sur l'événement [. . .] L'égalité que nous voulons, c'est l'égalité où 'un' égale 'un', mais où chaque 'un' est dessiné différement, autrement. (Rodgers, 1998: 155)[2]

Notes

1. Gisèle Halimi is a lawyer, onetime Deputy and UNESCO Ambassador as well as founder of the feminist pressure group, *Choisir* which has existed since 1971 to campaign for contraception, abortion and most recently, political parity. She was head of the Juppé government's commission into political parity from 1995–7.
3. 'Equality means having the same voice and the same importance – the same power to shape events [. . .] the sort of equality we want is an equality where "one" equals "one", but where each "one" is conceptualized differently and in new ways.'

References

Aulagnon, M. (1999) 'Tirs croisés contre la pilule abortive' in *Femmes, le mauvais genre?*, *Le Monde diplomatique*, 'Manière de voir', March–April, no. 44: 27–30.

Bourdieu, P. (1998) *La Domination masculine*, Paris: Seuil.

Cesbron, P. (1997) 'Menaces sur la liberté d'avorter', *Le Monde diplomatique*, February 1997: 14.

Frischer, D. (1997) *La Revanche des misogynes, où en sont les femmes après trente ans de féminisme?* Paris: Albin Michel.

Mossuz-Lavau, J. (1999) 'Résistantes face au Front national' in *Femmes, le mauvais genre?*, *Le Monde diplomatique*, 'Manière de voir', March–April, no. 44: 84–6.

Ozouf, M (1995) *Les mots des femmes*, Paris: Fayard.

Ramonet, I. (1999) 'La cause des femmes' in *Femmes, le mauvais genre?*, *Le Monde diplomatique*, 'Manière de voir', March-April, no. 44: 6–7.

Rodgers, C. (1998) *Le Deuxième Sexe de Simone de Beauvoir, un héritage admiré et contesté*, Paris: L'Harmattan.

Index

Index

Index

Index

see also press, alternative women's
Luxton, M., 48, 50

Mabile, S., 39n6
Mainstreaming, 38, 72
Majnnoni d'Intignano, B., 35
Mandraut, I., 39n5
Manifeste des 343, 9
Maquelle, S., 81
Marie Pas Claire, 75
  see also press, women's alternative
Marjollet, C., 180
Marry, C., 39n1
Marsden, D., 29
Martel, F., 178, 180–1, 183
Martin, A., 116
Martin, C., 23, 56, 59–60
Martin, J., 91, 95
Martin, M., 74
Martin, V., 100
Maruani, M., 2, 32
Massot, J., 94
materialist feminists, 10, 179
Mathieu, N-C., 178
Mauduit, L., 39n5
Maunaye, E., 59
May 1968, 8, 72, 174–5
McMillan, J., 97, 100
media professions
  place of women, 78–81
media stars, 81,
  see also Chazal, C., Ockrent, C.,
    Sinclair, A.
media, women in, 65–88
  see also press
  advertising, 68–70
  code of ethics, 68
  stereotyping, sexual, 68–9, 84
  frequency of appearances, 67
  representations of politicians, 76–8
  see also Aubry, M., Juppettes,
    Laguiller, A., Veil, S.
Mendras, H., 206
Meron, M., 29
Michon., F., 24, 27
Milroy, J., 124
Milroy, L., 124
Minni, C., 29
Mitchell, J., 148n9

Moi, T., 174
Montefiore, J., 133
Moreau, M-L., 124
Morokvasic, M., 57, 153, 155,
Mossuz-Lavau, J., 91, 95, 100–1, 214
Mouchtouris, A., 3, 199
Mouvement de libération des femmes
  (MLF), 9–10, 74
Mouvement d'Information et
  d'Expressions Lesbiennes (MIEL), 180
  see also lesbian and gay movement

Nanas Beurs, 158
  see also immigrant women,
    associations
Neale, J., 23
Neiertz, V., 70
Nicole-Drancourt, C., 22, 32, 38, 54–5
Nicollet, A., 155
non-kinship exchanges of labour
  definition of, 59–60
  men and women, by, 59–60
Nouvelles Questions Féministes (NQF),
  11, 69, 75, 179–81

occupational segregation, 34–6
  Rural women, 203
Ockrent, C., 81
  see also media stars
O'Reilly, J., 27, 30–1
Outin, J-L., 194
Ozouf, M., 213

Pacte Civil de Solidarité (PaCS), 182,
  183–4
Pacte d'Intérêt Commun (PIC), 182
paid work, 7
  characteristics of, 21–46
parité
  see parity
parity
  campaign, 92, 102–4, 214
  cohabitation, 94
  debate, 84
  political parties, 101–3
  women's groups, 101, 106
part-time work, 27–33
  age, by, 28–9
  definition of, 27, 39n5

Index

Index

Wright, V., 89, 94

Yaguello, M., 2, 114, 116–19, 121, 123, 126

Young, M., 52

Yuval-Davis, 153

Zelensky, A., 10

Zilberman, S., 24, 38

Zonabend, F., 191, 206